First World War
and Army of Occupation
War Diary
France, Belgium and Germany

17 DIVISION
Divisional Troops
Divisional Trench Mortar Batteries,
32 Trench Mortar Battery
and Divisional Ammunition Column
13 July 1915 - 31 December 1918

WO95/1992

The Naval & Military Press Ltd
www.nmarchive.com
Published in association with The National Archives

Published by

The Naval & Military Press Ltd

Unit 10 Ridgewood Industrial Park,

Uckfield, East Sussex,

TN22 5QE England

Tel: +44 (0) 1825 749494

www.naval-military-press.com

www.nmarchive.com

This diary has been reprinted in facsimile from the original. Any imperfections are inevitably reproduced and the quality may fall short of modern type and cartographic standards.

Contents

Document type	Place/Title	Date From	Date To
Heading	17th Division 17th Divl Ammn Colmn Jly 1915-May 1919		
Heading	Diary of 17th Divisional Ammunition Column & from 1.7.15 to 31.7.15		
Heading	17th Division 17th Divl Ammunition Column Vol I, II, III Jly Aug Feb 15		
Heading	Diary of 17th Divisional Ammunition Column From 1.8.15 to 31.8.15		
War Diary	Winchester	13/07/1915	15/07/1915
War Diary	Southampton	15/07/1915	15/07/1915
War Diary	Havre	16/07/1915	16/07/1915
War Diary	In Train	17/07/1915	17/07/1915
War Diary	Wirquin	18/07/1915	19/07/1915
War Diary	Arques	19/07/1915	20/07/1915
War Diary	Hondeghem	20/07/1915	05/08/1915
War Diary	Boeschepe	06/08/1915	31/08/1915
Heading	Diary of 17th Divisional Ammunition Column. & from 1.9.15 to 30.9.15		
War Diary	Boeschepe	16/09/1915	30/09/1915
War Diary	Boeschepe	01/09/1915	15/09/1915
Heading	17th Division 17th Div. A.C. Vol 4 Oct 15		
Heading	War Diary Of 17th Divisional Ammunition Column From 1.10.15 To 31.10.15		
War Diary	Boeschepe	01/10/1915	07/10/1915
War Diary	Steenvorde	08/10/1915	25/10/1915
War Diary	Poperinghe	26/10/1915	31/10/1915
Heading	17th Division 17th D.A.C Vol. 5 Vol 15		
Miscellaneous	War Diary Of 17th Divisional Ammunition Column From November 1st 1915 To November 30th 1915	01/12/1915	01/12/1915
War Diary	Poperinghe	01/11/1915	30/11/1915
Heading	17th D.A.C. Vol 6 121/7910		
Miscellaneous	War Diary Of 17th Divisional Ammunition Column From December 1st 1915 To December 31st 1915	31/12/1915	31/12/1915
War Diary	Poperinghe	01/12/1915	31/12/1915
Heading	17th D.A.C Vol 7 Jan 16		
Miscellaneous	War Diary Of 17th Divisional Ammunition Column From 1/1/16 To 31/1/16 Volume 7	31/01/1916	31/01/1916
War Diary	Poperinghe	01/01/1916	08/01/1916
War Diary	Zouafques	09/01/1916	31/01/1916
Heading	17th D.A.C. Vol:8		
War Diary	War Diary Of 17th Divisional Ammunition From 1/2/16 to 29/2/16 Volume 8		
War Diary	Zouafques	01/02/1916	12/02/1916
War Diary	Boeschepe	13/02/1916	29/02/1916
War Diary	War Diary Of 17th Divisional Ammunition Column From 1/3/16 To 31/3/16 Volume 9	31/03/1916	31/03/1916
War Diary	Borre	23/03/1916	31/03/1916
War Diary	Boeschepe	01/03/1916	11/03/1916
War Diary	Borre	12/03/1916	23/03/1916

War Diary	War Diaries For The Month Of April Of 17th Divisional Ammunition Column From 1/1/16 To 30/1/16 Volume.10	01/01/1916	30/01/1916
War Diary	Borre	01/04/1916	01/04/1916
War Diary	Armentieres	02/04/1916	30/04/1916
Miscellaneous	War Diaries For The Month Of May Of 17th Divisional Ammunition Column From 1/5/16 To 31/5/16 Volume 11	31/05/1916	31/05/1916
War Diary	Armentieres	01/05/1916	22/05/1916
War Diary	Seninghem	23/05/1916	31/05/1916
Miscellaneous	War Diaries For The Month Of June Of 17th Divisional Ammunition Column From 1/6/16 To 30/6/16 Volume 12	30/06/1916	30/06/1916
War Diary	Seninghem	01/06/1916	30/06/1916
Heading	17th Div. XV. Corps. War Diary 17th Divisional Ammunition Column. July 1916 17th Div. XV-Corps.		
Miscellaneous	War Diaries For The Month Of July Of 17th Divisional Ammunition Column From 1/7/16 To 31/7/16 Volume 13	31/07/1916	31/07/1916
War Diary		01/07/1916	31/07/1916
Miscellaneous	Wastage from Sickness (Other than battle Casualties) during past month Officers	31/07/1916	31/07/1916
Heading	17th Divisional Amm Column. 17th Divisional Ammunition Column August 1916		
Miscellaneous	War Diaries For The Month Of July Of 17th Divisional Ammunition Column From 1/8/16 To 31/8/16 Volume 14	31/08/1916	31/08/1916
War Diary	Dernancourt	01/08/1916	02/08/1916
War Diary	Near Albert	02/08/1916	23/08/1916
War Diary	Occoches	24/08/1916	30/08/1916
Miscellaneous	Casualties, Summary of animals. LD.10. Mules 4 Wastage from Sickness 6 Other Ranks Battle Casualties Nil		
Heading	War Diaries For The Month Of September 1/9/16 To 30/9/16 Of 17th Divisional Ammunition Column Volume 15		
War Diary	Henu	01/09/1916	22/09/1916
War Diary	Genne Ivergny	22/09/1916	30/09/1916
Heading	War Diaries Of The Divisional Ammunition Column For The Month Of October 1916		
War Diary	Pas	01/10/1916	18/10/1916
War Diary	Albert	19/10/1916	21/10/1916
War Diary	Near Albert	22/10/1916	30/10/1916
War Diary	Near Bouzincourt	31/10/1916	31/10/1916
Miscellaneous	Casualties		
Heading	War Diaries Of 17th Divisional Ammunition Column For The Month Of November 1916 Volume 17		
War Diary	N. Albert	01/11/1916	20/11/1916
War Diary	Meaulte	21/11/1916	25/11/1916
War Diary	Carnoy	26/11/1916	30/11/1916
Heading	War Diaries Of 17th Divisional Ammunition Column For The Month Of December 1916 31/12/16 Volume 18		
War Diary	Meaulte	01/12/1916	31/12/1916
Miscellaneous	Casualties	31/12/1916	31/12/1916

Heading	War Diaries Of 17th Divisional Ammunition Column For The Month Of January 1917 31/1/17 Volume 19		
Miscellaneous	Casualties	31/01/1917	31/01/1917
War Diary	Meaulte	01/01/1917	12/01/1917
War Diary	Carnoy	13/01/1917	31/01/1917
War Diary	Meaulte	01/01/1917	12/01/1917
War Diary	Carnoy	13/01/1917	31/01/1917
Miscellaneous	Casualties	31/01/1917	31/01/1917
Heading	War Diaries Of 17th Divisional Ammunition Column For The Month Of February 1917 28/2/17 Volume 20		
War Diary	Carnoy	01/02/1917	28/02/1917
Miscellaneous	Casualties	28/02/1917	28/02/1917
Heading	War Diaries Of 17th Divisional Ammunition Column For The Month Of March 1917 31/3/17 Volume 21		
War Diary	Carnoy	01/03/1917	04/03/1917
War Diary	Near. Albert	05/03/1917	16/03/1917
War Diary	Albert Puchvillers	17/03/1917	19/03/1917
War Diary	Heuzecourt	20/03/1917	23/03/1917
War Diary	On March	24/03/1917	31/03/1917
Heading	War Diaries 17th Divisional Ammunition Column For The Month Of April 1917 Volume 22		
Miscellaneous	Casualties	31/03/1917	31/03/1917
War Diary	Bray	01/04/1917	08/04/1917
War Diary	On March	09/04/1917	09/04/1917
War Diary	Agnez	10/04/1917	11/04/1917
War Diary	Arras	12/04/1917	30/04/1917
Heading	War Diary Of 17th Divisional Ammunition Column From 1/5/17 To 31/5/17 Volume 23		
War Diary	Arras	01/05/1917	31/05/1917
Miscellaneous	Casualties	01/06/1917	01/06/1917
Heading	War Diary Of 17th Divisional Ammunition Column From 1/6/17 To 30/6/17 Volume 24		
War Diary	Arras	01/06/1917	18/06/1917
War Diary	W Of Anzin	19/06/1917	30/06/1917
Miscellaneous	Casualties		
Heading	War Diary Of 17th Divisional Ammunition Column From 1/7/17 To 31/7/17 Volume 25		
War Diary	Anzin	01/07/1917	31/07/1917
Miscellaneous	Casualties	31/07/1917	31/07/1917
Heading	War Diary Of 17th Divisional Ammunition Column From 1/8/17 To 31/8/17 Volume 26		
War Diary	Anzin	01/08/1917	31/08/1917
Miscellaneous	Casualties	31/08/1917	31/08/1917
Heading	War Diary Of 17th Divisional Ammunition Column From 1/9/17 To 30/9/17 Volume 27		
War Diary	Anzin	01/09/1917	30/09/1917
Miscellaneous	Casualties	30/09/1917	30/09/1917
Heading	War Diary Of 17th Divisional Ammunition Column From 1/10/17 To 31/10/17 Volume 28		
War Diary	Anzin	01/10/1917	02/10/1917
War Diary	Proven	03/10/1917	31/10/1917
Miscellaneous	Casualties	31/10/1917	31/10/1917
Heading	War Diary Of 17th Divisional Ammunition Column From 1/11/17 To 30/11/17 Volume 29		
War Diary		01/11/1917	30/11/1917
Miscellaneous	Casualties	30/10/1917	30/10/1917

Miscellaneous	Return of Strength	30/11/1917	30/11/1917
Heading	War Diary Of 17th Divisional Ammunition Column From 1/12/17 To 30/12/17 Volume 30		
War Diary		01/12/1917	31/12/1917
Heading	War Diary Of 17th Divisional Ammunition Column From 1/1/18 To 31/1/18 Volume 31		
War Diary	In The Field	01/01/1918	31/01/1918
Miscellaneous	Casualties	31/01/1918	31/01/1918
Miscellaneous	Return of Strength	31/01/1918	31/01/1918
Heading	War Diary Of 17th Divisional Ammunition Column From 1/2/18 To 28/2/18		
Miscellaneous	Return of Strength	31/12/1917	31/12/1917
Miscellaneous	Casualties	31/12/1917	31/12/1917
War Diary	Beaucourt Sur Hallue	01/02/1918	28/02/1918
Miscellaneous	Casualties	28/02/1918	28/02/1918
Miscellaneous	Return of Strength	28/02/1918	28/02/1918
Heading	17th Div. 17th Divisional Ammunition Column, R.F.A. March 1918		
Heading	War Diary Of 17th Divisional Ammunition Column From 1/3/18 To 31/3/18		
War Diary	Bertincourt	21/03/1918	31/03/1918
Miscellaneous	Casualties	31/03/1918	31/03/1918
Heading	17th Divisional Artillery War Diary 17th Divisional Ammunition Column R.F.A. April 1918		
Heading	War Diary Of 17th Divisional Ammunition Column From 1/4/18 To 30/4/18		
War Diary	In The Field	01/04/1918	30/04/1918
Miscellaneous	Casualties	30/04/1918	30/04/1918
Miscellaneous	Return of Strength	30/04/1918	30/04/1918
Heading	War Diary Of 17th Divisional Ammunition Column From 1/5/18 To 31/5/18		
War Diary		01/05/1918	31/05/1918
Miscellaneous	Casualties	31/05/1918	31/05/1918
Miscellaneous	Return of Strength	31/05/1918	31/05/1918
Heading	War Diary 17th Divisional Ammunition Column From 1/6/18 To 30/6/18		
War Diary		01/06/1918	30/06/1918
Miscellaneous	Return of Strength	20/06/1918	20/06/1918
Miscellaneous	Casualties	30/06/1918	30/06/1918
Heading	War Diary Of 17th Divisional Ammunition Column From 1/7/18 To 31/7/18		
War Diary		01/07/1918	17/07/1918
War Diary	Field	18/07/1918	31/08/1918
Miscellaneous	Return of Strength	31/07/1918	31/07/1918
Miscellaneous	Casualties	31/07/1918	31/07/1918
Heading	17th Divl. Artillery 17th Divisional Ammunition Column. August 1918		
Heading	War Diary 17th Divisional Ammunition Column From 1/8/18 To 31/8/18		
War Diary		01/08/1918	31/08/1918
Miscellaneous	Casualties	31/08/1918	31/08/1918
Miscellaneous		31/08/1918	31/08/1918
Heading	War Diary Of 17th Divisional Ammunition Column From 1/9/18 To 30/9/18		
War Diary		01/09/1918	30/09/1918
Miscellaneous	Casualties	30/09/1918	30/09/1918

Miscellaneous	Strength Return	30/09/1918	30/09/1918
Heading	War Diary Of 17th Divisional Ammunition Column From 1/10/18 To 31/10/18		
War Diary		01/10/1918	31/10/1918
Miscellaneous	Casualties	31/10/1918	31/10/1918
Miscellaneous	Strength Return	31/10/1918	31/10/1918
Heading	War Diary Of 17th Divisional Ammunition From 1/11/18 To 30/11/18		
War Diary	In The Field	01/11/1918	30/11/1918
Miscellaneous	Strength	30/11/1918	30/11/1918
Miscellaneous	Casualties	30/11/1918	30/11/1918
Heading	War Diary Of 17th Divisional Ammunition Column From 1/121/18 To 31/12/18		
War Diary		01/12/1918	31/12/1918
Miscellaneous	Casualties	31/12/1918	31/12/1918
Miscellaneous	Strength Return	31/12/1918	31/12/1918
Heading	War Diary Of 17th Divisional Ammunition Column From 1/1/19 To 31/1/19		
Miscellaneous	Strength Return	31/01/1919	31/01/1919
Miscellaneous	Casualties		
War Diary		18/01/1919	31/01/1919
War Diary		01/01/1919	17/01/1919
Heading	War Diary Of 17th Divisional Ammunition Column From 1/2/19 To 28/2/19		
War Diary		01/02/1919	22/02/1919
War Diary	Bettencourt	23/02/1919	28/02/1919
Miscellaneous	Strength Return	28/02/1919	28/02/1919
Miscellaneous	Casualties	28/02/1919	28/02/1919
Heading	War Diary Of 17th Divisional Ammunition Column From 1/3/19 To 31/3/19		
War Diary	Bettencourt	01/03/1919	31/03/1919
Miscellaneous	Casualties	31/03/1919	31/03/1919
Miscellaneous	Strength Return	31/03/1919	31/03/1919
Heading	War Diary Of 17th Divisional Ammunition Column From 1/4/19 To 30/4/19		
Miscellaneous	Strength Return	30/01/1919	30/01/1919
Miscellaneous	Casualties	30/01/1919	30/01/1919
War Diary	Bettencourt	01/04/1919	26/05/1919
Miscellaneous	Strength Return	26/05/1919	26/05/1919
Miscellaneous	Casualties	26/05/1919	26/05/1919
Heading	War Diary Of 17th Divisional Ammunition Column From 1/5/19 To 26/5/19		
Heading	17 Div 32 Trench Mortar Bty 1915 Aug To 1916 Feb		
War Diary		02/08/1915	28/08/1915
War Diary		04/10/1915	31/10/1915
War Diary		01/00/1915	30/00/1915
War Diary		01/00/1915	03/00/1915
War Diary	Map Square J.19.a.43	06/11/1915	09/11/1915
War Diary	I.11.a	10/11/1915	20/11/1915
War Diary	Railway Wood. L.T.M, Group	05/12/1915	10/12/1915
War Diary	Railway Wood	11/12/1915	11/12/1915
War Diary	Railway Wood A.T.M. Group	14/12/1915	22/12/1915
Heading	32 Trench Mortar Battery Jan Vol II 17 Div		
War Diary	14th Div. Rest Area France	07/01/1916	24/01/1916
War Diary	Reserve Wood The Bluff	09/02/1916	21/02/1916

Heading	17th Division Trench Mortar Batteries Feb 1917 To Dec 1918		
War Diary		01/02/1917	28/02/1918
Heading	17th Div. 17th Divisional Trench Mortar Batteries. March 1918		
War Diary		01/03/1918	31/03/1918
Heading	17th Divisional Artillery War Diary 17th Divisional Trench Mortars April 1918		
War Diary	In The Field	01/04/1918	31/07/1918
Heading	17th Divl. Artillery. D.T.M.O. 17th Division, August 1918		
War Diary		01/08/1918	30/08/1918
War Diary	In The Field	01/10/1918	31/12/1918

17TH DIVISION

17TH DIVL AMMN COLMN

JLY 1915 - MAY 1919

CONFIDENTIAL DIARY

OF

17th DIVISIONAL AMMUNITION COLUMN.

From 1.7.15 to 31.7.15.

17th Division

121
7517

17th Divl: Ammunition Column
Vols I, II, III.

July Aug & Sep / 15

May '19

CONFIDENTIAL DIARY

OF

17th DIVISIONAL AMMUNITION COLUMN.

From 1.8.15 to 31.8.15.

Army Form C. 2118.

Instructions regarding War Diaries and Intelligence Summaries are contained in F. S. Regs., Part II. and the Staff Manual respectively. Title pages will be prepared in manuscript.

WAR DIARY
or
INTELLIGENCE SUMMARY.
(Erase heading not required.)

Hour, Date, Place	Summary of Events and Information	Remarks and references to Appendices
13 July 1915 WINCHESTER	Orders received to embark at SOUTHAMPTON on 15.7.15	RWD
15 do. WINCHESTER	Marched out of Camp at 5 am Strength as under 11 officers 540 O.R. 96 G.S. Waggons 2. Water Carts 1 Maltese Cart Officers Lt COL RWL Dunlop C.I.E. Commanding Lt F.C. COLLINS R.F.A. Adjt No 1 Section: Captain J J REILLY; 2/Lt A FITTES; 2/Lt W H THOMPSON No 2 Section: Major Warren; Lieut C.A GRUNCELL; 2/Lt J. RITCHIE No 3 Section: Capt. W. PRIESTLEY; 2/Lt C. J HENNING; 2/Lt H M TARRY LIEUT. C M TALBOT RAMC attached	RWD
9am do SOUTHAMPTON	Unit arrived at SOUTHAMPTON and commenced embarking H.Q. & No 3 Section SS BLACKWELL No 1 Section SS AFRICAN PRINCE No 2 Section S.S. HUANCHO. These transports sailed in order named at 1 hour intervals commencing 4 pm	RWD
16 July 1915 HAVRE.	SS BLACKWELL arrived at HAVRE at 1 am. African PRINCE and HUANCHO at about 10 am. Unit entrained in 5 trains as follows Part of No 3 section at 6.30pm Do No 2 " at 9.30pm Do No 1 " at 1.30 am (17.7.15) H.Q and details at 4.3 am Do Details at 5.0 am Do	RWD

R W L Dunlop
LT. COL. R.F.A.
COMMANDING 17th DIV. AMM. COLM.

(9 29 6) W4141—463 100,000 9/14 H W V Forms/C. 2118/10

Instructions regarding War Diaries and Intelligence Summaries are contained in F. S. Regs., Part II. and the Staff Manual respectively. Title pages will be prepared in manuscript.

WAR DIARY
or
INTELLIGENCE SUMMARY.
(Erase heading not required.)

Army Form C. 2118.

Hour, Date, Place	Summary of Events and Information	Remarks and references to Appendices
17 July 1915 INTRAIN +	Unit reaches destinations as follows 1st Train WIZERNES 8pm; 2nd ST OMER 1am; 3rd WIZERNES 4.30 am (18.7.15); 4th do 7.0 am do; 5th do 11.0 am do	RWSD
18 July 1915 WIRQUIN	In billets at WIRQUIN Dr Martin G. Burkinsley [?] and was sent to No. 10. F.A.	RWSD
19 July 1915 do ARQUES	Marched from WIRQUIN at 9 am reaching ARQUES at 1.15pm	RWSD
20 do " HONDEGHEM	Marches from ARQUES at 9.45am reaching HONDIGHEM at 1.15pm INBILLETS AT HONDEGHEM	RWSD
21 do do	Received from 17. D.A.P. 976000 SAA 5564 A 484 AX 765 BX	RWSD
22 do do	Major WARREN posted to C/79. Capt HOTCHKISS from C/79 to No 2 section	RWSD
23 do do	~~[illegible]~~ In billets at HONDEGHEM	RWSD
24 do do	do	RWSD
25 do do	do	RWSD
26 do do	Sent 114000 SAA to Railhead	RWSD
27 do do	Supplies 532 A to 78 Bde	RWSD
28 do do	" 39000 SAA to 9 Northumberland Fusiliers	RWSD
29 do do	In billets at Hondeghem	RWSD
30 do do	Do	RWSD
31 do do	Supplies 180 AX to 79 Bde	RWSD

[signature]
LT. COL. R.F.A.
COMMANDING 17th DIV. AMM. COLM.

(9 29 6) W4141—463 100,000 9/14 H W V Forms/C. 2118/10

Army Form C. 2118.

Instructions regarding War Diaries and Intelligence Summaries are contained in F. S. Regs., Part II. and the Staff Manual respectively. Title pages will be prepared in manuscript.

WAR DIARY
or
INTELLIGENCE SUMMARY.
(*Erase heading not required.*)

Hour, Date, Place		Summary of Events and Information	Remarks and references to Appendices
1st Aug 1915	HONDEGHEM	In billets at HONDEGHEM	RWRD
2 do	do	do	RWRD
3 do	do	do	RWRD
4 do	do	do	RWRD
5 do	do	Supplied 64000 SAA to 80 Bde, 100000 SAA + 148 A to 70 Bde	RWRD
6 do	BOESCHEPE	Marched to billets in BOESCHEPE	RWRD
7 do	do	In billets at BOESCHEPE	RWRD
8 do	do	Supplied 35000 SAA to 50th Bde	RWRD
9 do	do	" 416 BX to 81st Bde	RWRD
10 do	do	" 150 Br 98 BX to 81st Bde and 1064 A to 80th Bde	
11 do	do	In billets at BOESCHEPE	RWRD
12 do	do	do	RWRD
13 do	do	do	RWRD
14 do	do	do	RWRD
15 do	do	do	RWRD
16 do	do	do	RWRD
17 do	do	Supplied 68000 SAA to 80th Bde. No 72032 Br. Moffitt slightly wounded by Shrapnel at YPRES	RWRD
18 do	do	" 43,000 " " "	RWRD
19 do	do	" 158,000 " " "	RWRD
20 do	do	In billets at BOESCHEPE	RWRD
21 do	do	do	RWRD
22 do	do	do	RWRD

R W R Dunlop
LT. COL. R.F.A.
COMMANDING 17th DIV. AMM. COLM.

Instructions regarding War Diaries and Intelligence Summaries are contained in F. S. Regs., Part II. and the Staff Manual respectively. Title pages will be prepared in manuscript.

WAR DIARY
or
INTELLIGENCE SUMMARY.

(*Erase heading not required.*)

Army Form C. 2118.

Hour, Date, Place		Summary of Events and Information	Remarks and references to Appendices
23 Aug 1915	BOESCHEPE	Supplies 148 A to 79 Bde	[illegible]
24 do	do	" 10,000 SAA to 12 M.M.G.	[illegible]
25 do	do	" 192 A + 12 AX to 79 Bde 2/Lieut THOMPSON and 2/Lieut RITCHIE attached to 80th & 81st Bde respectively	[illegible] [illegible]
26 do	do	One mule wounded on fatigue at YPRES	[illegible]
27 do	do	In billets at BOESCHEPE	[illegible]
28 do	do	-do-	[illegible]
29 do	do	-do- Supplies 404 A to 79 Bde. 2/Lieut THOMPSON rejoined	[illegible]
30 do	do	-do- " 10000 SAA to 12 MMG & 152 A to 79 Bde	[illegible]
31 do	do	do -	[illegible]

[illegible]
LT. COL. R.F.A.
COMMANDING 17th DIV. AMM. COLM.

CONFIDENTIAL DIARY

OF

17th DIVISIONAL AMMUNITION COLUMN.

From 1.9.15 to 30.9.15.

Instructions regarding War Diaries and Intelligence Summaries are contained in F. S. Regs., Part II. and the Staff Manual respectively. Title pages will be prepared in manuscript.

WAR DIARY
or
INTELLIGENCE SUMMARY.
(*Erase heading not required.*)

Army Form C. 2118.

Hour, Date, Place	Summary of Events and Information	Remarks and references to Appendices
16 ~~[illegible]~~ September 1915 BOESCHEPE	IN BILLETS at BOESCHEPE - Supplied 30000 SAA & 76 A to 79 Bde	RHSD
17 Sept 1915 BOESCHEPE	No 79467 Dr J. SHIMMIN wounded in trenches Supplied 116 A & 200 AX to 79 Bde	RHSD
18 " " "	In billets at BOESCHEPE	RHSD
19 " " "	Supplied 6000 Saa 152 A to 79th Bde	RHSD
20 " " "	" 162 AX to 78 Bde + 36 AX to 79 Bde 16000 Saa to 12 MMG	RHSD
21 " " "	" 52 AX to 79 Bde and 40000 S.a.a. + 36 A to 79th Bde: to 80th Bde 18200 Saa + 84 A	RHSD
22 " " "	In billets at BOESCHEPE	RHSD
23 " " "	Supplied 50000 Saa + 192 A + 112 AX to 79 Bde	RHSD
24 " " "	" 65000 Saa 388 A + 72 AX to 79 Bde	RHSD
25 " " "	2/Lieut RITCHIE + 2/Lieut FITTES posted 81st Bde. Supplied 16000 Saa 316 A + 4 AX to 79 Bde and 30000 to 12 MMG	RHSD
26 " " "	In billets at BOESCHEPE	RHSD
27 " " "	Supplied 20000 Saa + 152 A to 79 Bde	RHSD
28 " " "	" 240000 Saa 132 A to -do-	RHSD
29 " " "	In billets at BOESCHEPE	RHSD
30 " " "	Supplied 10000 Saa + 116 A to 79 Bde	RHSD

RW [illegible]
Lt Col RFA
17 DAC.

Instructions regarding War Diaries and Intelligence Summaries are contained in F. S. Regs., Part II. and the Staff Manual respectively. Title pages will be prepared in manuscript.

WAR DIARY
or
INTELLIGENCE SUMMARY.
(Erase heading not required.)

Army Form C. 2118.

Hour, Date, Place	Summary of Events and Information	Remarks and references to Appendices
1 Sept 1915 BOESCHEPE	In billets at BOESCHEPE. Supplied 144 A to 79 Bde	RWAD
		RWAD
2 do do	Supplies 168 A to 79 Bde	
	In billets at BOESCHEPE	RWAD
3 do do		
4 do do	No 39367 Gr J. Butler & No 79091 Dr G. Green wounded by Shrapnel on trench fatigue. Supplied 20,000 SAA to 12 M.M.G. 74 A to 80 Bde	RWAD
		RWAD
5 do do	Supplies 128 A to 79 Bde	
6 do do	2/Lieuts WARD & WILSON joined. 296 A to 79 Bde and 23000 SAA to 12 MMG	RWAD
7 do do	2/Lieut THOMPSON posted D/79 Brigade. Supplied 17,000 SAA + 116 A to 79 Bde	RWAD
8 do do	" KING joined. Supplies 136 A to 80 Bde	RWAD
9 do do	LIEUT LEGROS joined " 30,000 SAA + 152 A to 79 Bde and 190 BX to 81st Bde	RWAD
10 do do	Supplied 26 BX to 81 Bde 23000 SAA and 36 A to 79 Bde and 280 A to 80 Bde	RWAD
11 do do	Supplied 2000 to 12 M.M.G. 20 A X 79th Bde & 70 BX to 81st Bde	RWAD
12 do do	In billets at BOESCHEPE	RWAD
13 do do	Supplied 3000 SAA + 36 A to 79 Bde	RWAD
14 do do	2/LIEUT TARRY & KING posted 81st Bde. 8000 SAA + 116 A to 79 Bde	RWAD
15 do do	2/LIEUT MORGAN joined. Supplied 8000 SAA 112 A to 79 Bde & 88 BX to 81st Bde	RWAD

[illegible]
RFA
178 BC

(9 29 6) W4141—463 100,000 9/14 H W V Forms/C. 2118/10

17th Division

121/7517

17th Div: A.C.

Vol 4

Oct 15

CONFIDENTIAL WAR DIARY

OF

17th DIVISIONAL AMMUNITION COLUMN.

From 1.10.15 to 31.10.15.

Instructions regarding War Diaries and Intelligence Summaries are contained in F. S. Regs., Part II. and the Staff Manual respectively. Title pages will be prepared in manuscript.

WAR DIARY
or
INTELLIGENCE SUMMARY.
(*Erase heading not required.*)

Army Form C. 2118.

Place	Date	Hour	Summary of Events and Information	Remarks and references to Appendices
	1915			
BOESCHEPE	1 Oct.		In billets at BOESCHEPE Supplied 20000 SAA to 12 M.M.G.	[illegible]
Do	2		Do. Supplied 304 A to 79 B.A.C., 78 BX to 81 BAC. 78857 Dr. Langley Slightly wounded on trench fatigue	[illegible]
Do	3		Supplied 148 A to 80 BAC	[illegible]
Do	4		" 20000 SAA to MMG. Lt GRUNCELL Slightly wounded by Shrapnel at KUMMEL	[illegible]
Do	5		In billets at BOESCHEPE	[illegible]
Do	6		Supplied 95 A to 80 BAC	[illegible]
Do	7		" 36 BX to 81 BAC	[illegible]
Do STEENVORDE	8		Proceeded by march route to STEENVORDE Commencing 5 pm	[illegible]
Do	9		In rest at STEENVORDE. HQ at PAMSGAT in P.1.c Nos 1 2 & 3 Sections in P 11 a Sheet 27	[illegible]
Do	10		Do	[illegible]
Do	11		Do.	[illegible]
Do	12		Captain W. PRIESTLEY posted to 81 BAC Capt. HOTCHKIS transferred to No 3 Lt GRUNCELL to No 2 Section in Command	[illegible]
Do	13		In rest at STEENVORDE	[illegible]
Do	14		Do.	[illegible]
Do	15		Do.	[illegible]
Do	16		Do.	[illegible]

[signature]
LT. COL. R.F.A.
COMMANDING 17th DIV. AMM. COLM.

T2134. Wt. W708-776. 500000. 4/15. Sir J. C. & S.

Instructions regarding War Diaries and Intelligence Summaries are contained in F. S. Regs., Part II. and the Staff Manual respectively. Title pages will be prepared in manuscript.

WAR DIARY
or
INTELLIGENCE SUMMARY.
(Erase heading not required.)

Army Form C. 2118.

Place	Date	Hour	Summary of Events and Information	Remarks and references to Appendices
~~[illegible]~~	1915			[illegible]
STEENVORDE	17 Oct		In rest at STEENVORDE	[illegible]
"	18		Do Supplied 25000 SAA to 79 BAC	[illegible]
"	19		Do	[illegible]
"	20		2/Lt FITTES RFA posted to unit and to No 1 Section	[illegible]
"			2/Lt WARD RFA posted from No 1 to No 2 Section	[illegible]
"	21		In rest at STEENVORDE	[illegible]
"	22		Do Supplied 70000 SAA to 79 BAC	[illegible]
"	23		Do Do 11498 BSM LILLIS promoted 2/Lieut Gazette 22.10.15 dated 22.9.15	[illegible]
"	24		Do Receives [illegible] from 79 BAC 2821 A 203 AX from 81st BAC 3266 A and 253 AX and [illegible] in H.Q.	[illegible]
"	25		Do	[illegible]
Do POPERINGHE	26		Supplied to 3 DAC 6591 A and 458 AX Marched into billets of 3 DAC near POPERINGHE. Received from 3 DAC	
"			286 BX 61 BX Marched into new billets in daylight commencing 2 pm	[illegible]
POPERINGHE	27		In billets at POPERINGHE in L 9 a & b Sheet 27	[illegible]
"	28		Do	[illegible]
"	29		Do	[illegible]
"	30		Do	[illegible]
"	31		Do	

[illegible signature]
LT. COL. R.F.A.
COMMANDING 17th DIV. AMM. COLM.

17th Division

17th D.A.C.
Vol: 5

121/7656

Nov. 15

Instructions regarding War Diaries and Intelligence Summaries are contained in F. S. Regs., Part II. and the Staff Manual respectively. Title pages will be prepared in manuscript.

WAR DIARY
or
INTELLIGENCE SUMMARY.
(Erase heading not required.)

Army Form C. 2118.

Place	Date	Hour	Summary of Events and Information	Remarks and references to Appendices
			Confidential.	
			War Diary	
			of	
			17th Divisional Ammunition Column.	
			from November 1st 1915 to November 30th 1915.	
			1/12/15. R. L. Dunlop [?] Lt Col R F A	
			Comd.g 17th Div. Amm. Column.	

2353 Wt. W2544/1454 700,000 5/15 D. D. & L. A.D.S.S./Forms/C. 2118.

Instructions regarding War Diaries and Intelligence Summaries are contained in F. S. Regs., Part II. and the Staff Manual respectively. Title pages will be prepared in manuscript.

WAR DIARY
or
INTELLIGENCE SUMMARY.
(Erase heading not required.)

Army Form C. 2118.

Place	Date 1915	Hour	Summary of Events and Information	Remarks and references to Appendices
Poperinghe	1-11		In billets at POPERINGHE in L.9.a.v.b. (sheet 27)	
			Captain J. J. Reilly, Lieut F. E. Collins & 10 other ranks proceeded on leave to	JCC
			England from 1st to 8th	
do	2.11		In billets as above.	
			Supplied 1216 rounds of "A" to 79th Bde RFA	JCC
			12 NCOs & men proceeded on leave to England for 2nd to 8th.	
-do	3-11		In billets as above.	
			Supplied following ammunition	
			To 79th Bde 5000 S.A.A. 1160 A	JCC
			To 80th Bde 1996 A	
			To 81st Bde 136 B 200 BX	
			Received 456 rounds A from Sub Park	
-do	4.11		Halted as above	
			Supplied following Ammunition	
			To 17 Sub Park 150 B 350 BX	JCC
			To 78 Bde RFA 76 A	
-do	5.11		Halted as above	
			2Lt W SKELTON joined from Base	JCC
			Supplied 79th Bde RFA with 1104 rounds A	
-do	6.11		Halted as above	
			Supplied 50000 rounds SAA & 252 A to 80 Bde	JCC
			Received 828 boxes pistol from Park	

2353 Wt. W2544/1454 700,000 5/15 D. D. & L. A.D.S.S./Forms/C. 2118.

Instructions regarding War Diaries and Intelligence Summaries are contained in F. S. Regs., Part II. and the Staff Manual respectively. Title pages will be prepared in manuscript.

WAR DIARY
or
INTELLIGENCE SUMMARY.
(Erase heading not required.)

Army Form C. 2118.

Place	Date 1915	Hour	Summary of Events and Information	Remarks and references to Appendices
POPERINGHE	7.11.15		Halted in Billets L9a & b (Sheet 27) Supplied 828 rounds pistol & 352 rounds A to 80th Bde RFA & 76 A to 78th Bde Received 228 rounds A & 360 BX from 17th Sub-Park	JCC
-do-	8.11.		Halted as above Received following ammunition from Sub Park:- 63000 saa 828 pistol 456 A 188 AX	JCC
do-	9.11		Halted as above 2Lt. W.SKELTON ordered to join 81st Bde RFA Issued 76 rounds BX to 81st Bde	JCC
do-	10.11		Halted as above LT.COL. R.W.L.DUNLOP and 1 other rank proceeded on leave to England from 10th to 17th 2Lt. LILLIS proceeded to Base in accordance with instructions that all Officers commissioned from ranks in RA are to proceed to Base Transferred a GS wagon and 4 mules to 140 Company ASC	JCC
-do-	11-11		Halted as above CAPT. J.N. HOTCHKIS & 10 other ranks proceeded on leave to England from 11th to 18th Following Amn received from 79th Bde 33000 saa from Park 684 A 188 AX Supplied 77000 saa & 552 Pistol to 79th Bde and 8000 saa to Park	JCC.

2353 Wt. W2544/1454 700,000 5/15 D. D. & L. A.D.S.S./Forms/C. 2118.

Army Form C. 2118.

WAR DIARY
or
INTELLIGENCE SUMMARY.
(Erase heading not required.)

Instructions regarding War Diaries and Intelligence Summaries are contained in F. S. Regs., Part II. and the Staff Manual respectively. Title pages will be prepared in manuscript.

Place	Date 1915	Hour	Summary of Events and Information	Remarks and references to Appendices
Poperinghe	12-11		Halted in billets at L9a7b (Sheet 27) Issued 228 A + 44 AX to 78th Bde A.C.	JCC
"	13 11		Halted in billets as above Under instructions from 17 D.A. 238 mules with harness were handed over for the MEERUT DIVISION and 64 Heavy & 90 light Draught horses were received with harness, also 4 mules with harness in exchange Issued 408 A to 80th Bde and 44 A to 78 Bde RFA and 2562 A & 304 AX to Batteries of 14th D. Arty. Received 44 rounds AX from C Battery 78th Bde RFA	JCC
"	14 11		Halted in billets as above. Received from Sub Park 912 A 564 AX Issued to 80th Bde RFA 192 A and 20 AX to 79th Bde RFA 1317 A to 81st Bde RFA 148 BX	JCC
"	15 11		Halted in billets as above Received from Sub Park 684 A & from 80 Bde RFA 8 A Issued to 80th Bde RFA 100 A 20 AX To 79th Bde 583 A To 80 Bde 20 AX To 81st Bde RFA 264 BX	JCC

Instructions regarding War Diaries and Intelligence Summaries are contained in F. S. Regs., Part II. and the Staff Manual respectively. Title pages will be prepared in manuscript.

WAR DIARY
or
INTELLIGENCE SUMMARY.
(Erase heading not required.)

Army Form C. 2118.

Place 1915	Date 1915	Hour	Summary of Events and Information	Remarks and references to Appendices
Polengle	16.11		Halted in billets at Lq a 7b (sheet 27) Received from Sut Park 52000 rounds saa 552 Pistol 496 A and 264 BX Issued to ~~80th~~ Bde A.C. 260 A Received 264 rounds BX & 1 B from 81st Bde Rest Kam to Park	JCC
do	17.11		Halted in billets as above Issued 4 rounds A to D.A.C, ~~and~~ 241 A to 80th Bde RFA & 122 BX to 81st Bde RFA	JCC
-do-	18.11		Halted as above. Received 9000 Mills Grenades	JCC
-do-	19.11		Halted as above Issued 9000 Mills Grenades to RE at H.16 d.1.1. (Sheet 28)	JCC JCC
-do-	20.11		Halted as above Issued 30000 saa to 79th Bde A.C	JCC
-do-	21.11		Halted as above	JCC
-do	22.11		-do- Supplied 108 rounds AX to 78th Bde A.C 108 " " " 79th " " 324 " " " 80th " "	

2353 Wt. W2544/1454 700,000 5/15 D. D. & L. A.D.S.S./Forms/C. 2118.

Instructions regarding War Diaries and Intelligence Summaries are contained in F. S. Regs., Part II. and the Staff Manual respectively. Title pages will be prepared in manuscript.

WAR DIARY
or
INTELLIGENCE SUMMARY.
(Erase heading not required.)

Army Form C. 2118.

Place 1915	Date 1915	Hour	Summary of Events and Information	Remarks and references to Appendices
Poperinghe ~~23.11.15~~	23.11		Halted in billets at L9 a & b (Sheet 27) Received 27 remounts for Divl Arty.	FCC
do	24.11		Halted as above ~~do~~ -	FCC
do	25.11		-do- Send 25 of the remounts recd. on 23/11/15 to HQ 17 Dvn for distribution	FCC
do	26.11		Halted as above.	FCC
do	27.11		-do- Supplied 36 rounds AX to 80th Bde RFA and 175 Rounds BX to 81st Bde RFA. Received 30000 SAA from Park one man joined from Base.	FCC
do	28.11		Halted as above	FCC
do	29.11		do	FCC
do	30.11		do.	FCC

Instructions regarding War Diaries and Intelligence Summaries are contained in F. S. Regs., Part II. and the Staff Manual respectively. Title Pages will be prepared in manuscript.

WAR DIARY
or
INTELLIGENCE SUMMARY
(Erase heading not required.)

Army Form C. 2118

Place	Date	Hour	Summary of Events and Information	Remarks and references to Appendices
			<u>Confidential.</u> War Diary of 17th Divisional Ammunition Column. from December 1st 1915 to December 31st 1915. [signature] Lt-Colonel R.F.A. Commanding 17th Div: Amm. Column. 31/12/15.	

1875 Wt. W593/826 1,000,000 4/15 J.B.C. & A. A.D.S.S./Forms/C. 2118.

Army Form C. 2118.

WAR DIARY
or
INTELLIGENCE SUMMARY.
(Erase heading not required.)

Instructions regarding War Diaries and Intelligence Summaries are contained in F. S. Regs., Part II. and the Staff Manual respectively. Title pages will be prepared in manuscript.

Place	Date 1915	Hour	Summary of Events and Information	Remarks and references to Appendices
1C				
POPERINGHE	1-12		Halted in billets near POPERINGHE at L9 a + b (Sheet 27) 21 men arrived from Base as re-inforcements to 17 D.A.	JCC
do.	2.12		Halted as above. Issued 100 rounds Trench Mortar Bombs 3.7".	JCC
do.	3.12		Halted as above. 20 re-inforcements who arrived on 1st were sent to various Batteries of the 17th D.A. 2 Lieut. P. O'Donnell R.F.A. reported his arrival on attachment to No 1 Section of this Unit under orders from 17 D.A.	JCC
do.	4.12		Halted as above	JCC JCC
do.	5.12		-do-	JCC
do	6-12		-do-	JCC
do.	7-12		-do-	JCC
do.	8-12		-do-	
do.	9-12		-do-	JCC

2353 Wt. W2544/1454 700,000 5/15 D. D. & L. A.D.S.S./Forms/C. 2118.

Instructions regarding War Diaries and Intelligence Summaries are contained in F. S. Regs., Part II. and the Staff Manual respectively. Title pages will be prepared in manuscript.

WAR DIARY
or
INTELLIGENCE SUMMARY.
(Erase heading not required.)

Army Form C. 2118.

Place	Date	Hour	Summary of Events and Information	Remarks and references to Appendices
	1915			
POPERINGHE	10-12		In billets at L 9 a & b (Sheet 27) 15 men (re-inforcements) joined from Base	FCC
do	11-12		In billets as above	FCC
do	12-12		-do- One man (re-inforcement) joined from Base	FCC
do	13-12		In Billets as above - Supplied 266000 rounds SAA to 78th Bde RFA, 267000 to 79th Bde RFA and 267000 to 80th Bde RFA	FCC
do-	14-12		In Billets as above -	FCC
do	15-12		-do-	FCC
do-	16-12		-do-	FCC
-do-	17-12		-do-	FCC
-do-	18-12		-do-	FCC
-do-	19-12		-do- No. 41840 Driver A. Hendley killed in action at Zillebeke Lake whilst working with 78th Bde R.F.A. and No 96442 Bdr. W. Burns was wounded at the same time & place	FCC
-do-	20-12		do-	FCC
do-	21-12		-do-	FCC
-do-	22-12		do.	FCC
do	23/12		In billets as above	FCC

2353 Wt. W2544/1454 700,000 5/15 D. D. & L. A.D.S.S./Forms/C. 2118.

Army Form C. 2118.

Instructions regarding War Diaries and Intelligence Summaries are contained in F. S. Regs., Part II. and the Staff Manual respectively. Title pages will be prepared in manuscript.

WAR DIARY
or
INTELLIGENCE SUMMARY.

(*Erase heading not required.*)

Place	Date 1915	Hour	Summary of Events and Information	Remarks and references to Appendices
POPERINGHE	24.12		In billets at L9a&b (Sheet 27)	FCC
do.	25.12		-do-	FCC
do.	26.12		-do-	FCC
do	27.12		-do-	FCC
do	28.12		-do- One horse wounded (shell fire) at VLAMERTINGHE	FCC
do	29.12		-do-	FCC
do.	30.12		-do-	FCC
do.	31.12		-do-	

[illegible signature]
LT. COL. R.F.A.
COMMANDING 17th DIV. AMM. COLM.

2353 Wt. W2544/1454 700,000 5/15 D. D. & L. A.D.S.S./Forms/C. 2118.

17th D.A.C.

Vol 7

Jan '16

Instructions regarding War Diaries and Intelligence Summaries are contained in F. S. Regs., Part II. and the Staff Manual respectively. Title Pages will be prepared in manuscript.

WAR DIARY
or
INTELLIGENCE SUMMARY
(Erase heading not required.)

Army Form C. 2118

Place	Date	Hour	Summary of Events and Information	Remarks and references to Appendices
			Confidential	
			War Diary	
			of	
			17th Divisional Ammunition Column	
			from 1/1/16 to 31/1/16.	
			J C Collins Lt RFA adjt for LT. COL. R.F.A. COMMANDING 17th DIV. AMM. COLM.	
	31/1/16		Volume 7	

1875 Wt. W593/826 1,000,000 4/15 J.B.C. & A. A.D.S.S./Forms/C. 2118.

Instructions regarding War Diaries and Intelligence Summaries are contained in F. S. Regs., Part II. and the Staff Manual respectively. Title pages will be prepared in manuscript.

WAR DIARY
or
INTELLIGENCE SUMMARY.
(Erase heading not required.)

Army Form C. 2118.

Place	Date 1916	Hour	Summary of Events and Information	Remarks and references to Appendices
POPERINGHE	1 Jany		In billets at L 9 a [illegible] (Sheet 27)	JCC
-do-	2 "		-do-	JCC
-do-	3 "		-do-	JCC
-do-	4 "		-do-	JCC
-do-	5 "		-do-	JCC
-do-	6		Unit marched to OCTHEZEELE en route to ZOUAFQUES. Drew 310000 rounds SAA and 52 BX from Park	JCC
-do-	7		Unit marched to ZOUAFQUES (10½ miles N.W. of ST. OMER) and went into billets there. No 1 Section occupied N end of village No 2 centre & No 3 South end of village. Took over ~~[illegible]~~ stock of ammunition left by 24th D.A.C. - This stack was badly arranged different natures of ammunition being mixed up. Too heavy rain to admit of it being taken out of the barn for counting.	JCC
-do-	8		In rest billets at ZOUAFQUES. Counting ammunition taken over from 24th D.A.C and found following Quantity*. Many of the boxes showed signs of exposure to weather & many boxes were opened. The ammunition was generally rusty and the boxes were very wet. * 523000 SAA 5375 A 778 A x 36 B 442 Bx 5836 Hand Grenades	JCC

Army Form C. 2118.

Instructions regarding War Diaries and Intelligence Summaries are contained in F. S. Regs., Part II. and the Staff Manual respectively. Title pages will be prepared in manuscript.

WAR DIARY
or
INTELLIGENCE SUMMARY.
(Erase heading not required.)

Place	Date	Hour	Summary of Events and Information	Remarks and references to Appendices
ZOUAFQUES	1915 9 Jany		In Rest billets at ZOUAFQUES. J.26.a.9.5 (sheet 27a) Continued inspection of ammunition. It was found that many boxes were not containing the ammunition marked on the lid eg 18pr H.E. were in shrapnel boxes & shrapnel in H.E. boxes in a few cases. The marking on some boxes could not be deciphered and these had to be opened to ascertain the nature of ammunition contained in them. In conducting this examination and also when ammunition has had to be handled at night the necessity for a different shaped box for 18pr H.E. from the box issued for shrapnel is very apparent. In the case of 4.5" How the shrapnel is packed in smaller boxes than lyddite or other H.E. while the handles on the shrapnel boxes are placed in the centre of the sides but at the ends of the sides in the H.E. boxes. A very large number of boxes of 18pr amm of US manufacture are being received. These boxes have no handles and are most difficult for rapid handling – otherwise this pattern box which opens at the end is far superior to the other patterns.	FCC
do	10 Jan		In Rest billets at ZOUAFQUES	FCC

2353 Wt. W2544/1454 700,000 5/15 D. D. & L. A.D.S.S./Forms/C. 2118.

Instructions regarding War Diaries and Intelligence Summaries are contained in F. S. Regs., Part II. and the Staff Manual respectively. Title pages will be prepared in manuscript.

WAR DIARY
or
INTELLIGENCE SUMMARY.
(*Erase heading not required.*)

Army Form C. 2118.

Place	Date 1916	Hour	Summary of Events and Information	Remarks and references to Appendices
ZOUAFQUES	Jan 11		In Rest billets at ZOUAFQUES J.26 a.0.5 (Sheet 27)	FCC
				FCC
-do-	Jan 12		-do-	FCC
			Lieut O'DONNELL left having been ordered to report to War Office. A Court of Enquiry ordered by GOCRA 17 Dv assembled to inspect the ammunition taken over from the 21st D.A.C. The Court in their finding expressed an opinion that the fuzes had probably deteriorated & should be handed back to the Park.	
-do-	Jan 13		In Rest billets at ZOUAFQUES	FCC
-do-	Jan 14		-do- Issued 76 rounds A to 78 Bde RFA and 50000 SAA to 7th East York Rgt.	FCC
-do-	Jan 15		In Rest billets at ZOUAFQUES. Issued 76A to 78 Bde RFA 96A and 45000 SAA to 80 Bde RFA 136000 SAA to 10 W Yorks 76A and 37000 SAA to 79 Bde RFA 38BX to 81st Bde RFA	FCC

Instructions regarding War Diaries and Intelligence Summaries are contained in F. S. Regs., Part II. and the Staff Manual respectively. Title pages will be prepared in manuscript.

WAR DIARY
or
INTELLIGENCE SUMMARY.
(Erase heading not required.)

Army Form C. 2118.

Place	Date 1916	Hour	Summary of Events and Information	Remarks and references to Appendices
ZOUAFQUES	16-1		In Rest billets at J.26.a.0.5 (Sheet 27 a) Issued 5000 saa + 552 pistol to 7 Border Rgt	JCC
do.	17.1		In Rest as above Issued to D.A.P. 3420 A and received 2508 A, 224 Bx and 360 Ax from D.A.P.	JCC
do.	18.1		In Rest as above Issued to D.A.P. 1946 A 776 Ax 36 B 84 Bx and received from D.A.P. 2184 A 556 Ax	JCC
do.	19.1.		In Rest as above Issued to B/78 14 A To 52 Infy Bde 80000 saa To D/78 - 70 A	JCC
do.	20.1		In Rest as above Issued 47 A to C/78 and 49 A to AC/80	JCC JCC
do.	21.1		In Rest as above.	JCC
do.	22.1		do.	JCC
do.	23.1		do.	JCC
do.	24.1		do. Issued 912 Ax to Park + 30 000 saa to Border Rgt Received 456 A 4 Ax from Park	
do.	25.1		In Rest as above.	JCC

2353 Wt. W2544/1454 700,000 5/15 D. D. & L. A.D.S.S./Forms/C. 2118.

Instructions regarding War Diaries and Intelligence Summaries are contained in F. S. Regs., Part II. and the Staff Manual respectively. Title Pages will be prepared in manuscript.

WAR DIARY
or
INTELLIGENCE SUMMARY
(Erase heading not required.)

Army Form C. 2118

Place	Date 1916	Hour	Summary of Events and Information	Remarks and references to Appendices
ZOUAFQUES	26.1		In Rest billets at J.26.a.0.5 (Sheet 27a) Issued 352 AX to D.A.P. received 568 A from D.A.P.	FCC
do.	27.1		In Rest billets as above	FCC
do.	28.1		In Rest as above. 13 Re-inforcements joined Issued 30000 SAA and 276 pistol to 7 Lincolns	FCC FCC
do.	29.1		In Rest as above. Issued 5000 SAA to 78 Coy R.E. 30000 SAA to Lincolns + 55000 to 7 Yorks	FCC
do.	30.1		In Rest as above. Issued 276 to 7 Lincolns, 25000 SAA to 7 Lincolns + 36000 SAA to 6 Dorsets	FCC FCC
do.	31.1		In Rest as above.	

F.C. Collins Lt R.F.A. Adjutant
for
LT. COL. R.F.A.
COMMANDING 17th DIV. AMM. COLM.

17th D AC

Vol: 8

Instructions regarding War Diaries and Intelligence Summaries are contained in F. S. Regs., Part II. and the Staff Manual respectively. Title pages will be prepared in manuscript.

WAR DIARY
or
INTELLIGENCE SUMMARY.
(Erase heading not required.)

Army Form C. 2118.

Place	Date	Hour	Summary of Events and Information	Remarks and references to Appendices
			Confidential War Diary of 17th Divisional Ammunition Column from 1/2/16 to 29/2/16 Volume 8 R W L Dunlop LT. COL. R.F.A. COMMANDING 17th DIV. AMM. COLM.	

T2134. Wt. W708—776. 500000. 4/15. Sir J. C. & S.

Army Form C. 2118

Instructions regarding War Diaries and Intelligence Summaries are contained in F. S. Regs., Part II. and the Staff Manual respectively. Title Pages will be prepared in manuscript.

WAR DIARY
or
INTELLIGENCE SUMMARY
(Erase heading not required.)

Place	Date 1916	Hour	Summary of Events and Information	Remarks and references to Appendices
ZOUAFQUES	1-2		In Rest at ZOUAFQUES (J.26.a.0.5 Sheet 27a) Issued 136000 rounds SAA to 78th Bde A.C.	FCC
do	2.2.		In Rest billets as above. Issued 20000 rounds SAA to 7: York Rgt	FCC
do.	3 2		In Rest billets as above. Issued 90000 SAA to 10 W. Yorks and 8000 SAA to 6 Dorsets	FCC FCC
do.	4 2		In Rest billets as above Received 20000 SAA from 7. Border Rgt Issued 95000 " to 52 Infy Bde 50000 " to 7 East Yorks	FCC
-do.	5.2		In Rest billets as above. Received from 78 Bde 3786 A, 246 AX, 405000 SAA " 79 " 3829 A, 201 AX, 345000 SAA for handing over to 3rd Dvnl. Arty. Issued 10000 SAA to York. Dragoons	FCC

1875 Wt. W593/826 1,000,000 4/15 J.B.C. & A. A.D.S.S./Forms/C. 2118.

Instructions regarding War Diaries and Intelligence Summaries are contained in F. S. Regs., Part II. and the Staff Manual respectively. Title Pages will be prepared in manuscript.

WAR DIARY
or
INTELLIGENCE SUMMARY
(Erase heading not required.)

Army Form C. 2118

Place	Date	Hour	Summary of Events and Information	Remarks and references to Appendices
	1916			
ZOUAFQUES	6.2		In Rest billets at ZOUAFQUES (J 26.a.0.5 Sheet 27A)	
			Received from 80th Bde RFA 3832 A 200 AX 355000 saa	JCC
			" 81st " " 84 B - 1786 BX	
			for handing over to 3rd Dvl Arty.	
			Recd from 17 Sub Park 80000 saa	
			Issued to AC/80th Bde. 1104 Pistol	JCC
-do-	7-2		In Rest billets as above-	
-do-	8-2		-do-	JCC
-do-	9-2		-do-	JCC
-do-	10-2		-do-	JCC
			Handed over following to 3rd D.A.C	
			1744000 saa 17193A 947 AX 84 B2316 BX 276 Pistol	JCC
do-	11-2		Marched to BUSSYCHEURE via SERQUES-St MOMELIN	
-do-	12-2		Marched to BOESCHEPE and occupied billets vacated by 3rd DAC as under:-	
			HQ. R.4.c.5.2 No1 Sec R9.b.6.5 No2 Sec R4.a.6.1 No.3 Sec R1.d.4.5 (Sheet 27)	JCC
			Took over 1086000 saa 2484 Pistol ~~876~~ 1120 AX and 216 BX from 3 DAC and issued 245000 saa and 2444 AX to 79th Bde AC	

1875 Wt. W593/826 1,000,000 4/15 J.B.C. & A. A.D.S.S./Forms/C. 2118.

Instructions regarding War Diaries and Intelligence Summaries are contained in F. S. Regs., Part II. and the Staff Manual respectively. Title Pages will be prepared in manuscript.

WAR DIARY
or
INTELLIGENCE SUMMARY
(Erase heading not required.)

Army Form C. 2118

Place	Date 1916	Hour	Summary of Events and Information	Remarks and references to Appendices
BOESCHEPE	13. 2		Billetted at Boeschepe	JCC
do	14. 2		" as above	JCC
			Received 1,488 Rds Mills Hand Grenades from 17th D.A.C.	
do	14-2		Issued 216 Rds BX to 81 Bde A/C	JCC
			Issued 876 Rds AX to 78 Bde RFA	
			Issued 1488 Rds Mills Hand Grenades to 51st Inf Bde	JCC
do	15. 2		Billetted as above	JCC
do	15-2		Issued 48,000 Rds SAA to Border Regiment	JCC
do	16-2		Billetted as above	
do	16-2		Issued 2484 Rds Pistol and 307,000 Rds SAA to 79 Amm Column	JCC
			Returned to Railhead 35,000 Rds "B" SAA and 6,000 Rds "N" SAA	JCC
do	16-2		Issued 20,000 Rds to 6th Dorset Regiment	JCC
do	17-2		Billetted as above.	JCC
do	17-2		Issued 40,000 Rds SAA to 76th Inf Bde	JCC
do	18. 2		Billetted as above.	
do	18. 2		30 Other Ranks Reinforcements joined from Base.	
do	18. 2		Issued 355,000 Rds SAA to 79th Bde Amm. Column.	

1875 Wt. W593/826 1,000,000 4/15 J.B.C. & A. A.D.S.S./Forms/C. 2118.

Army Form C. 2118.

Instructions regarding War Diaries and Intelligence Summaries are contained in F. S. Regs., Part II. and the Staff Manual respectively. Title pages will be prepared in manuscript.

WAR DIARY
or
INTELLIGENCE SUMMARY.
(Erase heading not required.)

Place	Date	Hour	Summary of Events and Information	Remarks and references to Appendices
BOESCHEPE	~~19.2.16~~ 19/2/16		Billetted at BOESCHEPE	
"	"		No 1 Section moved to R.7.b (Sheet 27)	
"	"		" 2 " " " R.1.d. -do-	FC
"	"		Issued 10,000 Rds SAA to 6th Dorset Regt	
"	"		" 40,000 Rds SAA to 76th Inf. Bde	
"	"		Received 8,556 Rds Pistol from 17th Amm Sub Park	
"	"		" 80,000 Rds SAA from 17th Amm Sub Park.	
"	20/2/16		Billetted as above	FC
"	"		Received from 17th D.A.P. 200,000 Rds SAA.	
"	21/2/16		" " " 240,000 Rds SAA.	
"	"		Issued to 19 Bde Amm Col 8,280 Rds Pistol Ammunition	FC
"	"		" " 180,000 Rds SAA	
"			Received from 17th DAP 240,000 Rds SAA	
"	22/2/16		Billetted as above	FC
"	"		Received from 17th D.A.P. 240,000 Rds SAA	
"	23/2/16		Billetted as above	FC

T2134. Wt. W708—776. 500000. 4/15. Sir J. C. & S.

Instructions regarding War Diaries and Intelligence Summaries are contained in F. S. Regs., Part II. and the Staff Manual respectively. Title pages will be prepared in manuscript.

WAR DIARY
or
INTELLIGENCE SUMMARY.
(Erase heading not required.)

Army Form C. 2118.

Place	Date	Hour	Summary of Events and Information	Remarks and references to Appendices
	1916			
BOESCHEPE	24.2		In billets as under H.Q. R.&.C.5.2 No1 Sec R.7.b. " 2. R.1.d. " 3. R.1.d.4.5	FCC
"	25.2		In billets as above Recd. 880000 saa from 17th A. S Park Issued 100000 saa to 76th Infy Bde	FCC
"	26.2		In billets as above Recd. 300000 saa from 17 S Park; Issued 500000 SAA to 76 Infy Bde	FCC
"	27.2		In billets as above. Issued 200000 saa to 79th Bde AC Recd 500000 saa from 17 Sub Park	FCC
"	28.2		In billets as above. Issued 200000 saa to 80th Bde AC Recd. 200000 saa from 17 Sub Park	FCC
"	29.2		In billets as above –	FCC

Instructions regarding War Diaries and Intelligence Summaries are contained in F. S. Regs., Part II. and the Staff Manual respectively. Title pages will be prepared in manuscript.

WAR DIARY
or
INTELLIGENCE SUMMARY.
(Erase heading not required.)

Army Form C. 2118.

Place	Date	Hour	Summary of Events and Information	Remarks and references to Appendices
	1916			
BOESCHEPE	29.2		200000 Rds. SAA supplied 80th Bde AC 300000 Rds. SAA recd 17th Sub Park	JCC.

1/3/16

J. C. Collins Lt RAfp

for LT. COL. R.F.A.
COMMANDING 17th DIV. AMM. COLM.

T2134. Wt. W708—776. 500000. 4/15. Sir J. C. & S.

Army Form C. 2118

Instructions regarding War Diaries and Intelligence Summaries are contained in F. S. Regs., Part II. and the Staff Manual respectively. Title Pages will be prepared in manuscript.

WAR DIARY
or
INTELLIGENCE SUMMARY
(Erase heading not required.)

Place	Date	Hour	Summary of Events and Information	Remarks and references to Appendices
			Confidential	17 Div A C Vol 9
			War Diary	
			of	
			17th Divisional Ammunition Column.	
			from 1/3/16 to 31/3/16.	
31/3/16.			Volume 9.	
			[signature] LT. COL. R.F.A. COMMANDING 17th DIV. AMM. COLM.	

1875 Wt. W593/826 1,000,000 4/15 J.B.C. & A. A.D.S.S./Forms/C. 2118.

Instructions regarding War Diaries and Intelligence Summaries are contained in F. S. Regs., Part II. and the Staff Manual respectively. Title pages will be prepared in manuscript.

WAR DIARY
or
INTELLIGENCE SUMMARY.
(Erase heading not required.)

Army Form C. 2118.

Place	Date	Hour	Summary of Events and Information	Remarks and references to Appendices
	1916			
BORRE	23-3		Issued to 21st D.A.C 216 Rds A 548 Rds AX 176 Rds BX	Rhes
"			" " 328,000 Rds SAA	
do	24-3		In billets at BORRE	Rhes
			Issued to 21st D.A.C 176 Rds BX	
do	25-3		No2 Section proceeded to ARMENTIERIES as advanced Section and occupied billets at B 15.d.8.0 Sheet (36)	Rhes
do	26.3		No3 Section marched to LA CRECHE and occupied billet as follows A 6.a.1.8. Sheet (36)	Rhes
do	27.3		H.Q. and No1 Section in billets at BORRE	Rhes
			Issued to No3 Section 21st Div. Amm Col.	
			246,000 Rds SAA 1,404 A 648 AX 176 BX	
do	28.3		In billets as above	Rhes
do	29.3		do	Rhes
do	30.3		do	Rhes
do	31.3		do	Rhes

T2134. Wt. W708—776. 500000. 4/15. Sir J. C. & S.

Instructions regarding War Diaries and Intelligence Summaries are contained in F. S. Regs., Part II. and the Staff Manual respectively. Title pages will be prepared in manuscript.

WAR DIARY
or
INTELLIGENCE SUMMARY.
(*Erase heading not required.*)

Army Form C. 2118.

Place	Date	Hour	Summary of Events and Information	Remarks and references to Appendices
	1916			
BOESCHEPE	1.3		In billets as follows:- (sheet 27)	
			H.Qrs R 9.b.2.8.	[illegible]
			No 1 Sec R.7.b.	
			" 2 " R.1.d.	
			" 3 " R.1.d.5.6	
			Issued 300000 Rds saa to 80th Bde A Col.	
			" 320000 Rds saa to 79th Bde A Col	
			Received 620000 Rds saa from 17 Sub Park	
-do-	2.3.		In billets as above.	[illegible]
do.			Issued 60000 to 8th S. Stafford Rgt	[illegible]
-do-	3.3		In billets as above.	[illegible]
-do-	4.3		-do-	[illegible]
			Received 80000 Rds SAA from Sub Park	
-do-	5.3.		In billets as above.	[illegible]
-do-	6.3.		-do-	[illegible]
-do-	7.3		-do-	[illegible]

T2134. Wt. W708—776. 500000. 4/15. Sir J. C. & S.

Instructions regarding War Diaries and Intelligence Summaries are contained in F. S. Regs., Part II. and the Staff Manual respectively. Title pages will be prepared in manuscript.

WAR DIARY
or
INTELLIGENCE SUMMARY.
(Erase heading not required.)

Army Form C. 2118.

Place	Date	Hour	Summary of Events and Information	Remarks and references to Appendices
	1916			
BOESCHEPE	8.3		In billets as follows:- (Sheet 27)	
			HQrs R.9.b.2.8., No 1 Sec. R.7.b., No 3 Sec R.1.d. 5-6	FC
			No 2 Sec. R.1.d.	
"	9.3		In billets as above	FC
"	10.3		do	FC
	11.3		do.	FC
BORRE	12.3		Marched to BORRE & went into billets as follows. - (Sheet 27)	FC
			HQ W.19.d.5.8	
			No 1 -do-	
			No 2 - W 20 c.1.8	
			No 3 W 20.b.0.6	
			Received 1844 AX and 20 A from Sub Park	
do-	13.3		In billets as above -	
			Received 3780 A from 3 D A C	FC
do	14.3		In billets as above	FC
do-	15.3		do-	FC

Army Form C. 2118.

Instructions regarding War Diaries and Intelligence Summaries are contained in F. S. Regs., Part II. and the Staff Manual respectively. Title pages will be prepared in manuscript.

WAR DIARY
or
INTELLIGENCE SUMMARY.
(*Erase heading not required.*)

Place	Date	Hour	Summary of Events and Information	Remarks and references to Appendices
	1916			
BORRE	16.3		In billets at BORRE	
			Received from 17th Sub Park 440 A and 74 BX	JCC
			Issued to 8/21. Bde AC 74 BX	
do.	17.3		In billets at BORRE	
			Issued to 79th Bde AC 40 A	JCC
do.	18.3		In billets at BORRE	JCC
do.	19.3		do.	JCC
do.	20.3		do.	JCC
do			Issued to 21st Div Amm Col 648 Rds A	RHR
			Received from 17th at SP 246,000 Rds SAA 4 Rds A	RHR
			Issued to 21st Div Amm Col 246,000 Rds SAA 4 Rds A	RHR
do	21.3		In billets at BORRE	RHR
			Issued to 21st Div. Amm. Col 648 Rds A	
do	22.3		In billets at BORRE	RHR
			Issued to 21st Div Amm Col 1284 Rds A 648 Rds AX	
do	23.3		In billets at BORRE	RHR

17 Div A C

Army Form C. 2118.

Vol 10

Instructions regarding War Diaries and Intelligence Summaries are contained in F. S. Regs., Part II. and the Staff Manual respectively. Title pages will be prepared in manuscript.

WAR DIARY
or
INTELLIGENCE SUMMARY.

(*Erase heading not required.*)

Place	Date	Hour	Summary of Events and Information	Remarks and references to Appendices
			Confidential	
			War Dairies for the month of April of	
			17th Divisional Ammunition Column.	
			from 1/4/16 to 30/4/16.	
			F.C. Collins Lt RFA Adjt for LT. COL. R.F.A. COMMANDING 17th DIV. AMM. COLM.	
30/4/16	Volume. 10.			

T2134. Wt. W708—776. 500000. 4/15. Sir J. C. & S.

Instructions regarding War Diaries and Intelligence Summaries are contained in F. S. Regs., Part II. and the Staff Manual respectively. Title pages will be prepared in manuscript.

WAR DIARY
or
INTELLIGENCE SUMMARY.
(Erase heading not required.)

Army Form C. 2118.

Place	Date	Hour	Summary of Events and Information	Remarks and references to Appendices
Borre	1/4/16		HQ vacated billets at Borre and marched to ARMENTIERES occupying billets at H 6a 9.9 (Sheet 36). No 1 Section vacated billets at BORRE and marched to ST JANS CAPPEL occupying billets at R 35 c 5.3 (Sheet 27) No 3 Section in billets at A 6 c 0 0 (LA CRECHE) Sheet 36, No 2 Section in billets at NIEPPE B15d 4.2 (Sheet 36)	Fcc
ARMENTIERES	2/4/16		In billets as above	Fcc
do	3/4/16		do	Fcc
do	4/4/16		do	Fcc
do	5/4/16		do	Fcc
do	6/4/16		do	Fcc
do	7/4/16		do	Fcc
do	8/4/16		do 12 Reinforcements joined No 3 Sec and 1 Reinforcement joined No 1 Sec from No 2 Depot Base.	Fcc
do	9/4/16		In billets as above	Fcc
do	10/4/16		do	Fcc
do	11/4/16		do	Fcc

Instructions regarding War Diaries and Intelligence Summaries are contained in F. S. Regs., Part II. and the Staff Manual respectively. Title pages will be prepared in manuscript.

WAR DIARY
or
INTELLIGENCE SUMMARY.
(Erase heading not required.)

Army Form C. 2118.

Place	Date	Hour	Summary of Events and Information	Remarks and references to Appendices
ARMENTIERES	12/4/16		In Billets as stated No1 Section R35C 5.3 Sheet 27 No 2 Section B15 d 4.2 NIEPPE Sheet 36 No3 Section A6C00 LA CRECHE Sheet 36, HQ H6A 9.9 ARMENIERES Sheet 36	FCC
do	13/4/16		In Billets as above	FCC
do	14/4/16		do 14 Reinforcements joined from No 2 Depot-Base	FCC
do	15/4/16		do	FCC
do	16/4/16		do	FCC
do	17/4/16		do	FCC
do	18/4/16		do	FCC
do	19/4/16		do	FCC
do	20/4/16		do	FCC
do	21/4/16		do	FCC
do	22/4/16		do	FCC
do	23/4/16		do	FCC
do	24/4/16		do	FCC
do	25/4/16		do	FCC
do	26/4/16		do	FCC

T2134. Wt. W708—776. 500000. 4/15. Sir J. C. & S.

Instructions regarding War Diaries and Intelligence Summaries are contained in F. S. Regs., Part II. and the Staff Manual respectively. Title pages will be prepared in manuscript.

WAR DIARY
or
INTELLIGENCE SUMMARY.
(Erase heading not required.)

Army Form C. 2118.

Place	Date	Hour	Summary of Events and Information	Remarks and references to Appendices
ARMENTIERES	27/6/16		In Billets as Stated No 1 Section R35c5.3 Sheet 27 No 2 Section B15d4.2 NIEPPE No 3 Section A6c0.0 LA CRECHE Sheet 36, HQ H6A9.9 ARMENTIERES Sheet 36.	HC
do	28/6/16		In Billets as above	HC
do	29/6/16		do	HC
do	30/6/16		do	HC

HC Collins Lt RFA
Adjt for
LT. COL. R.F.A.
COMMANDING 17th DIV. AMM. COLM.

T2134. Wt. W708—776. 500000. 4/15. Sir J. C. & S.

Instructions regarding War Diaries and Intelligence Summaries are contained in F. S. Regs., Part II. and the Staff Manual respectively. Title Pages will be prepared in manuscript.

WAR DIARY
or
INTELLIGENCE SUMMARY
(Erase heading not required.)

Army Form C. 2118

17th DAC

Vol 11

Place	Date	Hour	Summary of Events and Information	Remarks and references to Appendices
			Confidential	
			War Dairies for the month of May of 17th Divisional Ammunition Column. from 1/5/16 to 31/5/16.	
			[signature] LT. COL. R.F.A. COMMANDING 17th DIV. AMM. COLM.	
			31/5/16. Volume 11	

1875 Wt. W593/826 1,000,000 4/15 J.B.C. & A. A.D.S.S./Forms/C. 2118.

Instructions regarding War Diaries and Intelligence Summaries are contained in F. S. Regs., Part II. and the Staff Manual respectively. Title pages will be prepared in manuscript.

WAR DIARY
or
INTELLIGENCE SUMMARY.
(Erase heading not required.)

Army Form C. 2118.

Place	Date	Hour	Summary of Events and Information	Remarks and references to Appendices
ARMENTIERES	1/5/16.		In Billets as stated H.Q. H6a 9.9. Sheet 36, No1 Sect. R35 c 5.3 Sheet 27 ST JANS CAPPEL No2 Section B.15.d 4.2. Sheet 36 NIEPPE, No 3 Section A 6 C 0 0 Sheet 36 LA CRECHE	JCC
do	2/5/16		In billets as above	JCC
do	3/5/16		do	JCC
do	4/5/16		do	JCC
do	5/5/16		do	JCC
do	6/5/16		do	JCC
do	7/5/16		do	JCC
do	8/5/16		do	JCC
do	9/5/16		do	JCC
do	10/5/16		do	JCC
do	11/5/16		do.	JCC
do	13/5/16		do.	
			Re-organization of Unit ordered. A 4th Section to be formed from Bde A Colm of Div Arty.	JCC
			Re-organization commenced	

T2134. Wt. W708—776. 500000. 4/15. Sir J. C. & S.

Instructions regarding War Diaries and Intelligence Summaries are contained in F. S. Regs., Part II. and the Staff Manual respectively. Title pages will be prepared in manuscript.

WAR DIARY
or
INTELLIGENCE SUMMARY.
(Erase heading not required.)

Army Form C. 2118.

Place	Date	Hour	Summary of Events and Information	Remarks and references to Appendices
ARMENTIERES	13/5/16		In billets as follows:–	
			H.Q. H.6.a.9.9 Sheet 36	FCC
			No 1 Sec R.35.c.5.3 " 27	
			" 2 " B.15.d.4.2 " 36	
			" 3 " A.6.c.0.0 " 36	
			" 4 " " 36	
			Re-organization of Unit proceeding	
"	14/5/16		In billets as above.	FCC
			Re-organization completed	
			Following Officers posted to Unit to complete Estab:–	
			Capt H Morgan to command No 4 Section } from Bde A. Colm	
			Lt. A J Dainty } from Bde A. Colm	
			" J D Hindley Smith } posted No 4 Sec } from Bde A. Colm	
			J Snebbington } posted No 4 Sec } from Bde A. Colm	
			" N W Stocken } posted No 4 Sec } from Bde A. Colm	
			" W Skelton posted to No 1 Section } from Bde A. Colm	
			J G Sproule " " 2 " from Base	
			Lt. A B Haynes " " 3	

Instructions regarding War Diaries and Intelligence Summaries are contained in F. S. Regs., Part II. and the Staff Manual respectively. Title pages will be prepared in manuscript.

WAR DIARY
or
INTELLIGENCE SUMMARY.
(Erase heading not required.)

Army Form C. 2118.

Place	Date	Hour	Summary of Events and Information	Remarks and references to Appendices
ARMENTIERES	15 5/16		In Billets as follows:-	JCC
			HQrs H.6.a.9.9 Sheet 36	
			No 1 Sec R.35.c.5.3. " 27	
			2 " B.15.a.4.2 " 36	
			3 " A.6.c.0.0 " 36	
			4 " B.21.a.6.2 " 36	
			Capt. E C Ridout posted to No 1 Sect. vice Capt J J Reilly to Base	
"	16 5/16		In billets as above	JCC
	17 5/16		do	JCC
	18 5/16		do	JCC
	19 5/16		do Handed over all Ammunition to New Zealand Div. DAC	JCC
	20 5/16		Unit marched to billeting area around VIEUX-BERQUIN	JCC
	21 5/16		Unit marched to RENESCURE	JCC
	22 5/16		Unit marched to SENINGHEM and went into billets there	JCC
SENINGHEM	23 5/16		In billets at SENINGHEM	JCC
do.	24 5/16		do. Commenced Training with 17 Dvl. Arty	JCC

Instructions regarding War Diaries and Intelligence Summaries are contained in F. S. Regs., Part II. and the Staff Manual respectively. Title pages will be prepared in manuscript.

WAR DIARY
or
INTELLIGENCE SUMMARY.
(*Erase heading not required.*)

Army Form C. 2118.

Place	Date	Hour	Summary of Events and Information	Remarks and references to Appendices
SENINGHEM	25/5/11		In billets at SENINGHEM - Training with 17th D. Arty	FCe
do	26/5/11		— do —	FCe
do.	27/5/11		— do —	FCe
			Issued 80000 rds to 50 Infy Bde	
			" 80000 to 52 Infy Bde	
do.	28/5/11		In billets at SENINGHEM - Training with 17th D Arty.	FCe
d.	29		Issued 1000 rds SAA to 77 Coy RE	
			" 30000 " " to 7 York & Lancs Rgt & 1 box pistol Amn	
			" 68000 " " to 52 Infy Bde	
			40000 " " to 50 " "	
do.	29/5/11		In billets at SENINGHEM - Training with 17th D. Arty	FCe
			Issued 12000 rds SAA to 7 Border Rgt	
			Recd 197000 rds SAA from 17 Sub Park	
d.	30/5/11		In billets at SENINGHEM - Training with 17 D Arty	FCe
			Issued 16000 rds SAA to S. Stafford Rgt	
			Recd 15000 rds SAA & 3312 pistol Amn from 17 Sub Park	

T2134. Wt. W708—776. 500000. 4/15. Sir J. C. & S.

Instructions regarding War Diaries and Intelligence Summaries are contained in F. S. Regs., Part II. and the Staff Manual respectively. Title pages will be prepared in manuscript.

WAR DIARY
or
INTELLIGENCE SUMMARY.
(Erase heading not required.)

Army Form C. 2118.

Place	Date	Hour	Summary of Events and Information	Remarks and references to Appendices
SENINGHEM	31/5/16		In billets at SENINGHEM – Training with 17th D. Arty Issued 1000 rds S.A.A. to C/79 Bde RFA	FCC

F. C. Collins Lt RFA
for LT. COL. R.F.A.
COMMANDING 17th DIV. AMM. COLM.

T2134. Wt. W708—776. 500000. 4/15. Sir J. C. & S.

17 Div AC

Army Form C. 2118

Vol 12
June

Instructions regarding War Diaries and Intelligence Summaries are contained in F. S. Regs., Part II. and the Staff Manual respectively. Title Pages will be prepared in manuscript.

WAR DIARY
or
INTELLIGENCE SUMMARY
(Erase heading not required.)

Place	Date	Hour	Summary of Events and Information	Remarks and references to Appendices
			Confidential War Diaries for the month of June of 17th Divisional Ammunition Column from 1/6/16 to 30/6/16. R W L Dunlop LT. COL. R.F.A. COMMANDING 17th DIV. AMM. COLM	
		30/6/16	Volume 12	

1875 Wt. W593/826 1,000,000 4/15 J.B.C. & A. A.D.S.S./Forms/C. 2118.

Instructions regarding War Diaries and Intelligence Summaries are contained in F. S. Regs., Part II. and the Staff Manual respectively. Title pages will be prepared in manuscript.

WAR DIARY
or
INTELLIGENCE SUMMARY.
(Erase heading not required.)

Army Form C. 2118.

Place	Date	Hour	Summary of Events and Information	Remarks and references to Appendices
	1916			
SENINGHEM	1-6		In billets at SENINGHEM (Sheet 5A). - Training with 17th Dvn.	FCC
"			Lieut. F J Barrett joined on posting.	
"	2 6		In billets + training as above.	FCC
			Issued 100 Rds A' to 'A' Bty 80 Bde RFA & 20000 Rds SAA to 10th Sherwood Forsters	
"	3.6		In billets & training as above.	FCC
"	4.6		- do -	
			Issued 14000 Rds SAA to Y & L. Rgt	FCC
"	5.6		In billets & training as above.	FCC
			Issued 60000 SAA to 52 Infy Bde + 17000 SAA to 8th S Staffs	
"	6 6		In billets & training as above	FCC
			Issued 30000 rds SAA to 7 Border Rgt. - Lt A Fitter to Anti Aircraft (17th D)	
"	7.6		In billets & training as above.	FCC
"	8 6		- do -	FCC
"	9.6		In billets as above	FCC
"	10.6		- do -	FCC
"	11-6 } 12-6 }		During the night 11-12 June 1916 the unit marched to THEROUANNE.	FCC

Army Form C. 2118.

Instructions regarding War Diaries and Intelligence Summaries are contained in F. S. Regs., Part II. and the Staff Manual respectively. Title pages will be prepared in manuscript.

WAR DIARY
or
INTELLIGENCE SUMMARY.
(Erase heading not required.)

Place	Date	Hour	Summary of Events and Information	Remarks and references to Appendices
	1916			
	12.6 / 13.6		During the night 12-13 June the unit marched to ANVIN and WAVRANS.	F.C.
	13.6 / 14.6		During the night 13-14 June the unit marched to BOUQUETMAISON and NOUVELLETTE	F.C.
	14.6 / 15.6		During the night 14-15 June the unit marched to TALMAS and VILLERS BOCAGE	F.C.
	15.6 / 16.6		During the night 15-16 June the unit marched to HEILLY. During the 16th final arrangements were made for the unit to be attached to the 7th & 21st Div. Arty.	F.C.
	17.6		Sections marched as follows:- No 1 Sec. less 1 subsection, " 2 " — " —, ½ How Section (3 subsections) } to a camp 500 W of Church at VILLE-SUR-CORBIE on attachment to the 21st D.A.C. No 3 Sec less 1 subsection, Three subsections of 1, 2 & 3 sections } to a camp at the village of MORLANCOURT on attachment to the 7th D.A.C. ½ How Section to a camp at TREUX on attachment to the 7th D.A.C. Head Quarters remained at HEILLY.	F.C.

Instructions regarding War Diaries and Intelligence Summaries are contained in F. S. Regs., Part II. and the Staff Manual respectively. Title pages will be prepared in manuscript.

WAR DIARY
or
INTELLIGENCE SUMMARY.
(*Erase heading not required.*)

Army Form C. 2118.

Place	Date	Hour	Summary of Events and Information	Remarks and references to Appendices
	1916			
	18.6		No change. Sections attached 7 & 21st D.A. - HQ at J.7.d.3.8 (Sheet 62D)	FCC
	19.6		-do- -do-	FCC
	20.6		-do- -do-	FCC
	21.6		-do- -do-	
	22.6		-do- -do-	
	23.6		-do- -do-	
	24.6		-do- -do-	
	25.6		-do- HQs moved to J.6.a.0.5	FCC
	26.6		-do- -do-	FCC
	27.6		-do- do-	FCC
	28.6		-do- -do-	FCC
	29.6		-do- -do-	FCC
	30.6		do- -do	FCC

FC Collins Lt RFA & Adjt
for Comdg 17 D.A.C

T2134. Wt. W708—776. 500000. 4/15. Sir J. C. & S.

17th Div.
XV.Corps.

WAR DIARY

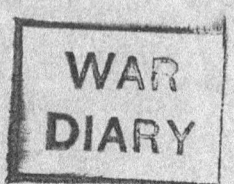

17th DIVISIONAL AMMUNITION COLUMN.

J U L Y

1 9 1 6

Army Form C. 2118.

Instructions regarding War Diaries and Intelligence Summaries are contained in F. S. Regs., Part II. and the Staff Manual respectively. Title Pages will be prepared in manuscript.

WAR DIARY
or
INTELLIGENCE SUMMARY

(Erase heading not required.)

17 D A C

Vol 13

Place	Date	Hour	Summary of Events and Information	Remarks and references to Appendices
			Confidential	
			War Diaries for the month of July of 17th Divisional Ammunition Column from 1/7/16 to 31/7/16.	
			Volume 13.	
			R H Smith LT. COL. R.F.A. COMMANDING 17th DIV. AMM. COLM.	
	31/7/16.			

2449 Wt. W14957/M90 750,000 1/16 J.B.C. & A. Forms/C.2118/12.

Instructions regarding War Diaries and Intelligence Summaries are contained in F. S. Regs., Part II. and the Staff Manual respectively. Title pages will be prepared in manuscript.

WAR DIARY
or
INTELLIGENCE SUMMARY.
(Erase heading not required.)

Army Form C. 2118.

Place	Date	Hour	Summary of Events and Information	Remarks and references to Appendices
	1916			
	1-7		Unit split up as under:-	
			No 1 & No 2 Sections less 1 Subsection of each } attached to 21st DAC &	
			Three subsections No 4 Section } under orders of 21st D.A.	
			No 3 Section less 1 subsection } Attached to 7th DAC &	JCC
			One subsection from each of Nos 1, 2 & 3 Sections } under orders of 7th D.A.	
			Three subsections No 4 Section }	
			Head Quarters at J.6 a.6.4 (Sheet 62D)	
	2.7		As above	JCC
	3.7		do.	JCC
	4.7		do.	JCC
	5.7		do.	JCC
			1 Saddler, 3 Grs. 9 Drs. Reinforcements received from Base	
	6.7		No change	JCC
	7.7		do.	JCC
	8.7		do.	
			1 Saddler, 2 Grs. Killed in action and 1 Gr. severely wounded	JC

T2134. Wt. W708—776. 500000. 4/15. Sir J. C. & S.

Instructions regarding War Diaries and Intelligence Summaries are contained in F. S. Regs., Part II. and the Staff Manual respectively. Title pages will be prepared in manuscript.

WAR DIARY
or
INTELLIGENCE SUMMARY.
(Erase heading not required.)

Army Form C. 2118.

Place	Date	Hour	Summary of Events and Information	Remarks and references to Appendices
	1916			
	9.7		Unit remains as on 1st	FCC
	10.7		No Change	FCC
	11.7		do	FCC
	12.7		do	FCC
	13.7		do. 1 Bdr. wounded in action	FCC
			2 S.S Corpls., 2 Bdrs., 1 Fitter, 1 Wheeler, 31 Grs., 12 Drs. reinforcements received from Base.	
			7 L.D. Horses posted to 78th Bde R.F.A	
	14.7		No change	FCC
	15.7		do.	
			2 S.S Cpls, 2 Bdrs, 1 Fitter, 31 Grs, 12 Drs. posted to 17th D.A. Brigades	
	16.7		No Change	FCC
	18.7		do.	FCC
	19.7		do	
			3 Grs posted to 17th D.A Brigades	FCC
	20.7		No change as regards detail attached 21st D.A	FCC

T2134. Wt. W708—776. 500000. 4/15. Sir J. C. & S.

WAR DIARY
or
INTELLIGENCE SUMMARY.
(Erase heading not required.)

Army Form C. 2118.

Instructions regarding War Diaries and Intelligence Summaries are contained in F. S. Regs., Part II. and the Staff Manual respectively. Title pages will be prepared in manuscript.

Place	Date	Hour	Summary of Events and Information	Remarks and references to Appendices
	1916			
	20.5		The detail attached 17 D.A. viz	FCC
			No 3 Section less 1 Subsection	
			One Subsection from each of Nos. 1, 2 & 3 Sections	
			Three Subsections No 4 Section	
			now attached to 5th D.A.	
			2 Corpls 1 a/Br posted to 17th D.A. Brigades also 31 Grs & 19 Drs	
	21.5		No change in distribution	FCC
			2Lt Hindley Smith No 4 Sec. to 80th Bde as Actg. Adjt.	
			1 Fitter Staff Sergt, 5 Sergts, 2 a/Br 6 Grs 2 Drs posted to 17 D.A. Brigades	
			8 ~~LD~~ Riders & 20 L.D. Horses posted to 17 D.A. Brigades	
	22.5		No change in distribution	FCC
			3 Bdrs joined from Base	
	23.5		No change in distribution	FCC
			3 Bdrs posted to 17 D.A. Brigades	
	24.5		No change in distribution	FCC
			40 Grs & 30 Drs reinforcements received from Base	

T2134. Wt. W708—776. 500000. 4/15. Sir J. C. & S.

Army Form C. 2118.

Instructions regarding War Diaries and Intelligence Summaries are contained in F. S. Regs., Part II. and the Staff Manual respectively. Title pages will be prepared in manuscript.

WAR DIARY
or
INTELLIGENCE SUMMARY.
(Erase heading not required.)

Place	Date	Hour	Summary of Events and Information	Remarks and references to Appendices
	1916			
	25.7		Sections ceased attachment to 5th & 21st Divisions and marching from their bivouacks in action bivouacked as follows:–	
			HQrs. at D.30.d.4.3 Sheet 62D	FCo
			No 1 Sec at D.30.d.5.7 do.	
			" 2 " at D.30.d.5.7 do.	
			" 3 " at J.6.a.6.4 do.	
			" 4 " at D.30.d.4.3. do.	
	26.7		As above	FCo
			Lieut E.H.T Bartlett joined & posted to No 4 Sec	
	27.7		As above	FCo
			2Lt. E.B MIRGAN joined & posted to No 1 Sec	
			1 NCO wounded in action	
			1 NCO + 1 man accidentally wounded	
	28.7		No change	FCo
	29.7		Unit marched to E.20.a.3.3 & bivouacked there	FCo

T2134. Wt. W708—776. 500000. 4/15. Sir J. C. & S.

Instructions regarding War Diaries and Intelligence Summaries are contained in F. S. Regs., Part II. and the Staff Manual respectively. Title pages will be prepared in manuscript.

WAR DIARY
or
INTELLIGENCE SUMMARY.
(Erase heading not required.)

Army Form C. 2118.

Place	Date	Hour	Summary of Events and Information	Remarks and references to Appendices
	1916			
	30.7		In bivouacks at E 20 a 3.3.	Fee
	31.7		do	Fee
			Summary of Casualties July 1916	
			Killed / Wounded in action / Wounded accidentally	
	17480		Saddler Griffiths J. 41397 Bdr. Tee J. 38517 Bdr Gainger J	Fee
	7135		Gnr. Barlow J. 77098 " Shaw H. 18834 Gr Sharpe J	
	42554		" Hoskins J.A 31197 Gnr Goodspeed C.H.	
			R.A.S. Drake (?) Lt. Col.	
			LT. COL. R.F.A. COMMANDING 17th DIV. AMM. COLM.	
			31/7/16	

T2134. Wt. W708—776. 500000. 4/15. Sir J. C. & S.

Wastage from Sickness
(other than battle casualties)
during past month.

Officers 1

O. Ranks. 3.

R W L Dunlop

3/7/16

LT. COL. R.F.A.
COMMANDING 17th DIV. AMM. COLM.

17th Divisional Amm Column.

17th DIVISIONAL AMMUNITION COLUMN

AUGUST 1 9 1 6

Army Form C. 2118.

VOL 14

D.A.C.

Instructions regarding War Diaries and Intelligence Summaries are contained in F. S. Regs., Part II. and the Staff Manual respectively. Title Pages will be prepared in manuscript.

WAR DIARY
or
INTELLIGENCE SUMMARY

(Erase heading not required.)

Place	Date	Hour	Summary of Events and Information	Remarks and references to Appendices
			Confidential.	
			War Diaries for the month of July of 17th Divisional Ammunition Column from 1/8/16 to 31/8/16	
			Volume 14	
			[illegible] LT. COL. R.F.A. COMMANDING 17th DIV. AMM. COLM.	
			31/8/16	

2449 Wt. W14957/M90 750,000 1/16 J.B.C. & A. Forms/C.2118/12.

Army Form C. 2118.

Instructions regarding War Diaries and Intelligence Summaries are contained in F. S. Regs., Part II. and the Staff Manual respectively. Title Pages will be prepared in manuscript.

WAR DIARY
or
INTELLIGENCE SUMMARY
(Erase heading not required.)

Place	Date 1916	Hour	Summary of Events and Information	Remarks and references to Appendices
DERNANCOURT	1-8		In bivouacks at E 20.a.3.3 Took over an Ammunition Dump near BECORDEL at E 12.b.9.2 Lieut Haynes posted to C/80 Bde RFA 2/Lieuts Officer, Simpson & Strickland joined from Base 32 remounts (LD horses) received	FCC
do near ALBERT	2-8		Moved to E 16.b.0.8 2/Lieut Reed joined from Base	FCC
do	3-8		In bivouacs at E.16.b.0.8 Captain Priestley & 28 men joined from Base	FCC
do	4-8		In bivouacs at E 16.b.0.8	FCC
do	5-8		-do-	FCC
do	6-8		-do- 2/Lieut D Henderson joined from Base	FCC
do	7-8		In bivouacs at E 16.b.0.8 30 Remounts (LD horses) received Capt. Priestly left for Base – 2Lts Sproule & Strickland to 81st Bde	FCC

Army Form C. 2118.

WAR DIARY
or
INTELLIGENCE SUMMARY
(Erase heading not required.)

Instructions regarding War Diaries and Intelligence Summaries are contained in F. S. Regs., Part II. and the Staff Manual respectively. Title Pages will be prepared in manuscript.

Place	Date 1916	Hour	Summary of Events and Information	Remarks and references to Appendices
near ALBERT	8-8		In bivouacs at E 16. d. 0. 8 2Lt Alder joined from 79th Bde R.F.A.	FCC
"	9-8		-do- CRA inspected the camp 17 Drivers - reinforcements - joined from Base	FCC
"	10-8		In bivouacs as above. 2Lt Offer and 2Lt Stocking posted to 78 Bde R.F.A. 2Lt Reed and 2Lt Simpson posted to 79 Bde R.F.A. Capt. W. Priestley rejoined, not having proceeded to Base Lieut. I Martin joined from 79th Bde R.F.A.	FCC
"	11-8		In bivouacs as above	FCC
"	12-8		do- Captain W Priestley to 53rd Field Ambulance	FCC
"	13.8		In camp as above 2Lt Stubbington rejoined from the Base.-	FCC
"	14-8		No change	FCC
"	15.8		No change	FCC

Army Form C. 2118.

Instructions regarding War Diaries and Intelligence Summaries are contained in F. S. Regs., Part II. and the Staff Manual respectively. Title Pages will be prepared in manuscript.

WAR DIARY
or
INTELLIGENCE SUMMARY

(Erase heading not required.)

Place	Date 1916	Hour	Summary of Events and Information	Remarks and references to Appendices
Nr. ALBERT	16-8		In camp at E 26 b 0 8	JCC
do	17-8		No change	JCC
do	18-8		No change	JCC
do	19-8		No change	JCC
do	20-8		In camp at E 26 b 0 8	JCC
			Handed over Dump to 7th D.A.C. –	
			During the period the Dump has been on charge of 17th D.A.Col. – the following amm. was received 97342 rounds A, 33334 AX, 8 B, 22580 BX	1696000 SAA
			And the following issues were made 1207000 SAA 96146 A 31793 AX 22568 BX –	
			Marched to BONNAY	
do.	21-8		In camp at BONNAY – ~~[illegible]~~	JCC
do.	22-8		Marched to RAINNEVILLE – Received 20 remounts (L.D. Horses)	JCC
do.	23-8		Marched to OCCOCHES	JCC

2449 Wt. W14957/M90 750,000 1/16 J.B.C. & A. Forms/C.2118/12.

Army Form C. 2118.

Instructions regarding War Diaries and Intelligence Summaries are contained in F. S. Regs., Part II. and the Staff Manual respectively. Title Pages will be prepared in manuscript.

WAR DIARY
or
INTELLIGENCE SUMMARY

(Erase heading not required.)

Place	Date	Hour	Summary of Events and Information	Remarks and references to Appendices
24-8-16 OCCOCHES			In rest	FCC
OCCOCHES	25.8.16		do	FCC
do	26.8.16		do Received 22 Gunners and 36 Drivers reinforcements from the Base	FCC FCC
do	27.8.16		In rest Lts STUBBINGTON, MARTIN and HENDERSON left for 6th D.A. on posting	FCC
do	28.8.16		do	FCC
do	29.8.16		do. Lieut TOLHURST joined from 78th Bde RFA	FCC
do	30.8.16		Moved to HENU 'A' echelon only with Head Quarters and took over Camp, Huts etc from 56th D.A.C Took over following Ammunition 2396 A, 700 AX 780 BX, 42 BX, 385 D 27 DX Lieut JOHNSTON joined from 78th Bde RFA	
do			In camp at HENU	FCC

2449 Wt. W14957/M90 750,000 1/16 J.B.C. & A. Forms/C.2118/12.

Army Form C. 2118.

WAR DIARY
or
INTELLIGENCE SUMMARY

(Erase heading not required.)

Instructions regarding War Diaries and Intelligence Summaries are contained in F. S. Regs., Part II. and the Staff Manual respectively. Title Pages will be prepared in manuscript.

Place	Date	Hour	Summary of Events and Information	Remarks and references to Appendices
			Casualties, Sumary F.	
			Animals. L.D. 10. Mules 4.	
			Wastage from Sickness. 6 Other Ranks	
			Battle Casualties. Nil.	
			[signature] LT. COL. R.F.A. COMMANDING 17th DIV. AMM. COLM.	

2449 Wt. W14957/M90 750,000 1/16 J.B.C. & A. Forms/C.2118/12.

Instructions regarding War Diaries and Intelligence Summaries are contained in F. S. Regs., Part II. and the Staff Manual respectively. Title Pages will be prepared in manuscript.

WAR DIARY
or
INTELLIGENCE SUMMARY
(Erase heading not required.)

Army Form C. 2118.

Vol 15

Place	Date	Hour	Summary of Events and Information	Remarks and references to Appendices
	30/9/16.		Confidential. War Diaries for the month of September 1/9/16 to 30/9/16 of 17th Divisional Ammunition Column Volume 15 R W [illegible] LT. COL. R.F.A. COMMANDING 17th DIV. AMM. COLM.	

2449 Wt. W14957/M90 750,000 1/16 J.B.C. & A. Forms/C.2118/12.

Army Form C. 2118.

Instructions regarding War Diaries and Intelligence Summaries are contained in F. S. Regs., Part II. and the Staff Manual respectively. Title Pages will be prepared in manuscript.

WAR DIARY
or
INTELLIGENCE SUMMARY
(Erase heading not required.)

Place	Date 1916	Hour	Summary of Events and Information	Remarks and references to Appendices
HENU	1-9		'A' Echelon camped at D.19.a.5.2 } sheet 57D 'B' " " " C.10.b.8.8 }	FCC
do.	2.9		As above	FCC
do.	3.9		As above	FCC
do	4.9		As above	FCC
do	5.9		As above	FCC
do.	6.9		As above	FCC
do.	7.9		As above 2 Lieuts Strangman, Farrington & Chirnside joined from 17 DA on attachment	FCC

[signature]

LT. COL. R.F.A.
COMMANDING 17th DIV. AMM. COLM.

2449 Wt. W14957/M90 750,000 1/16 J.B.C. & A. Forms/C.2118/12.

Army Form C. 2118.

WAR DIARY
or
INTELLIGENCE SUMMARY
(Erase heading not required.)

Instructions regarding War Diaries and Intelligence Summaries are contained in F. S. Regs., Part II. and the Staff Manual respectively. Title Pages will be prepared in manuscript.

Place	Date 1916	Hour	Summary of Events and Information	Remarks and references to Appendices
HENN	8.9		A Echelon camped at D.19 a 5 2 } Sheet 57D B " " C.10 b 8 8 } 2Lieut Tatem joined from 17th D.A. on attachment	JCC JCC
do.	9.9		As above	JCC
do	10.9		As above	JCC
do	11.9		As above	JCC
do	12.9		As above – Lt Johnston admitted to Hospital	JCC
do	13.9		As above –	JCC
do.	14.9		As above – 49 other ranks joined from Base.	JCC
do.	15.9		As above – Lieut Nicholl joined from Base and 2Lieut Parrington returned from duty at the Base. 8 O.Ranks reinforcements joined from Base.	

2449 Wt. W14957/M90 750,000 1/16 J.B.C. & A. Forms/C.2118/12.

Army Form C. 2118.

WAR DIARY
or
INTELLIGENCE SUMMARY
(Erase heading not required.)

Instructions regarding War Diaries and Intelligence Summaries are contained in F. S. Regs., Part II. and the Staff Manual respectively. Title Pages will be prepared in manuscript.

Place	Date 1916	Hour	Summary of Events and Information	Remarks and references to Appendices
HENU	16.9		A Echelon camped at D 19 a 5 2 } Sheet 57 D B " C 10 b 8 8 }	JCC
				JCC
do.	17.9		As above	JCC
do	18.9		do.	JCC
do	19.9		do.	JCC
do.	20.9		do	JCC
do	21.9		Handed over to 33rd D.A.C. and marched to BEAUVOIS. Following rounds handed over to 33 D.A.C 3439 A.X. 2281 B.X. 22 D. 1178 D.X. During the period 1-9-16 to 20-9-16 the following issues of amm were made	

A	AX	B	BX	BF7	D.	DX	WX
24511	20215	310	6349	460	1688	1805	350

2449 Wt. W14957/M90 750,000 1/16 J.B.C. & A. Forms/C.2118/12.

Instructions regarding War Diaries and Intelligence Summaries are contained in F. S. Regs., Part II. and the Staff Manual respectively. Title Pages will be prepared in manuscript.

WAR DIARY
or
INTELLIGENCE SUMMARY

(Erase heading not required.)

Army Form C. 2118.

Place	Date 1916	Hour	Summary of Events and Information	Remarks and references to Appendices
—	22.9		Marched to GENNE IVERGNY west of Auxi-le-Chateau	JCC
GENNE IVERGNY	23.9		In rest	JCC
do	24.9		-do- 5 mules received	JCC
do	25.9		-do-	JCC
do	26.9		-do- 48 O.R reinforcements received	JCC
do	27.9		do-	JCC
do	28.9		do	RWD
do	29-9		Marched to REMAISNEL 2 OR reinforcements received.	RWD
do	30-9		Marched to PAS.	RWD
			Casualties. Animals LD Mules 21 5 Casualties:- Wastage from Sickness 1 Officer Lt. J.S. Johnston & 17 Other Ranks.	

2449 Wt. W14957/M90 750,000 1/16 J.B.C. & A. Forms/C.2118/12.

Army Form C. 2118.

Vol 16

Instructions regarding War Diaries and Intelligence Summaries are contained in F. S. Regs., Part II. and the Staff Manual respectively. Title Pages will be prepared in manuscript.

WAR DIARY
or
INTELLIGENCE SUMMARY
(Erase heading not required.)

Place	Date	Hour	Summary of Events and Information	Remarks and references to Appendices
	1/11/16		Confidential War Diaries of 17th Divisional Ammunition Column for the month of October 1916. Volume 16. [signature] LT. COL. R.F.A. COMMANDING 17th DIV. AMM. COLM.	

2449 Wt. W14957/M90 750,000 1/16 J.B.C. & A. Forms/C.2118/12.

Army Form C. 2118.

Instructions regarding War Diaries and Intelligence Summaries are contained in F. S. Regs., Part II. and the Staff Manual respectively. Title Pages will be prepared in manuscript.

WAR DIARY
or
INTELLIGENCE SUMMARY
(Erase heading not required.)

Place	Date	Hour	Summary of Events and Information	Remarks and references to Appendices
PAS.	1/10/16.		"A" Echelon camped at C 15 ~~b~~ 8.2 } Sheet 57 D.	JCC
			"B" Echelon camped at C 10 D 8.4 }	JCC
do	2/10/16		do	
do.	3/10/16.		do Took over Ammunition Dump from 33rd DAC at HENU A 26917 AX 17468 BX 993. 1/2 D 528 DX WX 153 Grenades N.P. 1900 9.45 TM 36 2" T.M. 858. 50 Other Ranks R.F.A. Reinforcements joined from No 2 G.B.D. Base.	JCC
do	4/10/16		do.	JCC
do	5/10/16		do	JCC
do	6/10/16		do Ammunition Dump HENU divided between 17th D.A.C. and 48th DAC but controlled by 48th D.A.C. 17th DAC only responsible for issues of ammunition to units of 17th D.A. 2.O.R Wounded. No 93249 Dr COCKBURN. J 2 Mules Killed " 24919 Dr WALKER W 2 " Wounded	JCC

Army Form C. 2118.

Instructions regarding War Diaries and Intelligence Summaries are contained in F. S. Regs., Part II. and the Staff Manual respectively. Title Pages will be prepared in manuscript.

WAR DIARY
or
INTELLIGENCE SUMMARY

(Erase heading not required.)

Place	Date	Hour	Summary of Events and Information	Remarks and references to Appendices
Pas	4/10/16		"A" Echelon camped at C 15 b 8.2 } Shut 57D.	
			"B" Echelon camped at C 10 a 8.4 }	[illegible]
"	"		2500 2" T.M. Bombs received from Railhead and issued as follows:- 1500 to 17th Div. T.M. and 1,000 to 48th DA.	
"	8/10/16	do	2/Lt E.B. MORGAN to Hospital (sick).	[illegible]
"	"	do	200 Boxes S.A.A. delivered to 51st Inf Bde.	[illegible]
"	"	do	Eight 2" T.M. Guns received from T.M. School 3rd Army	[illegible]
"	"	do	and issued to 17th Div. T.M.	
"	9/10/16	do	No 135189. Dr LAWTON. T. Accidentally injured (Thrown from	
"	do	do	G.S. Wagon through mules shying at bursting of a shell. 1 Mule killed.	[illegible]
"	do	do	200 Boxes SAA delivered to 51st Inf Bde.	
"	10/10/16	do	500 Boxes SAA delivered to 51st Inf Bde.	[illegible]
"	11/10/16	do	447 Boxes SAA " " 50th Inf Bde	[illegible]

2449 Wt. W14957/M90 750,000 1/16 J.B.C. & A. Forms/C.2118/12.

Instructions regarding War Diaries and Intelligence Summaries are contained in F. S. Regs., Part II. and the Staff Manual respectively. Title Pages will be prepared in manuscript.

WAR DIARY
or
INTELLIGENCE SUMMARY
(Erase heading not required.)

Army Form C. 2118.

Place	Date	Hour	Summary of Events and Information	Remarks and references to Appendices
PAS	11/10/16		"A" Echelon Camped at C15 b. 8 2 } Sheet 57D "B" Echelon Camped at C10 D 8. 4 }	JCC
do	do		do 20 Boxes SAA to 50th M. G. C 10 " " " 8th South Staffs 300 Mills Hand Grenades to 50 Inf Bde. 500 Boxes SAA from 4th O.S.P.	JCC
do	12/10/16		do 9 Boxes SAA to 7th East Yorks 18 Boxes SAA to 10th West Yorks.	JCC
do	13/10/16		do 30 Boxes SAA to 51st M. G. C 500 Boxes SAA from 4/4 O.A.S.P.	JCC
do	15/10/16		do 6 Boxes SAA to 7th East Yorks	JCC
do	15/10/16		do 300 Mills Hand Grenades from O.R. Train P.A.S.	JCC

2449 Wt. W14957/M90 750,000 1/16 J.B.C. & A. Forms/C.2118/12.

Army Form C. 2118.

Instructions regarding War Diaries and Intelligence Summaries are contained in F. S. Regs., Part II. and the Staff Manual respectively. Title Pages will be prepared in manuscript.

WAR DIARY
or
INTELLIGENCE SUMMARY
(Erase heading not required.)

Place	Date	Hour	Summary of Events and Information	Remarks and references to Appendices
Pas.	16/10/16	—	"A" Echelon Camped at C 15 b. 8. 2 } Sheet 57 D. D Echelon Camped at C 10 D 8. 4 }	JCC
do	do		do 34 Boxes SAA to 8th South Staffs.	JCC
do	do		do 500 Boxes SAA to 50 Inf Bde.	JCC
do	do		do 1848 A 3084 AX 1368 BX from Dump HENU	JCC
do	17/10/16		do 60 OR reinforcements from No 2 G.B.D Base.	
do	18/10/16		Unit marched to ALBERT. and camped as follows:- "A" Echelon camped at W. 24. c. Sheet 57 D "B" Echelon camped at W. 24 c -do-	JCC
ALBERT	19/10/16		do Took over refilling point at W. 20. a. central (Sheet 57 D	JCC
do.	20/10/16		A & B Echelons camped as above. Formed Ammunition Dump at W. 18. b. central (Sheet 57 D)	JCC
do.	21/10/16		Unit shifted camp to E 5. a & b (Sheet 62 D) and was heavily engaged in moving ammunition from Refilling point to Dump.	JCC.

Instructions regarding War Diaries and Intelligence Summaries are contained in F. S. Regs., Part II. and the Staff Manual respectively. Title Pages will be prepared in manuscript.

WAR DIARY
or
INTELLIGENCE SUMMARY
(Erase heading not required.)

Army Form C. 2118.

Place	Date	Hour	Summary of Events and Information	Remarks and references to Appendices
Near ALBERT	22 10/16		"A" Echelon camped at E.5. a+b. (Sheet 62 D) "B" Echelon moved camp to a site about W. 20. a. central (Sheet 57 D) Unit engaged in filling up Batteries in action	JCC
"	23 10/16		Unit camped as above. Very heavy ammunition work Posted O.R. to Brigades 17 R.D.A. as follows:- 78th Bde - 38, 79th Bde - 36, 81st Bde - 25	JCC
"	24 10/16		No change	JCC
"	25 10/16		No change 18 O.R. reinforcements arrived	JCC
"	26 10/16		No change One man of No 3 Section wounded in action	JCC
"	27 10/16		No change	JCC
"	28 10/16		No change	JCC
"	29 10/16		"A" Echelon moved camp to W. 20. a. central "B" Echelon remained at W. 20. a. central Otherwise no change	JCC
"	30 10/16		No change	JCC

2449 Wt. W14957/M90 750,000 1/16 J.B.C. & A. Forms/C.2118/12.

Instructions regarding War Diaries and Intelligence Summaries are contained in F. S. Regs., Part II. and the Staff Manual respectively. Title Pages will be prepared in manuscript.

WAR DIARY
or
INTELLIGENCE SUMMARY
(Erase heading not required.)

Army Form C. 2118.

Place	Date	Hour	Summary of Events and Information	Remarks and references to Appendices
near BOUZINCOURT	31/10/16		All sections camped at W. 20. a. central (Sheet 57 D)	[illegible]
			During the period the Unit has been on the THIEPVAL – COURCELLETTE front the following ammunition has been received	X.
			4299 A, 22480 AX 6612 BX	
			and the following number of rounds issued to Brigades	
			36061 A 20980 AX 7158 BX	
			The difficulties of supplying ammunition to gun positions are very great owing to the absence of roads and the presence of deep mud. It has been found practically impossible to supply by limbers, even using teams of 10 and 12 horses or mules has been such a strain on the animals that this practice has been discontinued – A tramline exists and passes close to certain battery positions, and whenever possible this tramline has been used to supply these Batteries. The distance others are from the nearest place on the tramline	

2449 Wt. W14957/M90 750,000 1/16 J.B.C. & A. Forms/C.2118/12.

Instructions regarding War Diaries and Intelligence Summaries are contained in F. S. Regs., Part II. and the Staff Manual respectively. Title Pages will be prepared in manuscript.

WAR DIARY
or
INTELLIGENCE SUMMARY
(Erase heading not required.)

Army Form C. 2118.

Place	Date	Hour	Summary of Events and Information	Remarks and references to Appendices
			renders it ~~as~~ a doubtful advantage to them. It has been found from experience that the tramline is only useable to a certain point and that some batteries are a very considerable distance from this point. Experiments have been tried of adapting ~~a~~ the saddle into a sort of pack saddle for the carrying of ammunition to gun positions and the most useful way has been found to strap or tie 2 boxes to the saddle one of each side, thus carrying ~~eight~~ rounds 18pr. per horse and four rounds 4.5 per horse direct to the guns from the dump. Thus the ten horses formerly put in a wagon limber which holds 38 rounds, 18pr. or 16 rounds 4.5" have been made to take 80 rounds 18pr or 40 rounds 4.5. Some means of supply must be discovered before long, and it is recommended that a carrier similar to two Carriers Amm. Q.F. 18pr. sewn together be issued to D.A.Cols at the rate of 100 per section of 'A' Echelon.	F.E.

2449 Wt. W14957/M90 750,000 1/16 J.B.C. & A. Forms/C.2118/12.

Army Form C. 2118.

Instructions regarding War Diaries and Intelligence Summaries are contained in F. S. Regs., Part II. and the Staff Manual respectively. Title Pages will be prepared in manuscript.

WAR DIARY
or
INTELLIGENCE SUMMARY
(Erase heading not required.)

Place	Date	Hour	Summary of Events and Information	Remarks and references to Appendices
			Casualties	
			Wastage from Sickness. Officers 1, O.R. 20	&c
			Casualties to Animals. Mules 6, Horses 17.	
			Accidentally Injured. Officers Nil. O.R. 6.	
			Wounded. Officers Nil. O.R. 3.	

R W L Dunlop
LT. COL. R.F.A.
COMMANDING 17th DIV. AMM. COLM.

2449 Wt. W14957/M90 750,000 1/16 J.B.C. & A. Forms/C.2118/12.

Army Form C. 2118.

Vol 17

Instructions regarding War Diaries and Intelligence Summaries are contained in F. S. Regs., Part II. and the Staff Manual respectively. Title pages will be prepared in manuscript.

WAR DIARY
or
INTELLIGENCE SUMMARY.
(Erase heading not required.)

Place	Date	Hour	Summary of Events and Information	Remarks and references to Appendices
			Confidential War Diaries of 17th. Divisional Ammunition Column for the month of November 1916. [signature] LT. COL. R.F.A. COMMANDING 17th DIV. AMM. COLM.	
	30/11/16		Volume 17.	

1577 Wt. W10791/1773 500,000 1/15 D. D. & L. A.D.S.S./Forms/C. 2118.

Instructions regarding War Diaries and Intelligence Summaries are contained in F. S. Regs., Part II. and the Staff Manual respectively. Title Pages will be prepared in manuscript.

WAR DIARY
or
~~INTELLIGENCE SUMMARY~~

(Erase heading not required.)

Army Form C. 2118.

Place	Date 1916	Hour	Summary of Events and Information	Remarks and references to Appendices
N. ALBERT	1-11		Unit camped at W.20 a. central (Sheet 57D on the BOUZINCOURT - ALBERT Road Supplying 17th D.A. in action near THIEPVAL - MOUQUET FARM	JCC
do.	2.11.		No. change.	JCC
do	3.11		No change No. 68283 Driver J Weir wounded in action	JCC
do.	4.11		No change No 97423 D. J Murphy wounded in action	JCC
do.	5.11		No change	JCC
do.	6.11		No change	JCC
do.	7.11		No change Posted 53 O.R. to Brigades 17th D.A	JCC
do.	8.11		No change 2/Lt. STOCKEN joined from 78th Bde H.Qrs.	JCC

2449 Wt. W14957/M90 750,000 1/16 J.B.C. & A. Forms/C.2118/12.

Instructions regarding War Diaries and Intelligence Summaries are contained in F. S. Regs., Part II. and the Staff Manual respectively. Title pages will be prepared in manuscript.

WAR DIARY
or
~~INTELLIGENCE SUMMARY.~~
(Erase heading not required.)

Army Form C. 2118.

Place	Date 1916	Hour	Summary of Events and Information	Remarks and references to Appendices
Nr ALBERT	9.11		Camped at W 20 central (Sheet 57 D)	FCC
			Lieut Moie RFA admitted to Hospital	
do.	10.11		no change	FCC
do	11.11		no change	FCC
do	12.11		no change	FCC
do	13.11		no change	FCC
do	14.11		No change	FCC
do	15.11		no change	FCC
do	16.11		no change	FCC
do	17.11		no change	FCC
			No 21671 Dr A LORRIMAN wounded in action	
do	18.11		no change	FCC
			No 73353 Dr J. RAINE wounded	
			" 106618 " F. WANSTELL do.	
do.	19.11		no change	FCC

T2134. Wt. W708—776. 500000. 4/15. Sir J. C. & S.

Instructions regarding War Diaries and Intelligence Summaries are contained in F. S. Regs., Part II. and the Staff Manual respectively. Title pages will be prepared in manuscript.

WAR DIARY
or
INTELLIGENCE SUMMARY.
(Erase heading not required.)

Army Form C. 2118.

Place	Date	Hour	Summary of Events and Information	Remarks and references to Appendices
Nr	1916			
ALBERT	20-11		In camp at W.a.20 central (sheet 57D)	FCC
			Handed over Ammunition Dump + Ammunition to II Corps Dump at DONNETTS Post	
			During the period the Unit has been in this Area the following no. of rounds have been issued to Brigades of 17th D.A.:- (from 21-10-16 to 19-11-16)	
			83922 A - 43952 AX - 18790 BX - 100 BT. 810 BSK - 354 BCBR - 86 BJ.	
MEAULTE	21-11		Unit moved to camps near MEAULTE as follows	FCC
			No 1, 2 + 3 Sections E 22.d.8.4 } sheet 62 D	
			" 4 Section E 28 a.0.0. }	
			HQrs E 28 a.2.4 }	
do	22-11		No change	FCC
do	23-11		do	FCC
do	24-11		do	FCC
do	25-11		No 1 Section & part of HQrs have moved into action & camped as follows	FCC
			No 1 Section at ~~A.b.6.6~~ A 13 b 6.6	
			Part of HQrs at A 4 b 6 6	

1577 Wt. W10791/1773 500,000 1/15 D. D. & L. A.D.S.S./Forms/C. 2118.

Instructions regarding War Diaries and Intelligence Summaries are contained in F. S. Regs., Part II. and the Staff Manual respectively. Title pages will be prepared in manuscript.

WAR DIARY
or
INTELLIGENCE SUMMARY.
(Erase heading not required.)

Army Form C. 2118.

Place	Date	Hour	Summary of Events and Information	Remarks and references to Appendices
	1916			
CARNOY etc	26.11		No 3 Sec. moved to a camp at A.13.b.8.3 (sheet 62 C)	FCC
			Remainder of No 2 Sec moved to camp at A.13.b.8.2.	
			Took over a gun amm Dump at GUILLEMONT STATION at T.19.c.1.10 and formed a Dump for Infy ammunition at S.29.c.6.2.	
do	27.11		Units are now camped as follows:- (No 2 moved to present camp yesterday)	FCC
			No 1 Sec A 13 b.6.6 (sheet 62 C)	
			" 2 " E 25 a.2.4 (sheet 62 D)	
			" 3 " A 13 b.8.3 (sheet 62C)	
			" 4 " part at A.13 b.8.2 (including O.C. section) } sheet 62C	
			" " A 4 b.5.6	
			Commenced supply of S A A to Guards Divn at about T.23.b.4.0 (Sheet 62C)	
			Following Officer reinforcements joined from Base:-	
			2Lieuts J. J. COULTHARD, S H STROUD, G R MOFFAT, W D MORGAN and Lieut. PARRY	
do	28.11		No change	
			The Officers who joined yesterday were posted to X Bde except ...	FCC

...uctions regarding War Diaries and Intelligence Summaries are contained in F. S. Regs., Part II. and the Staff Manual respectively. Title pages will be prepared in manuscript.

WAR DIARY
or
INTELLIGENCE SUMMARY.
(Erase heading not required.)

Army Form C. 2118.

Place	Date	Hour	Summary of Events and Information	Remarks and references to Appendices
	1916			
	28.11 (continued)		MORGAN who was posted to 79 Bde RFA	JCC
	29-11		No change	
	30-11		do	
			Casualties.	
			Wastage from Sickness. 30 O.R. 1 Officer	
			Horses. 21	
			Mules 17	
			R L Dunlop LT. COL. R.F.A. COMMANDING 17th DIV. AMM. COLM.	

1577 Wt. W10791/1773 500,000 1/15 D. D. & L. A.D.S.S./Forms/C. 2118.

Army Form C. 2118.

Instructions regarding War Diaries and Intelligence Summaries are contained in F. S. Regs., Part II. and the Staff Manual respectively. Title pages will be prepared in manuscript.

WAR DIARY
or
INTELLIGENCE SUMMARY.
(Erase heading not required.)

Vol 18

Place	Date	Hour	Summary of Events and Information	Remarks and references to Appendices
			Confidential War Diaries of 17th Divisional Ammunition Column for the month of December 1916 31/12/16 Volume. 18. [illegible] Captain ~~Lt. Col.~~ R.F.A. COMMANDING 17th DIV. AMM. COLM.	

1577 Wt. W10791/1773 500,000 1/15 D. D. & L. A.D.S.S./Forms/C. 2118.

Instructions regarding War Diaries and Intelligence Summaries are contained in F. S. Regs., Part II. and the Staff Manual respectively. Title pages will be prepared in manuscript.

WAR DIARY
or
INTELLIGENCE SUMMARY.
(Erase heading not required.)

Army Form C. 2118.

Place	Date	Hour	Summary of Events and Information	Remarks and references to Appendices
MEAULTE	1 12/16		Units camped as follows:-	L.L.
			9/61 Section at A 13 b 6.6 (Sheet 62 c)	L.L.
			2 " " E 28 a 2.4 (Sheet 62 D)	L.L.
			3 " " A 13 b 8.3 (Sheet 62 c)	L.L.
			4 " part " A 13 b 8.2 (including O.C. Section } Sheet 62 c	L.L.
			" " A 4 b 5.6	L.L.
			HQ E 28 2.4	
do	2 12/16		No change 37 O.R. joined from 9/G 2 GBD.	L.L.
do	3 12/16		No change	L.L.
			2/Lts ABRAHAM A.R FOSKETT B. HARPER R.W, HESLOP G.R, MOLLETT J.	L.L.
			WALKER R.M, HUDSON S. BOWMAN R & Lt BEAKBANE joined from Base	L.L.
do	4 12/16		No change	L.L.
do	5 12/16		No change	L.L.
do	6 12/16		2/Lts HESLOP C.R. HUDSON S. FOSKETT B. posted 78th Bde RFA	L.L.
			2/Lt BOWMAN R. to 79 Bde RFA, & 2/Lt WALKER R.M to 79 Bde RFA	L.L.
			2/Lts MOLLETT J, ABRAHAM A.R & Lt BEAKBANE to 81st Bde RFA	L.L.
do	7 12/16		No change 5 ORs posted to 78 Bde RFA	L.L.
			8 ORs posted to 79 Bde RFA	
			4 ORs posted to 81st Bde RFA	

1577 Wt. W10791/1773 500,000 1/15 D. D. & L. A.D.S.S./Forms/C. 2118.

Army Form C. 2118.

WAR DIARY
or
INTELLIGENCE SUMMARY.
(Erase heading not required.)

Instructions regarding War Diaries and Intelligence Summaries are contained in F. S. Regs., Part II. and the Staff Manual respectively. Title pages will be prepared in manuscript.

Place	Date	Hour	Summary of Events and Information	Remarks and references to Appendices
MEAULTE	8/12/16		Units camped as follows:–	
			No 1 HQ Section at E.28.a 2.4 / A.13.b.6.6 (Sheet 62 C)	
			2 " " E 28.a 2.4 (Sheet 62 D)	
			3 " " A 13.b.8.3 (Sheet 62 C)	
			4 " part " A 13.b.8.2 (including O6 Section) } Sheet 62 C.	
			" " A. 4.b.5.6	
do	9/12/16		No change 2/Lt GREGORY R.V. & 2/Lt URQUHART A.R joined from Base	
			Lt HALLWARD B.M. from 81st Bde RFA	
do	10/12/16		No change 2/Lt MARTLEY J.F & Lt SHEFFIELD R. from Base	
			2/Lt GREGORY R.V. to 79 Bde RFA, 2/Lt URQUHART A.R to 79 Bde RFA	
do	11/12/16		No change 2/Lt MARTLEY J.F to 81st Bde RFA	
do	12/12/16		No change Lt SHEFFIELD D.R. to 78 Bde RFA	
do	13/12/16		No change	
do	14/12/16		No change No 77412 Dvr KNIGHT W.H. Wounded	
do	15/12/16		No change	
do	16/12/16		No change	

1577 Wt. W10791/1773 500,000 1/15 D. D. & L. A.D.S.S./Forms/C. 2118.

Instructions regarding War Diaries and Intelligence Summaries are contained in F. S. Regs., Part II. and the Staff Manual respectively. Title pages will be prepared in manuscript.

WAR DIARY
or
INTELLIGENCE SUMMARY.
(Erase heading not required.)

Army Form C. 2118.

Place	Date	Hour	Summary of Events and Information	Remarks and references to Appendices
MEHUNTE	17/12/16		Units camped as follows :-	L.G.
			4th No 1 Section at E.28.a.2.4 Sheet 62D / A.13.b.6.6 (Sheet 62.C)	L.G.
			2 " " E.28.a.2.4 (Sheet 62 D)	L.G.
			3 " " A.13.b.8.3 (Sheet 62 C)	L.G.
			4 " part " A.13.b.8.2 (including O.C. Section) Sheet 62C)	L.G.
			" " A.4.b.5.6	L.G.
do	18/12/16		No change	L.G.
do	19/12/16		No change	L.G.
do	20/12/16		No change	L.G.
do	21/12/16		No change	L.G.
do	22/12/16		No change 35 O.R. Reinforcements joined from Base. (No 2 G.B.D)	L.G.
do	23/12/16		No change 2/Lt H G FRANKLIN (Somerset Yeomanry) joined from Base and	L.G.
do	24/12/16		No change attached to No 4 Section	L.G.
do	25/12/16		No change The following reinforcements were posted to Brigades :-	L.G.
			15 O.R. to 48 Bde RFA, 5 O.R. to 49 Bde & 6 O.R. to 81 A Bde	L.G.
			Captain H MORGAN O.C. No 4 Section to Hospital (Sick)	L.G.

1577 Wt. W10791/1773 500,000 1/15 D. D. & L. A.D.S.S./Forms/C. 2118.

Instructions regarding War Diaries and Intelligence Summaries are contained in F. S. Regs., Part II. and the Staff Manual respectively. Title pages will be prepared in manuscript.

WAR DIARY
or
INTELLIGENCE SUMMARY.

(*Erase heading not required.*)

Army Form C. 2118.

Place	Date	Hour	Summary of Events and Information	Remarks and references to Appendices
MEAULTE	26/12/16		Units camped as follows :-	
			HQ at E.28.a.2.4 (Sheet 62D)	
			No 1 Sec " A.13.b.6.6 (Sheet 62D)	
			2 " " E.28.a.2.4 (Sheet 62D)	
			3 " " A.13.b.8.3 (Sheet 62D)	
			4 " part " A.13.b.8.2 (including OC Section) Sheet 62D	
			" " A.4.b.5.6	
do	27/12/16		No change. 35 O.R. Reinforcements joined from No 2 GBD Base	
do	28/12/16		No change 23 O.R Reinforcements posted to 48th Bde RFA	
do	29/12/16		No change	
do	30/12/16		No change Lieut O.C.H. RILEY, Lieut A.W. DAVIES & 2/Lt J. NEALE joined from Base.	
do	31/12/16		No change	

1577 Wt. W10791/1773 500,000 1/15 D. D. & L. A.D.S.S./Forms/C. 2118.

...ions regarding War Diaries and Intelligence Summaries are contained in F. S. Regs., Part II. and the Staff Manual respectively. Title pages will be prepared in manuscript.

WAR DIARY
or
INTELLIGENCE SUMMARY.
(Erase heading not required.)

Army Form C. 2118.

Place	Date	Hour	Summary of Events and Information	Remarks and references to Appendices
			Casualties	
			Wastage from Sickness — Officers: 2/Lt. W. TIPPLE, Captain. H MORGAN. — Other Ranks: 46	
			Animals. — Horses: 23 — Mules: 63	
			Casualties in action. — Killed: Nil. — Wounded: Hosptl Dvr W. H. KNIGHT.	
			Ammunition on hand — A: 1714 — AX: 1006 — B: - — BX: 576 — SAA: 960,000 — Grenades: 3480	
			31/12/16.	
			[illegible signature] Captain ~~LT. COL.~~ R.F.A. COMMANDING 17th DIV. AMM. COLM.	

1577 Wt. W10791/1773 500,000 1/15 D. D. & L. A.D.S.S./Forms/C. 2118.

Instructions regarding War Diaries and Intelligence Summaries are contained in F. S. Regs., Part II. and the Staff Manual respectively. Title pages will be prepared in manuscript.

WAR DIARY
or
INTELLIGENCE SUMMARY.
(Erase heading not required.)

Army Form C. 2118.

Vol 19

Place	Date	Hour	Summary of Events and Information	Remarks and references to Appendices
			Confidential War Diaries of 17th Divisional Ammunition Column for the month of January 1917. 31/1/17 [illegible signature] LT. COL. R.F.A. COMMANDING 17th DIV. AMM. COLM. Volume 19	

1577 Wt. W10791/1773 500,000 1/15 D. D. & L. A.D.S.S./Forms/C. 2118.

Army Form C. 2118.

WAR DIARY
or
INTELLIGENCE SUMMARY.
(Erase heading not required.)

Instructions regarding War Diaries and Intelligence Summaries are contained in F. S. Regs., Part II. and the Staff Manual respectively. Title pages will be prepared in manuscript.

Place	Date	Hour	Summary of Events and Information	Remarks and references to Appendices
			<u>Casualties.</u>	
			Wastage from Sickness. Officers: 2/Lt. H Chermside. Other Ranks: 51	
			Animals. Horses: 47. Mules: 22.	
			Casualties in action. Killed. Nil. Wounded Nil.	
			Ammunition on hand. A: 1714, AX: 1006, B: -, BX: 576, S.A.A.: 960,000, Grenades: 3480.	
			31/1/17	
			[illegible] LT. COL. R.F.A. COMMANDING 17th DIV. AMM. COLM.	

Army Form C. 2118.

Instructions regarding War Diaries and Intelligence Summaries are contained in F. S. Regs., Part II. and the Staff Manual respectively. Title pages will be prepared in manuscript.

WAR DIARY
or
INTELLIGENCE SUMMARY.
(Erase heading not required.)

Place	Date	Hour	Summary of Events and Information	Remarks and references to Appendices
MEAULTE	1/1/17		Unit camped as follows :-	M.P.T.
			No 1 Section at A. 13. b. 6.6 (Sheet 62D)	M.P.T.
			" 2 " " E. 28. a. 2.4 (Sheet 62D)	M.P.T.
			" 3 " " A. 13. b. 8. 3 (Sheet 62D)	M.P.T.
			" 4 " part " A. 13. b. 8. 2 (including 06 Section) } Sheet 62D	M.P.T.
			" " A. 4. b. 5.6	M.P.T.
			HQ " E. 28. a. 2.4	M.P.T.
do	2/1/17		No change	M.P.T.
do	3/1/17		No change.	M.P.T.
do	4/1/17		No change	M.P.T.
do	5/1/17		No change. 60. O.R. Reinforcements from Base (No 2 G B D.)	M.P.T.
do	6/1/17		No change.	M.P.T.
do	7/1/17		No change	M.P.T.
do	8/1/17		No change. 7 O.R. Reinforcements to 78 Bde RFA + 21 O.R. to 79th Bde	M.P.T.
do	9/1/17		No change	M.P.T.
				M.P.T.

Army Form C. 2118.

Instructions regarding War Diaries and Intelligence Summaries are contained in F. S. Regs., Part II. and the Staff Manual respectively. Title pages will be prepared in manuscript.

WAR DIARY
or
INTELLIGENCE SUMMARY.
(Erase heading not required.)

Place	Date	Hour	Summary of Events and Information	Remarks and references to Appendices
MEAULTE		10/1/17	Unit camped as follows:-	M.P.T.
			No 1 Sec at A.13. b.6.6. (Sheet 62c)	M.P.T.
			2 " E.28. a.2.4. (Sheet 62D)	M.P.T.
			3 " A.13. b.8.3. (Sheet 62c)	M.P.T.
			4 part " A.13. b.8.2 (including O.C. Section) } Sheet 62c.	M.P.T.
			" " A.4. b.5.6.	M.P.T.
			HQ " E.28. a.2.4. 47 OR Reinforcements joined from No 2 GBD. 2/Lt E.B. REED joined from No 2 GBD.	M.P.T.
do		11/1/17	No change.	M.P.T.
do		12/1/17	HQ & No 2 Section marched to CARNOY and occupied camps as follows:-	M.P.T.
			HQ at A 13 b. 8.2 Sheet 62c	M.P.T.
			No 2 Section at A 13 b. 8.3. Sheet 62c.	M.P.T.
			No 1 Section at A 13 b. 2.4 Sheet 62c	M.P.T.
			No 4 " at A.13 b 8.2 Sheet 62c.	M.P.T.
			Reorganization of 14th D.A.C. was carried out as follows:- No 3 Section was	M.P.T.
			disbanded & Nos 1 & 2 Sections were increased to a strength of 214 all ranks.	M.P.T.
			No 4 Section remained the same with the exception that 3 G.S. Wagons with teams	M.P.T.

1577 Wt. W10791/1773 500,000 1/15 D. D. & L. A.D.S.S./Forms/C. 2118.

Instructions regarding War Diaries and Intelligence Summaries are contained in F. S. Regs., Part II. and the Staff Manual respectively. Title pages will be prepared in manuscript.

WAR DIARY
or
INTELLIGENCE SUMMARY.
(Erase heading not required.)

Army Form C. 2118.

Place	Date	Hour	Summary of Events and Information	Remarks and references to Appendices
			complete & 9 Drivers became surplus to their establishment & were posted to the	
			A Echelon. The surplus details from No 3 Section on disbandment were	
			posted to 147th Brigade & 76th Brigade R.F.A.	M.A.S.
CARNOY	13th		Units camped as follows :- A & B Echelons at A136 82 Sheet 62C.	M.A.S.
			No change.	M.A.S.
"	14th		" 26 O.R. reinforcements posted to 49th Brigade & 16 to 78th Brigade.	M.A.S.
	1		" 2nd Lt Reed C. B. to hospital sick.	M.A.S.
"	15th		"	M.A.S.
"	16th		12 Reinforcements to 78th Brigade & 19 to 49th Brigade.	M.A.S.
"			The Rev. A. B. CARTER to England.	M.A.S.
"	17th		7 men to T. Ms.	M.A.S.
"	18th			M.A.S.
"	19th		36 Reinforcements arrived from Base.	M.A.S.
"	20		2nd Lt. W.P.A. TULLOCH from Base & 2nd Lt A. J. HIBBERT from Base.	M.A.S.
"	21			M.A.S.
"	22		2nd Lt H. CHERMSIDE to hospital sick.	M.A.S.

1577 Wt. W10791/1773 500,000 1/15 D. D. & L. A.D.S.S./Forms/C. 2118.

Instructions regarding War Diaries and Intelligence Summaries are contained in F. S. Regs., Part II. and the Staff Manual respectively. Title pages will be prepared in manuscript.

WAR DIARY
or
INTELLIGENCE SUMMARY.
(Erase heading not required.)

Army Form C. 2118.

Place	Date	Hour	Summary of Events and Information	Remarks and references to Appendices
CARNOY	23		Captain H. MORGAN to England sick. 23 Reinforcements to 78th Brigade.	MHT
"			12 to 79th Brigade. 1 to 81st Brigade	MHT
"	24		2nd Lts. R. NEUMAN-BOTLER, W. H. SOTHERAN, J.E. JACKSON, N. P. MORGATHROYD,	MHT
			J. H. KERSHAW. from Base. 34 reinforcements from Base. Rev Capt. SINCLAIR SMITH arrives.	MHT
	25		No change.	MHT
	26		2nd Lt. H. J. HIBBERT to 79th Brigade.	MHT
	27		No change	MHT
	28		"	MHT
	29		"	MHT
	30		"	MHT
	31		14 Reinforcements to 78th Brigade. 7 to 79th Brigade.	MHT

Instructions regarding War Diaries and Intelligence Summaries are contained in F. S. Regs., Part II. and the Staff Manual respectively. Title pages will be prepared in manuscript.

WAR DIARY
or
INTELLIGENCE SUMMARY.
(Erase heading not required.)

17th Div Amm Col

Army Form C. 2118.

549

Place	Date	Hour	Summary of Events and Information	Remarks and references to Appendices
MEAULTE	1/7		Unit camped as follows:–	
			1st Section at A.13.b.6.6. (Sheet 62d)	
			2 " " E.25.a.2.4. (Sheet 62D)	
			3 " " A.13.b.8.3 (Sheet 62d)	
			4 " part " A.13.b.9.2. (including of Section) Sheet 62d	
			" " A.4.1.5.6.	
			HQ " E.28.a.2.2.	
do	2/7		No change.	
do	3/7		No change.	
do	4/7		No change.	
do	5/7		No change. 60 O.R. Reinforcements from Base (to 2nd B.D.)	
[illegible]	[illegible]		No change [illegible] Reinforcements [illegible]	
[illegible]	[illegible]		No change [illegible]	
[illegible]	[illegible]		No change	

1577 Wt. W10791/1773 500,000 1/15 D. D. & L. A.D.S.S./Forms/C. 2118.

Instructions regarding War Diaries and Intelligence Summaries are contained in F. S. Regs., Part II. and the Staff Manual respectively. Title pages will be prepared in manuscript.

WAR DIARY
or
INTELLIGENCE SUMMARY.
(Erase heading not required.)

Army Form C. 2118.

550

Place	Date	Hour	Summary of Events and Information	Remarks and references to Appendices
MEAULTE		10th	Unit camped as follows:-	
			No 1 Sec at A 13. b. 6. 6 (Sheet 62 d)	
			2 " " B 28 a 2. 4. (Sheet 62 D)	
			3 " A 13. b. 7. 3. (Sheet 62 d)	
			4 [illegible] A 13. b. 8. 2 (including [illegible] Section) } Sheet 62 d	
			" A 14 b. 5. 6	
			HQ " E. [illegible] 47 [illegible] reinforcements [illegible]	
do		11th	No change	
do		12th	HQ & No 2 Section marched to CARNOY and occupied camps as follows	
			HQ at [illegible] Sheet 62 d	
			No 2 Section at A 13 [illegible] Sheet 62 d	
			No 1 Section at A 13 b 2. 4 Sheet 62 d	
			No 4 " at A [illegible] Sheet 62 d	
			Reorganization of 17th D A C was carried out as follows:- No 3 Section was disbanded & Nos. 1 & 2 Sections were increased to a Strength of 214 all ranks No 4 Section ~~remained~~ remained the same with the exception that 3 G.S. Wagons with teams	

Instructions regarding War Diaries and Intelligence Summaries are contained in F. S. Regs., Part II. and the Staff Manual respectively. Title pages will be prepared in manuscript.

WAR DIARY
or
INTELLIGENCE SUMMARY.
(Erase heading not required.)

Army Form C. 2118.

551

Place	Date	Hour	Summary of Events and Information	Remarks and references to Appendices
			complete & 9 Drivers became surplus to their establishment & were posted to the A Echelon. The surplus details from No 3 Section on disbandment were posted to 147th Brigade & 276 Brigade RFA	
CARNOY	13		Unit camped as follows A+B Echelon at A13 b 32 Sheet 62C no change	
"	14		26 OR reinforcements posted to 79th Bde & 16 to 78 Bde	
"			2 Lt Reed CB to Hospital Sick	
"	15			
	16		12 Reinforcements to 78 Bde & 19 to 79 Bde.	
			The Rev A B Carter to England.	
	17		7 men to T M	
	18			
	19		36 Reinforcements arrived from Base	
	20		2nd Lt WPA TULLOCH from Base & 2nd Lt AJ HIBBERT from Base	
	21			
	22		2nd Lt A CHERMSIDE to Hospital Sick	

1577 Wt. W10791/1773 500,000 1/15 D. D. & L. A.D.S.S./Forms/C. 2118.

Army Form C. 2118.

WAR DIARY
or
INTELLIGENCE SUMMARY.
(Erase heading not required.)

Instructions regarding War Diaries and Intelligence Summaries are contained in F. S. Regs., Part II. and the Staff Manual respectively. Title pages will be prepared in manuscript.

552

Place	Date	Hour	Summary of Events and Information	Remarks and references to Appendices
CARNOY	23		Capt H MORGAN to England Sick 23 Reinforcements to 78 Bde 12 to 79 Bde. 1 to 81st Bde	
	24		2 Lts R NEWMAN-BUTLER W.H. SOTHERAN J.E. JACKSON N.N. MURGATHROYD J.H. KERSHAM from Base 34 reinforcements from Base. Lt. Capt. SINCLAIR SMITH arrives	
	25		No change	
	26		2nd Lt. A.J. HIBBERT to 79th Brigade	
	27		No change	
	28			
	29			
	30			
	31		14 Reinforcements 7 to 78th Brigade 7 to 79th Brigade	

Lt & Adjutant
Commanding

Instructions regarding War Diaries and Intelligence Summaries are contained in F. S. Regs., Part II. and the Staff Manual respectively. Title pages will be prepared in manuscript.

WAR DIARY
or
INTELLIGENCE SUMMARY.
(Erase heading not required.)

Army Form C. 2118.

Place	Date	Hour	Summary of Events and Information	Remarks and references to Appendices
			553	
			Casualties	
			Wastage from Sickness. Officers: 2/Lt H. Chermside. Other Ranks: 51	
			Animals. Horses: 47. Mules: 22	
			Casualties in action. Killed Nil. Wounded Nil.	
			Ammunition on hand. A: 1714. AX: 1006. B: –. BX: 576. S.A.A.: 960,000. Grenades: 3480	
			31/7/17 — L G Allen Lt & Adjutant	

1577 Wt. W10791/1773 500,000 1/15 D. D. & L. A.D.S.S./Forms/C. 2118.

Instructions regarding War Diaries and Intelligence Summaries are contained in F. S. Regs., Part II. and the Staff Manual respectively. Title pages will be prepared in manuscript.

WAR DIARY
or
INTELLIGENCE SUMMARY.
(Erase heading not required.)

Army Form C. 2118.

Vol 20

Place	Date	Hour	Summary of Events and Information	Remarks and references to Appendices
			Confidential War Diaries of 17th Divisional Ammunition Column for the month of February 1917. 28/2/17. Volume 20. [signature] LT. COL. R.F.A. COMMANDING 17th DIV. AMM. COLM.	

1577 Wt. W10791/1773 500,000 1/15 D. D. & L. A.D.S.S./Forms/C. 2118.

Instructions regarding War Diaries and Intelligence Summaries are contained in F. S. Regs., Part II. and the Staff Manual respectively. Title pages will be prepared in manuscript.

WAR DIARY
or
~~INTELLIGENCE SUMMARY.~~
(Erase heading not required.)

Army Form C. 2118.

Place	Date	Hour	Summary of Events and Information	Remarks and references to Appendices
	1917			
CARNOY	1.2.		Unit camped on CARNOY – MAMETZ Road as follows:–	
			H.Qrs at A.13.b.8.2 } Sheet 62^c	
			No 1 Sec " A.13.b.6.6 }	
			" 2 " " A.13.b.8.3 }	
			B.Ech. " A.13.b.8.2 }	FCC
do.	2.2		No change	
			Lt H Clemside from Hospital	FCC
do.	3.2		No change	FCC
do.	4.2		do	
			Lieut W.P. Tullock posted to 17th Div Trench Mortars	FCC
do.	5.2		No change	
			BSM CRANE commissioned and posted to 48th D.A.C	
			During the night 4–5 an enemy aeroplane bombed No 1 Sec Camp and 9 horses and 22 mules of the section were killed outright	FCC
do.	6.2		No change	FCC
do.	7.2		do – Capt G. Jongler R.A.M.C admitted to Hospital	FCC

1577 Wt. W10791/1773 500,000 1/15 D. D. & L. A.D.S.S./Forms/C. 2118.

Army Form C. 2118.

WAR DIARY
or
~~INTELLIGENCE SUMMARY.~~
(Erase heading not required.)

Instructions regarding War Diaries and Intelligence Summaries are contained in F. S. Regs., Part II. and the Staff Manual respectively. Title pages will be prepared in manuscript.

Place	Date	Hour	Summary of Events and Information	Remarks and references to Appendices
	1917			
CARNOY	8.2		No change	JCC
"	9.2		do	
"	10.2		do	
"	11.2		do	
"	12.2		do. 2 Lieut W.A. Carne and 45 O.R. Reinforcements joined from Base also Lieuts L.H. Maddams, A.G. McClellan, H.G. Huckstead, H.W. Gordon, G. Colman, J.S. Franklin	JCC
"	13.2		No change. No 38171 Dr J. Cooper and 68235 Dr W.A. Tuckey were killed today in a railway smash at SERQUES.	JCC
"	14.2		No change. 2Lt H.G. Huckstead posted to 17th Div T. Mortars " L.H. Maddams " " 78th Bde R.F.A. " J.S. Franklin " " " H.W. Gordon " " 79 Bde R.F.A.	JCC

1577 Wt. W10791/1773 500,000 1/15 D. D. & L. A.D.S.S./Forms/C. 2118.

Instructions regarding War Diaries and Intelligence Summaries are contained in F. S. Regs., Part II. and the Staff Manual respectively. Title pages will be prepared in manuscript.

WAR DIARY
or
~~INTELLIGENCE SUMMARY.~~
(Erase heading not required.)

Army Form C. 2118.

Place	Date	Hour	Summary of Events and Information	Remarks and references to Appendices
	1917			
CARNOY	15.2		No change.	
			21 O.R. Reinforcements to 78 Bde. R.F.A.	
			19 " " " 79 " "	FCC
"	16.2		No change	FCC
			2 Lt. G. Coleman to Hospital	
"	17.2		No change	FCC
"	18.2		do.	FCC
"	19.2		do.	FCC
"	20.2		do.	FCC
			Captain G. Joughin RAMC discharged from Hospital	
			Lieut. C.N. Woodland joined from Base	
"	21.2		No change	FCC
			108 O.R. Reinforcement from Base	
"	22.2		No change	FCC
"	23.2		do.	FCC
"	24.2		do.	FCC

1577 Wt. W10791/1773 500,000 1/15 D. D. & L. A.D.S.S./Forms/C. 2118.

Instructions regarding War Diaries and Intelligence Summaries are contained in F. S. Regs., Part II. and the Staff Manual respectively. Title pages will be prepared in manuscript.

WAR DIARY
or
~~INTELLIGENCE~~ SUMMARY.
(Erase heading not required.)

Army Form C. 2118.

Place	Date	Hour	Summary of Events and Information	Remarks and references to Appendices
	1917			
CARNOY	25.2		no change.	FCC
"	26.2		no change.	FCC
"	27.2		do.	FCC
"	28.2		do.	FCC
			36 OR Reinforcements to 78 Bde RFA	
			49 " " " 79 "	
			1714 rounds + 1006 AX issued to Dump GUILLEMONT by order of 20: D.A.	
			28/2/17	
			R W L Dunlop Lt Col R.F.A. Comdg 17: D.A.C	

1577 Wt. W10791/1773 500,000 1/15 D. D. & L. A.D.S.S./Forms/C. 2118.

Instructions regarding War Diaries and Intelligence Summaries are contained in F. S. Regs., Part II. and the Staff Manual respectively. Title pages will be prepared in manuscript.

WAR DIARY
or
INTELLIGENCE SUMMARY.
(Erase heading not required.)

Army Form C. 2118.

Place	Date	Hour	Summary of Events and Information	Remarks and references to Appendices
			Casualties.	
			Wastage from Sickness Officers – . Other Ranks 23.	
			Animals. Horses 27 Mules 28	
			Casualties in action Killed – Wounded 2 Other Ranks	
			Casualties (accidental) Train smash. Killed No 38771 Dvr Cooper T. No 68235 Dvr Tuckey W.A.	
			28/2/17.	
			[signature] LT. COL. R.F.A. COMMANDING 17th DIV. AMM. COLM.	

1577 Wt. W10791/1773 500,000 1/15 D. D. & L. A.D.S.S./Forms/C. 2118.

Army Form C. 2118.

Instructions regarding War Diaries and Intelligence Summaries are contained in F. S. Regs., Part II. and the Staff Manual respectively. Title pages will be prepared in manuscript.

WAR DIARY
or
INTELLIGENCE SUMMARY.
(Erase heading not required.)

Place	Date	Hour	Summary of Events and Information	Remarks and references to Appendices
			vol 21	

Confidential

War Diaries
of
17th Divisional Ammunition Column,
for the month of March 1917.

31/3/17 Volume 21.

H C Collyer Lieut & adj.
LT. COL. R.F.A.
COMMANDING 17th DIV. AMM. COLM.

Instructions regarding War Diaries and Intelligence Summaries are contained in F. S. Regs., Part II. and the Staff Manual respectively. Title pages will be prepared in manuscript.

WAR DIARY
or
INTELLIGENCE SUMMARY.
(Erase heading not required.)

Army Form C. 2118.

Place	Date	Hour	Summary of Events and Information	Remarks and references to Appendices
	1917			
CARNOY	1-3		In camp as follows:-	
			H Qrs A.13.b.8.2 } Sheet 62C	
			No 1 Sec A.13.b.6.6 }	
			" 2 " A.13.b.8.3 }	
			B/ich A.13.b.8.2 }	JCC
			2Lieut M.P. Inteur admitted to Hospital	
"	2.3		No change in distribution of Unit	JCC
			2Lieut R.W. HARPER admitted to Hospital	
"	3.3		No change-	JCC
"	4.3		do	JCC
Nr ALBERT	5.3		Unit marched by road to W.24.C. Central (Albert combined sheet)	JCC
"	6.3		Unit began supply of Ammunition to 17th D.A. in action about M.27 b. - M.28.a (Albert combined sheet)	JCC
"	7.3		No change-	
			56 O.R. Reinforcements joined from Base	JCC

1577 Wt. W10791/1773 500,000 1/15 D. D. & L. A.D.S.S./Forms/C. 2118.

Instructions regarding War Diaries and Intelligence Summaries are contained in F. S. Regs., Part II. and the Staff Manual respectively. Title pages will be prepared in manuscript.

WAR DIARY
or
INTELLIGENCE SUMMARY.
(Erase heading not required.)

Army Form C. 2118.

Place	Date	Hour	Summary of Events and Information	Remarks and references to Appendices
Near ALBERT	1917 8.3		No change 9 O.R. Reinforcements joined from Base	JCC JCC
"	9.3		No change	
"	10.3		do 2 Lieut M.P. TUTEUR from Hospital	JCC
"	11.3		No change 2 Lieut R.W. HARPER from Hospital 2 Lieut M.J. TARRY joined as reinforcement from Base	JCC
"	12.3		No change 2 Lieut M.J. TARRY ~~joined~~ JCC posted to 78' Bde R.F.A. 25 reinforcements posted to 78' Bde R.F.A. 30 " " " 79 "	JCC
"	13.3		No change	JCC
"	14.3		do	JCC
"	15.3		do	JCC
"	16.3		do	JCC

1577 Wt. W10791/1773 500,000 1/15 D. D. & L. A.D.S.S./Forms/C. 2118.

Army Form C. 2118.

Instructions regarding War Diaries and Intelligence Summaries are contained in F. S. Regs., Part II. and the Staff Manual respectively. Title pages will be prepared in manuscript.

WAR DIARY
or
INTELLIGENCE SUMMARY.
(Erase heading not required.)

Place	Date 1917	Hour	Summary of Events and Information	Remarks and references to Appendices
ALBERT	17.3		No change	FCC
PUCHVILLERS	18.3		Unit marched to PUCHVILLERS & went into billets there	FCC
do	19.3		Unit camped & billetted at PUCHVILLERS.	FCC
HEUZECOURT	20.3		Unit marched to HEUZECOURT and ~~went~~ went into camp & billets there	FCC
"	21.3		Camped & billetted at HEUZECOURT	FCC
"	22.3		No change	FCC
			57 OR Reinforcements joined from Base	
			2Lt. C D MORGAN R.F.A, M.C. and Lieut J. F. Rowland joined as reinforcements from Base Depot	
			RSM W Burton joined from "B" Bty 84th Bde R.F.A. on appointment	
"	23.3		No change	FCC
			2Lt G. COLEMAN posted to 33rd D.A.	
			2Lt ~~JB~~ F. ROWLAND posted to 78th Bde RFA	
			2Lt C. D. MORGAN. M.C. posted to 17th Dvl Trench Mortars	
			22 GUNNERS posted to 17th Dvl T. Mortars	
On March	24.3		Unit marched to AUBROMETZ & went into camp & billets there.	FCC

1577 Wt. W10791/1773 500,000 1/15 D. D. & L. A.D.S.S./Forms/C. 2118.

Instructions regarding War Diaries and Intelligence Summaries are contained in F. S. Regs., Part II. and the Staff Manual respectively. Title pages will be prepared in manuscript.

WAR DIARY
or
INTELLIGENCE SUMMARY.
(Erase heading not required.)

Army Form C. 2118.

Place	Date 1917	Hour	Summary of Events and Information	Remarks and references to Appendices
In March	25.3		Unit marched to St MICHAEL (near St POL) and went into camp there	JCC
"	26.3		Unit marched to BRAY and went into camp there	JCC
"	27.3		Unit camped at BRAY at F.20.A.5.8. (Sheet 51C.)	JCC
"	28.3		No change	JCC
"	29.3		No change	JCC
"	30.3		No change	JCC
"	31.3		No change	JCC

J.C. Collins Lieut & Adj
for LT. COL. R.F.A.
COMMANDING 17th DIV. AMM. COLM.

1577 Wt. W10791/1773 500,000 1/15 D. D. & L. A.D.S.S./Forms/C. 2118.

Instructions regarding War Diaries and Intelligence Summaries are contained in F. S. Regs., Part II. and the Staff Manual respectively. Title pages will be prepared in manuscript.

WAR DIARY
or
INTELLIGENCE SUMMARY.
(Erase heading not required.)

Army Form C. 2118.

17th DAC
Vol 22

Place	Date	Hour	Summary of Events and Information	Remarks and references to Appendices
			Confidential War Diaries of 17th Divisional Ammunition Column for the month of April 1917. Volume 22	

R W [illegible]
COMMANDING 17th D[illegible]

1577 Wt. W10791/1773 500,000 1/15 D. D. & L. A.D.S.S./Forms/C. 2118.

Instructions regarding War Diaries and Intelligence Summaries are contained in F. S. Regs., Part II. and the Staff Manual respectively. Title pages will be prepared in manuscript.

WAR DIARY
or
INTELLIGENCE SUMMARY.

(*Erase heading not required.*)

Army Form C. 2118.

Place	Date	Hour	Summary of Events and Information	Remarks and references to Appendices
			Casualties.	
			Wastage from Sickness. Officers Nil. Other Ranks 12.	
			Animals Horses 14 Mules 1	
			Casualties in action Killed Nil Wounded Nil.	
			Casualties (Accidental) Killed Nil Injured Nil.	

31/3/17.

[illegible signature] Lieut & adjutant for LT. COL. R.F.A. COMMANDING 17th DIV. AMM. COLM.

1577 Wt. W10791/1773 500,000 1/15 D. D. & L. A.D.S.S./Forms/C. 2118.

Instructions regarding War Diaries and Intelligence Summaries are contained in F. S. Regs., Part II. and the Staff Manual respectively. Title pages will be prepared in manuscript.

WAR DIARY
or
~~INTELLIGENCE SUMMARY.~~

(Erase heading not required.)

Army Form C. 2118.

Volume 22.

Place	Date 1917	Hour	Summary of Events and Information	Remarks and references to Appendices
BRAY	1-4.		Unit camped at F. 20 a 5 8 (Sheet 51C) A detachment consisting of 5 Officers 160 O Ranks 345 animals 31 G S wagons 12 Limbered G S wagons 3 S A A Carts was formed into a S A A Section to work with 17th Dvl. Infy This S A A Section marched to LE CHUROY today, strength as above. 37 O.R. Reinforcements joined from Base	JCC
"	2.4.		Unit, less S A A Section, camped at F. 20. a. 5. 8. (Sheet 51C)	JCC
"	3.4.		no change.	JCC
"	4.4.		Lieut URQUHART joined as a Reinforcement from Base and was posted to 79 Bde R F A The following detail to form a 'B' Echelon was this day attached to 17 DA	JCC

1577 Wt. W10791/1773 500,000 1/15 D. D. & L. A.D.S.S./Forms/C. 2118.

Instructions regarding War Diaries and Intelligence Summaries are contained in F. S. Regs., Part II. and the Staff Manual respectively. Title pages will be prepared in manuscript.

WAR DIARY
or
INTELLIGENCE SUMMARY.
(Erase heading not required.)

Army Form C. 2118.

Place ~~1917~~	Date 1917	Hour	Summary of Events and Information	Remarks and references to Appendices
BRAY	4.4.		and joined Bdes accordingly:- To 78 Bde RFA — 4 Officers, 118 O.R., 155 Animals, 18 Wagons Amm QF 18pr, 6 " " " 4.5" How To 79 Bde RFA — 4 Officers, 117 O.R., 155 Animals, 18 Wagons Amm QF 18pr, 6 " " " 4.5 How.	JCC
"	5.4.		Unit less SAA Section and detail attached to Bdes. camped at F. 20. a. 5. 8 (Sheet 57c) 14 O.R. Reinforcements posted to 78 Bde RFA and 14 O.R. posted to 79 Bde RFA.	JCC
"	6.4.		No change	JCC
"	7.4		No change	JCC
"	8.4		No change. 2Lt ALDER and 67 O.R. Reinforcements joined from Base - 20 O.R. posted to 78 Bde 20 O.R. posted to 79 Bde. 2Lt ALDER posted to 78 Bde RFA No 39325 a/Br. F. G. Jarrold wounded (slight) in action.	JCC

1577 Wt. W10791/1773 500,000 1/15 D. D. & L. A.D.S.S./Forms/C. 2118.

Army Form C. 2118.

Instructions regarding War Diaries and Intelligence Summaries are contained in F. S. Regs., Part II. and the Staff Manual respectively. Title pages will be prepared in manuscript.

WAR DIARY
or
INTELLIGENCE SUMMARY.
(*Erase heading not required.*)

Place	Date 1917	Hour	Summary of Events and Information	Remarks and references to Appendices
On march	9.4		Following additional detail attached to Brigades from the DAC :-	FCC
			78th Bde RFA 18 Drivers 36 L D horses or mules	
			79 Bde RFA 15 " 30 — " —	
			Remainder of unit moved to AGNEZ lez DUISANS and went into camp and billets there.	
AGNEZ	10.4		In camp at AGNEZ lez DUISANS	FCC
"	11.4		-do-	FCC
ARRAS	12.4		Unit marched to camp just W of ARRAS (G.20. central - Sheet 51b)	FCC
"	13.4		In camp near ARRAS	FCC
"	14.4		do-	FCC
"	15.4		do-	FCC
			86 O.R. reinforcements joined from Base	
"	16.4		In camp near ARRAS	FCC
"	17.4		-do-	FCC
			50 Reinforcements posted to 78th Bde RFA	
			34 " " " 79	

1577 Wt. W10791/1773 500,000 1/15 D. D. & L. A.D.S.S./Forms/C. 2118.

Army Form C. 2118.

Instructions regarding War Diaries and Intelligence Summaries are contained in F. S. Regs., Part II. and the Staff Manual respectively. Title pages will be prepared in manuscript.

WAR DIARY
or
INTELLIGENCE SUMMARY.
(Erase heading not required.)

Place	Date 1917	Hour	Summary of Events and Information	Remarks and references to Appendices
ARRAS	18 4		In camp near ARRAS	
			2Lt. A.C. TOLHURST attached to 78th Bde RFA	FCC
"	19.4		In camp near ARRAS	FCC
			2 O.R. reinforcements posted to 47th Amm Sub Park	
"	20.4		In camp near ARRAS - 38135 Dr. J. HARRISON wounded (at duty) taking amm to gun positions of 17th D.A. in action near FEUCHY CAPEL	FCC
"	21.4		-do-	FCC
			39 O.R. reinforcements joined from Base	
			6 L D horses and 4 L D mules No 2 Section wounded on ammunition carrying fatigue	
			Report received from O.C. S.A.A. Section that during last few days 14 mules have been killed in action	
"	22.4		In camp near ARRAS	FCC
"	23.4		No change	
			No 84243 Sergt. C. GOOCH wounded (at duty) in action - Taking up amm to 17th D.A. in action near ~~FUSHY~~ FEUCHY CAPEL	FCC
			No 114870 Dr. A. LIPSCOMBE was also wounded at the same time	

1577 Wt. W10791/1773 500,000 1/15 D. D. & L. A.D.S.S./Forms/C. 2118.

Army Form C. 2118.

Instructions regarding War Diaries and Intelligence Summaries are contained in F. S. Regs., Part II. and the Staff Manual respectively. Title pages will be prepared in manuscript.

WAR DIARY
or
INTELLIGENCE SUMMARY.

(Erase heading not required.)

Place	Date 1917	Hour	Summary of Events and Information	Remarks and references to Appendices
ARRAS	24.4		In camp near ARRAS No 93176 Dr J. RICHARDSON killed in action at BATTERY VALLEY Sheet 51 b N.W.	JCC
"	25.4		In camp near ARRAS 6 OR reinforcements posted to 78th Bde R.F.A. 7 " " " 79th " 23 " " " 17th Div Trench Mortars	JCC
"	26.4		In camp near ARRAS.	JCC
(Sheet 51 b)			At about noon hostile shell fire was opened on an Ammunition Dump at G 29. C. 4.9, held on charge by this unit and known as "E" Dump 17th Group VI Corps. The second shell dropped on a dump of AX and set alight to the boxes. An ammunition wagon belonging to a Battery of the 79th Brigade R.F.A. was destroyed by a direct hit - the horses of the team being killed. No 1246 Dr. R. ATKINSON of this unit was wounded (at duty). Approximately the following ammunition was destroyed. - 11428 A, 11880 AX, 4752 BX 500 A Smoke, 300 BCBR, 518 BSK, 1472 DX, 1650 DPS, 220 DSK	

Instructions regarding War Diaries and Intelligence Summaries are contained in F. S. Regs., Part II. and the Staff Manual respectively. Title pages will be prepared in manuscript.

WAR DIARY
or
INTELLIGENCE SUMMARY.
(Erase heading not required.)

Army Form C. 2118.

Place	Date 1917	Hour	Summary of Events and Information	Remarks and references to Appendices
ARRAS	27.4		In camp near ARRAS	FCC
"	28.4		-do-	FCC
"	29.4		-do-	FCC
"	30.4		-do-	FCC
			Casualties.	
			Wastage from Sickness Officers Nil. Other Ranks 30.	
			Animals:- Killed: Horses. Mules. Wounded: Horses. Mules.	
			Casualties in Action: Killed Horses 2, Mules 21; Wounded Horses 8, Mules 12	
			Casualties (Evacuations). Horses 21, Mules 9	
			Casualties:- Officers Nil	
			Other Ranks:- Killed 1 (L/093176 Dvr Richardson G)	
			Wounded 5.	
			[signature]	
			Lt. Col. R.F.A. Commanding 17th Div. Am. Coln.	

Instructions regarding War Diaries and Intelligence Summaries are contained in F. S. Regs., Part II. and the Staff Manual respectively. Title pages will be prepared in manuscript.

WAR DIARY
or
INTELLIGENCE SUMMARY.
(Erase heading not required.)

Army Form C. 2118.

Vol 23

Place	Date	Hour	Summary of Events and Information	Remarks and references to Appendices
			Confidential War Diary of 17th Divisional Ammunition Column from 1/5/17 to 31/5/17	
			1/6/17. Volume 23.	
			H. C. Collins Lt. (?) for LT. COL. R.F.A. COMMANDING 17th DIV. AMM. COLM.	

1577 Wt. W10791/1773 500,000 1/15 D. D. & L. A.D.S.S./Forms/C. 2118.

Instructions regarding War Diaries and Intelligence Summaries are contained in F. S. Regs., Part II. and the Staff Manual respectively. Title pages will be prepared in manuscript.

WAR DIARY
or
INTELLIGENCE SUMMARY.
(Erase heading not required.)

Army Form C. 2118.

Place	Date 1917	Hour	Summary of Events and Information	Remarks and references to Appendices
ARRAS	1-5		Unit camped at G.20 central (Sheet 51b) near ARRAS except S.A.A. Section attached to, and working with, 17th Divl Infy.	JCC
"	2-5		No change	JCC
"	3.5		do	
			4 O.R. reinforcements joined from Base	JCC
"	4.5		No change	JCC
			2 O.R. posted to 78th Bde R.F.A.	
			2 O.R. posted to 79th Bde R.F.A.	
"	5.5		No change	
			No 46716 Gunner A. J. WILKINS wounded whilst conveying ammunition to Gun Positions 17th D.A. near FEUCHY CAPEL (sheet 51b) also 2 mules killed and 3 wounded.	JCC
"	6.5		No change.	JCC
"	7.5		No change.	JCC
			13 O.R. Reinforcements joined from Base	
"	8.5		No change	JCC

Instructions regarding War Diaries and Intelligence Summaries are contained in F. S. Regs., Part II. and the Staff Manual respectively. Title pages will be prepared in manuscript.

WAR DIARY
or
INTELLIGENCE SUMMARY.
(Erase heading not required.)

Army Form C. 2118.

Place	Date 1917	Hour	Summary of Events and Information	Remarks and references to Appendices
ARRAS	9-5		In camp at G 20 central (sheet 51b)	JCC
			5 O.R. posted to 78th Bde RFA	
			7 " " " 79 "	
			1 " " " 17 Divl T. Mortars	
"	10.5		No change	JCC
			No. 72028 Whlr Corpl W Jackson / 96362 Gunr L Day / 76646 Drvr L Birchall } accidentally wounded through the explosion of a German Time fuze they were taking to pieces	
"	11-5		No change	
			No 96362 Gnr L Day / 76646 D L Birchall } Died of wounds accidentally received.	JCC
"	12.5		No change	JCC
			107 O.R. reinforcements joined from Base	
"	13.5		No change.	JCC
"	14.5		No change.	JCC
"	15.5		No change. 38 O.R posted to 78th Bde RFA & 53 O.R to 79 Bde RFA	JCC

1577 Wt. W10791/1773 500,000 1/15 D. D. & L. A.D.S.S./Forms/C. 2118.

Instructions regarding War Diaries and Intelligence Summaries are contained in F. S. Regs., Part II. and the Staff Manual respectively. Title pages will be prepared in manuscript.

WAR DIARY
or
INTELLIGENCE SUMMARY.
(Erase heading not required.)

Army Form C. 2118.

Place	Date 1917	Hour	Summary of Events and Information	Remarks and references to Appendices
ARRAS	16.5		In camp at G.20 central (sheet 51 b)	FCC
"	17.5		No change	FCC
"	18.5		No 2 Section moved to AYETTE (Lens Sheet 11) S of ARRAS and became attached to 37th Div Arty. for supply to 79th Bde RFA. 39 O.R joined from Base	FCC
			The Unit is now encamped as follows	
			H.Q & No 1 Sec } G.20 central (sheet 51 b)	
			No 2 " AYETTE (Lens sheet 11)	
			" 3 " G.11 b 5 7 (sheet 51 b)	
"	19.5		No change	FCC
"	20.5		No change	FCC
			16 O.R. posted to 78th Bde RFA	
			17 O.R. posted to 79th Bde RFA	
			2/Lieut R.G. NEWMAN BUTLER posted to C/79 Bde RFA	
"	21.5		No change	FCC
"	22.5		do	FCC

1577 Wt. W10791/1773 500,000 1/15 D. D. & L. A.D.S.S./Forms/C. 2118.

Instructions regarding War Diaries and Intelligence Summaries are contained in F. S. Regs., Part II. and the Staff Manual respectively. Title pages will be prepared in manuscript.

WAR DIARY
or
INTELLIGENCE SUMMARY.
(Erase heading not required.)

Army Form C. 2118.

Place	Date 1917	Hour	Summary of Events and Information	Remarks and references to Appendices
ARRAS	21-5		No change	FCC
"	22.5		do	FCC
"	23.5		No 2 Section returned to Camp at G 20 Central today	FCC
"	24.5		No change	FCC
"	25.5		No change - Lt L.M. WOODLAND admitted to hospital (sick)	FCC
"	26.5		No change 27 O.R. reinforcements arrived from Base & were posted as follows :- 15 to 78 Bde RFA 10 to 79 Bde RFA 1 to Trench Mortars & the remaining man remaining with DAC	FCC
"	27.5		No change	FCC
"	28.5		No change	FCC
"	29.5		No change	FCC
"	30.5		No change	FCC
	31.5		No change	FCC

F C Collins
Lieut. R.F.A.
Adjt. 17th Div. Amm. Coln
Lieut. R.F.A.

1577 Wt. W10791/1773 500,000 1/15 D. D. & L. A.D.S.S./Forms/C. 2118.

Instructions regarding War Diaries and Intelligence Summaries are contained in F. S. Regs., Part II. and the Staff Manual respectively. Title pages will be prepared in manuscript.

WAR DIARY
or
INTELLIGENCE SUMMARY.
(Erase heading not required.)

Army Form C. 2118.

Place	Date	Hour	Summary of Events and Information	Remarks and references to Appendices
			Casualties	
			Officers (Sick). 1 Officer.	
			Other Ranks (Sick). 12	
			Officers Killed Nil Wounded Nil	
			Other Ranks Killed Nil Wounded No 46796 Gnr WILKINS A.J. (Accidental)	
			Accidentally Injured (Not on duty). No 42078 Whlr Cpl JACKSON W	
			96362 Gnr. DAY L.	
			46646 Dr BIRCHALL L.	
			Horses. Killed by shell fire. 2. Died in Hospital.	
			Evacuated 7. No 21144 Bdr Gaunt W	
			Mules Evacuated 4 No 96362 Gnr DAY L	
			No 46646 Dr BIRCHALL L	
	1/6/17		F.C. Collins Lt & Adjt for	

1577 Wt. W10791/1773 500,000 1/15 D. D. & L. A.D.S.S./Forms/C. 2118.

Instructions regarding War Diaries and Intelligence Summaries are contained in F. S. Regs., Part II. and the Staff Manual respectively. Title pages will be prepared in manuscript.

WAR DIARY
or
INTELLIGENCE SUMMARY.
(Erase heading not required.)

Army Form C. 2118.

Vol 24

Place	Date	Hour	Summary of Events and Information	Remarks and references to Appendices
			Confidential War Diary of 17th Divisional Ammunition Column from 1/6/17 to 30/6/17 30/6/17. Volume 24. [illegible] LT. COL. R.F.A. COMMANDING 17th DIV. AMM. COLM.	

1577 Wt. W10791/1773 500,000 1/15 D. D. & L. A.D.S.S./Forms/C. 2118.

Instructions regarding War Diaries and Intelligence Summaries are contained in F. S. Regs., Part II. and the Staff Manual respectively. Title pages will be prepared in manuscript.

WAR DIARY
or
INTELLIGENCE SUMMARY.
(*Erase heading not required.*)

Army Form C. 2118.

Place	Date 1917	Hour	Summary of Events and Information	Remarks and references to Appendices
ARRAS	1.6		Unit camped as follows:-	FCC
			"A" Echelon at G. 20 central (Sheet 51b)	
			"B" " " G. 11.a.9.4 -do-	
			"B" Echelon rejoined the 17th Dvl Arty. from attachment to 17th Dvl. Infy.	
			3 O.R. reinforcements joined from Base	
			2 O.R. posted to 78th Bde. R.F.A	
			1 O.R. posted to 17th Trench Mortars (Med)	
"	2.6.		No change	FCC
"	3.6		No change	FCC
"	4.6		No change	FCC
"	5.6		No change	FCC
			12 O.R. reinforcements joined from Base	
"	6.6		No change	FCC
			2 O.R. posted to 78th Bde R.F.A	
"	7.6		No change	FCC
			6 O.R. posted to 79 Bde R.F.A	

1577 Wt. W10791/1773 500,000 1/15 D. D. & L. A.D.S.S./Forms/C. 2118.

Instructions regarding War Diaries and Intelligence Summaries are contained in F. S. Regs., Part II. and the Staff Manual respectively. Title pages will be prepared in manuscript.

WAR DIARY
or
INTELLIGENCE SUMMARY.
(Erase heading not required.)

Army Form C. 2118.

Place	Date 1917	Hour	Summary of Events and Information	Remarks and references to Appendices
ARRAS	8.6		Unit camped as follows:-	JCC
			A echelon at G.20. central (sheet 51b)	
			B echelon at G.11.a.9.4 do.	
			2 O.R. reinforcements posted from Base	
			1 O.R. posted to 79th Bde. R.F.A.	
			1 O.R. posted to 78th Bde. R.F.A.	
do.	9.6.		No change	JCC
do	10.6		No change	
			Lieut. L. M. WOODLAND rejoined from Hospital	JCC
do.	11.6		No change	JCC
do	12.6		No change	JCC
			21 O.R. reinforcements joined from Base	
			No 58935 BQMS A. BAREHAM Commissioned and posted to 33rd. Divl. Arty as 2Lieut.	
do	13.6		No change	JCC

1577 Wt. W10791/1773 500,000 1/15 D. D. & L. A.D.S.S./Forms/C. 2118.

Instructions regarding War Diaries and Intelligence Summaries are contained in F. S. Regs., Part II. and the Staff Manual respectively. Title pages will be prepared in manuscript.

WAR DIARY
or
INTELLIGENCE SUMMARY.
(Erase heading not required.)

Army Form C. 2118.

Place	Date 1917	Hour	Summary of Events and Information	Remarks and references to Appendices
ARRAS	14.6		Unit camped as follows:-	
			A echelon at G.20. central (sheet 51b)	FCL
			B " at G.11.a.9.4 -do-	
			6 O.R. posted to 78 Bde RFA	
			13 O.R. posted to 79 Bde RFA	
do	15.6		No change	FCL
do	16.6		No1 Section moved to camp at G.1.d.0.7 (sheet 51b) being relieved by 20th DAC	FCL
			and relieving No1 Sect. 51st DAC.	FCL
do	17.6		No change	FCL
do	18.6		H.Qrs. moved to camp at F.22.C.4.0 (sheet 51c)	FCL
			No2 Section moved camp to G.1.d.0.7 (sheet 51d) being relieved by 293 BAC	FCL
			in relief of No2 Sec. 51 DAC	
			Handed over E Dump to 293 DAC	
			The Unit is now camped as follows	
			H.Qrs. F.22.C.4.0 (sheet 51c)	
			Remainder A Echelon G.1.d.0.7	
			B " G.11.a.9.4	

1577 Wt. W10791/1773 500,000 1/15 D. D. & L. A.D.S.S./Forms/C. 2118.

Army Form C. 2118.

WAR DIARY
or
INTELLIGENCE SUMMARY.
(Erase heading not required.)

Instructions regarding War Diaries and Intelligence Summaries are contained in F. S. Regs., Part II. and the Staff Manual respectively. Title pages will be prepared in manuscript.

Place	Date 1917	Hour	Summary of Events and Information	Remarks and references to Appendices
W of ANZIN	19.6		No change	[initials]
do	20.6		No change	[initials]
			2Lt. H. CHERMSIDE to Base for dental treatment	
do	21-6		No change	[initials]
			37 O.R. reinforcements joined from Base	
do	22-6		No change	
do	23-6		No change	
do	24-6		No change 13 OR posted to 78 Bde RFA, 17 OR posted 79 Bde RFA, 10 OR to Trench Mortars	
do	25-6		No change	
do	26-6		No change	
do	27-6		No change	
do	28-6		No change 13 O Ranks reinforcements from Base	
do	29-6		No change	
do	30-6		No change	

[signature]
LT. COL. R.F.A.
COMMANDING 17th DIV. AMM. COLM.

1577 Wt. W10791/1773 500,000 1/15 D. D. & L. A.D.S.S./Forms/C. 2118.

Army Form C. 2118.

Instructions regarding War Diaries and Intelligence Summaries are contained in F. S. Regs., Part II. and the Staff Manual respectively. Title pages will be prepared in manuscript.

WAR DIARY
or
INTELLIGENCE SUMMARY.
(*Erase heading not required.*)

Place	Date	Hour	Summary of Events and Information	Remarks and references to Appendices
			Casualties.	
			Officers (Sick) 2 Officers	
			Other Ranks (Sick) 13 O/Rs	
			Officers Killed Nil Wounded Nil.	
			Other Rank. Killed Nil Wounded Nil.	
			Horses. Evacuated. 3	
			Mules. Evacuated. 6	
			[signature] LT. COL. R.F.A. COMMANDING 17th DIV. AMM. COLM.	

30/4/7

1577 Wt. W10791/1773 500,000 1/15 D. D. & L. A.D.S.S./Forms/C. 2118.

Instructions regarding War Diaries and Intelligence Summaries are contained in F. S. Regs., Part II. and the Staff Manual respectively. Title pages will be prepared in manuscript.

WAR DIARY
or
INTELLIGENCE SUMMARY.
(Erase heading not required.)

Army Form C. 2118.

Place	Date	Hour	Summary of Events and Information	Remarks and references to Appendices
			VH 25	
			Confidential	
			War Diary	
			of	
			17th Divisional Ammunition Column	
			from 1/7/17 to 31/7/17.	
			31/7/17. Volume 25	
			R. [signature]	
			LT. COL. R.F.A. COMMANDING ... AMM. COLM.	

1577 Wt. W10791/1773 500,000 1/15 D. D. & L. A.D.S.S./Forms/C. 2118.

Instructions regarding War Diaries and Intelligence Summaries are contained in F. S. Regs., Part II. and the Staff Manual respectively. Title pages will be prepared in manuscript.

WAR DIARY
or
INTELLIGENCE SUMMARY.
(Erase heading not required.)

Army Form C. 2118.

Place	Date	Hour	Summary of Events and Information	Remarks and references to Appendices
ANZIN	1.7.17		Unit camped as follows: A Echelon G.1.d.0.7. B Echelon G.11.a.9.4. (Sheet 51b)	M.A.T.
			H.Q. F.22.c.4.0. (Sheet 51C)	M.A.T.
			1 O.R. posted to H.Q. 17th D.A. 4 O.R. to 78th Brigade. 7 OR	M.A.T.
			to 79th Brigade.	M.A.T.
	2		No change.	M.A.T.
	3		" " 2/Lieut H. Chermside from hospital	M.A.T.
	4		" " "	M.A.T.
	5		" "	M.A.T.
	6		" "	HCC
	7		" "	
			12 O.R reinforcements joined from Base	HCC
	8		No change	HCC
	9		No change	HCC
	10		No change	HCC
	11		No Change	HCC

1577 Wt. W10791/1773 500,000 1/15 D. D. & L. A.D.S.S./Forms/C. 2118.

Instructions regarding War Diaries and Intelligence Summaries are contained in F. S. Regs., Part II. and the Staff Manual respectively. Title pages will be prepared in manuscript.

WAR DIARY
or
INTELLIGENCE SUMMARY.
(Erase heading not required.)

Army Form C. 2118.

Place	Date 1917	Hour	Summary of Events and Information	Remarks and references to Appendices
ANZIN	12.7		No change	
			5 O.R. posted to 78th Bde RFA	FCC
			4 O.R. posted to 79 Bde RFA	
			4 O.R. posted to 17th Div. Trench Mortars	
	13.7		No change	
			No 7774 Sergt C. DEAR AVC posted from No 13 Vety Hospl	FCC
	14.7		No change - 9 O.R. reinforcements joined from Base	FCC
	15.7		No change -	FCC
			8 O.R. posted to 79 BdeRFA	
	16.7		No change.	FCC
	17.7		No change.	FCC
	18.7		No change -	FCC
	19		No 18939 Dr L. ROBINSON No 3 Sec. wounded in action near FAMPOUX & 2 mules killed.	
	19.7		No change	FCC
			No 3971 BQMS J. HANNAH posted from C/63 BdeRFA	

1577 Wt. W10791/1773 500,000 1/15 D. D. & L. A.D.S.S./Forms/C. 2118.

Instructions regarding War Diaries and Intelligence Summaries are contained in F. S. Regs., Part II. and the Staff Manual respectively. Title pages will be prepared in manuscript.

WAR DIARY
or
INTELLIGENCE SUMMARY.
(Erase heading not required.)

Army Form C. 2118.

Place	Date 1917	Hour	Summary of Events and Information	Remarks and references to Appendices
ANZIN	20.7		No change -	FCC
	21.7		No change -	FCC
	22.7		No change - 14 Remounts received from Adv. Remount Depot	FCC
	23.7		No change -	FCC
	24.7		No change - 26 Remounts received from Adv. Remount Depot	FCC
	25.7		No change -	FCC
	26.7		No change - 2 Remounts posted to 17th Div. Signals	FCC
	27.7		No change -	FCC
	28.7		No change -	FCC
	29.7		No change -	FCC
	30.7		No change -	FCC
	31.7		No change -	FCC

R. [illegible] Lt. Col. R.F.A.

1577 Wt. W10791/1773 500,000 1/15 D. D. & L. A.D.S.S./Forms/C. 2118.

Instructions regarding War Diaries and Intelligence Summaries are contained in F. S. Regs., Part II. and the Staff Manual respectively. Title pages will be prepared in manuscript.

WAR DIARY
or
INTELLIGENCE SUMMARY.
(Erase heading not required.)

Army Form C. 2118.

Place	Date	Hour	Summary of Events and Information	Remarks and references to Appendices
			Casualties	
			Officers (Sick) 2	
			Other Ranks (Sick) 9	
			Officers. Killed Nil Wounded Nil	
			Other Ranks Killed Nil Wounded No 18939 D. L. ROBINSON. at Duty.	
			Horses Evacuated 5	
			Mules Evacuated 4	
			31/7/17	
			[signature] LT. COL. R.F.A. COMMANDING 17th DIV. AMM. COLM.	

1577 Wt. W10791/1773 500,000 1/15 D. D. & L. A.D.S.S./Forms/C. 2118.

Army Form C. 2118.

WAR DIARY
or
INTELLIGENCE SUMMARY.
(Erase heading not required.)

Instructions regarding War Diaries and Intelligence Summaries are contained in F. S. Regs., Part II. and the Staff Manual respectively. Title pages will be prepared in manuscript.

Vol 26

Place	Date	Hour	Summary of Events and Information	Remarks and references to Appendices
			Confidential War Diary of 17th Divisional Ammunition Column from 1/8/17 to 31/8/17. 31/8/17 Volume 26 [signature] LT. COL. R.F.A. COMMANDING 17th DIV. AMM. COLM	

1577 Wt. W10791/1773 500,000 1/15 D. D. & L. A.D.S.S./Forms/C. 2118.

Instructions regarding War Diaries and Intelligence Summaries are contained in F. S. Regs., Part II. and the Staff Manual respectively. Title pages will be prepared in manuscript.

WAR DIARY
or
INTELLIGENCE SUMMARY.
(Erase heading not required.)

Army Form C. 2118.

Place	Date 1917	Hour	Summary of Events and Information	Remarks and references to Appendices
ANZIN	1-8.		Unit in camp as follows:-	
			H.Qrs. F. 22 C.4.0. (sheet 51c)	FCC
			No.1 & No.2 Sections G.1.d.0.7 (sheet 51b)	
			No.3 Section G.11 a 9.4 (sheet 51b)	
"	2.8		No change -	FCC
			1 O.R. to 29th Mobile Vety. Section	
"	3.8		No change	FCC
"	4.8		No change.	
			7 O.R. reinforcements from Base	
			5 O.R. posted to 78th Bde R.F.A. and 7 O.R. posted to 17th Div. T.M.	FCC
"	5.8		No change	FCC
			1 O.R. to Base Detail	
			1 O.R. from Base	
			1 O.R. posted to 7?th Bde R.F.A.	
"	6.8		No change	FCC
"			1 O.R. posted to 5th D.A.C.	

Army Form C. 2118.

Instructions regarding War Diaries and Intelligence Summaries are contained in F. S. Regs., Part II. and the Staff Manual respectively. Title pages will be prepared in manuscript.

WAR DIARY
or
INTELLIGENCE SUMMARY.
(Erase heading not required.)

Place	Date 1917	Hour	Summary of Events and Information	Remarks and references to Appendices
ANZIN	7.8		No change	JCC
"	8.8		No change	JCC
			1 O.R. posted from Base	
"	9.8		No change	JCC
"	10.8		No change.	JCC
"	11.8		No change.	JCC
			1 O.R. posted from H.Q. 17th D. Arty.	
"	12.8		No change	JCC
"	13.8		No change	JCC
"	14.8		No change.	JCC
"	15.8		No change.	JCC
"	16.8		No change –	JCC
			1 O.R. posted from 17th Div T. M.	
"	17.8		No change	JCC
"	18.8		No change	JCC
"	19.8		No change	JCC

1577 Wt. W10791/1773 500,000 1/15 D. D. & L. A.D.S.S./Forms/C. 2118.

Army Form C. 2118.

WAR DIARY
or
INTELLIGENCE SUMMARY.
(Erase heading not required.)

Instructions regarding War Diaries and Intelligence Summaries are contained in F. S. Regs., Part II. and the Staff Manual respectively. Title pages will be prepared in manuscript.

Place	Date 1917	Hour	Summary of Events and Information	Remarks and references to Appendices
ANZIN	20.8		No change.	JCC
do	21.8		No change.	JCC
do	22.8		No change.	JCC
do	23.8		No change	JCC
do	24.8		No change.	JCC
do	25.8		No change.	JCC
do	26.8		No change.	JCC
do.	27.8		No change.	JCC
do	28.8		Re-organization of the Unit begun.	
			The Unit is now organized as A Echelon, consisting of H.Qrs. & Nos 1 & 2 Sections & S.A.A. Section.	JCC
			A portion of the surplus establishment was today transferred to the Advanced H.T Depot, Abbeville & consisted of the following:–	
			19 Drivers	
			38 L.D Horses	
			18 G.S. Wagons & 1 Maltese Cart	

Instructions regarding War Diaries and Intelligence Summaries are contained in F. S. Regs., Part II. and the Staff Manual respectively. Title pages will be prepared in manuscript.

WAR DIARY
or
INTELLIGENCE SUMMARY.
(*Erase heading not required.*)

Army Form C. 2118.

Place	Date 1917	Hour	Summary of Events and Information	Remarks and references to Appendices
ANZIN	29-8		No change.	JCC
do	30-8		No change. 8 L.D. horses and 19 mules to 29th Mobile Vety Section on reduction of establishment.	JCC
do	31-8		No change	JCC

[signature] LT. COL. R.F.A.
COMMANDING 17th DIV. AMM. COLM.

1577 Wt. W10791/1773 500,000 1/15 D. D. & L. A.D.S.S./Forms/C. 2118.

Instructions regarding War Diaries and Intelligence Summaries are contained in F. S. Regs., Part II. and the Staff Manual respectively. Title pages will be prepared in manuscript.

WAR DIARY
or
INTELLIGENCE SUMMARY.
(Erase heading not required.)

Army Form C. 2118.

Place	Date	Hour	Summary of Events and Information	Remarks and references to Appendices
			Casualties	
			Officers (Sick) Nil	
			Other Ranks (Sick) 7	
			Officers. Killed Nil	
			Officers Wounded Nil	
			Other Ranks Killed Nil	
			Other Ranks Wounded Nil	
			Horses Evacuated 5 ~~44~~ Prisr Transferred 48 Died 1	
			Mules Evacuated 6 ~~28~~ Prisr " 30 " 2	
			31/8/17	
			[signature] Lt. Col. R.F.A. Commanding 17th Div. Amm. Col.	

1577 Wt. W10791/1773 500,000 1/15 D. D. & L. A.D.S.S./Forms/C. 2118.

Instructions regarding War Diaries and Intelligence Summaries are contained in F. S. Regs., Part II. and the Staff Manual respectively. Title pages will be prepared in manuscript.

WAR DIARY
or
INTELLIGENCE SUMMARY.
(Erase heading not required.)

Army Form C. 2118.

Place	Date	Hour	Summary of Events and Information	Remarks and references to Appendices
			Vol 27	
			Confidential	
			War Diary	
			of	
			17th Divisional Ammunition Column	
			from 1/9/17 to 30/9/17	
	30/9/17		Volume 27	
			J C Allen CAPTAIN, R.F.A. ADJUTANT 17TH DIV. AMN. COL.	

2353 Wt. W2544/1454 700,000 5/15 D. D. & L. A.D.S.S./Forms/C. 2118.

Instructions regarding War Diaries and Intelligence Summaries are contained in F. S. Regs., Part II. and the Staff Manual respectively. Title pages will be prepared in manuscript.

WAR DIARY
or
INTELLIGENCE SUMMARY.

(Erase heading not required.)

Army Form C. 2118.

Place	Date	Hour	Summary of Events and Information	Remarks and references to Appendices
	1917			
ANZIN	1-9		Unit in camp as follows:-	
			HQrs. F. 22 c. 4. 0 (Sheet 51C)	JCC
			Nos. 1 & No 2 Sections G. 1. d. 0. 7 (Sheet 51b)	
			No 3 Section G. 11. a 9. 4 (Sheet 51b)	
"	2.9		No change	JCC
"	3.9		No change	JCC
"	4.9		No change	JCC
"	5.9		No change	JCC
"	6.9		2 Lieut. [illegible] CLOUDESLY RFA posted from D/78 Bde RFA	JCC
"	7.9		No change	JCC
"	8.9		No change	JCC
"	9.9		No change	JCC
"	10.9		No change - No 111878 Driver J. ROBSON No 3 Sect. wounded.	JCC
"	11-9		No change - 2Lt. W. A. CARNE posted to D/78 Bde RFA	JCC
"	12.9		No change -	JCC
"	13.9		No change.	JCC

1577 Wt. W10791/1773 500,000 1/15 D. D. & L. A.D.S.S./Forms/C. 2118.

Instructions regarding War Diaries and Intelligence Summaries are contained in F. S. Regs., Part II. and the Staff Manual respectively. Title pages will be prepared in manuscript.

WAR DIARY
or
INTELLIGENCE SUMMARY.
(Erase heading not required.)

Army Form C. 2118.

Place	Date	Hour	Summary of Events and Information	Remarks and references to Appendices
			No change	
ANZIN	14 9/17		The following Animals were posted to Bdes of 17th D.A. 37 to 78 Bde RFA + 23 to 79th Bde RFA.	HCC
				HCC
do	15 9/17		No change	HCC
do	16 9/17		do	HCC
do	17 9/17		do	HCC
do	18 9/17		do	HCC
do	19 9/17		do	HCC
do	20 9/17		do	HCC
do	21 9/17		do	HCC
do	22 9/17		do	HCC
do	23 9/17		do	HCC
do	24 9/17		do - Lt H. CHERMSIDE to Hospital	HCC
do	25 9/17		do	HCC
do	26 9/17		do	HCC
do	27 9/17		do	HCC
do	28 9/17		do	HCC

2353 Wt. W2544/1454 700,000 5/15 D. D. & L. A.D.S.S./Forms/C. 2118.

Instructions regarding War Diaries and Intelligence Summaries are contained in F. S. Regs., Part II. and the Staff Manual respectively. Title pages will be prepared in manuscript.

WAR DIARY

or

INTELLIGENCE SUMMARY.

(Erase heading not required.)

Army Form C. 2118.

Place	Date	Hour	Summary of Events and Information	Remarks and references to Appendices
ANZIN	29/9/17		No change	[initials]
do	30/9/17		No change	[initials]

[signature]
CAPTAIN. R.F.A.
ADJUTANT 17th DIV. AMM. COL.

2353 Wt. W2544/1454 700,000 5/15 D. D. & L. A.D.S.S./Forms/C. 2118.

Instructions regarding War Diaries and Intelligence Summaries are contained in F. S. Regs., Part II. and the Staff Manual respectively. Title pages will be prepared in manuscript.

WAR DIARY
or
INTELLIGENCE SUMMARY.
(Erase heading not required.)

Army Form C. 2118.

Place	Date	Hour	Summary of Events and Information	Remarks and references to Appendices
			Casualties	
			Officers (Sick) 2/Lt H. Chermside	
			Other Ranks (Sick). 10.	
			Officers Killed Nil	
			Officers Wounded Nil	
			Other Ranks Killed Nil	
			Other Ranks Wounded 1 Other Ranks	
			Horses Evacuated 2	
			Mules Evacuated —	
			30/9/17	H C Allen CAPTAIN. R.F.A. ADJUTANT 17th DIV. AMM. COL.

2353 Wt. W2544/1454 700,000 5/15 D. D. & L. A.D.S.S./Forms/C. 2118.

Instructions regarding War Diaries and Intelligence Summaries are contained in F. S. Regs., Part II. and the Staff Manual respectively. Title pages will be prepared in manuscript.

WAR DIARY
or
INTELLIGENCE SUMMARY.
(Erase heading not required.)

Army Form C. 2118.

Vol 28

Place	Date	Hour	Summary of Events and Information	Remarks and references to Appendices
			Confidential War Diary of 17th Divisional Ammunition Column from 1/10/17 to 31/10/17	

31/10/17 Volume 28

[signature]
LT. COL. R.F.A.
COMMANDING 17th DIV: AMM. COL

2353 Wt. W2544/1454 700,000 5/15 D. D. & L. A.D.S.S./Forms/C. 2118.

Army Form C. 2118.

Instructions regarding War Diaries and Intelligence Summaries are contained in F. S. Regs., Part II. and the Staff Manual respectively. Title pages will be prepared in manuscript.

WAR DIARY
or
INTELLIGENCE SUMMARY.
(Erase heading not required.)

Place	Date 1917	Hour	Summary of Events and Information	Remarks and references to Appendices
ANZIN	1-10		Unit camped at	
			H.Qrs. F.22 c.4.0 (Sheet 51c)	KCC
			Nos 1 & 2 Sections G.1.d 0.7 (Sheet 51b)	
			No. 3 Sec. G.11.a 9.4 (Sheet 51b)	
			H.Qrs & No 1 Section entrained at Arras to proceed North	
	2-10		No 2 Section & No 3 Sec. entrained at Arras to proceed North	
			H.Qrs. No 2 Section & half No 3 Sec. detrained at CASSEL	KCC
			No 1 Section & half No 3 Section detrained at GODEWAERSVELDE	
			and the Unit marched in that order to camp at F.1.b. (Sheet 27) PROVEN	
PROVEN	3-10		Unit in camp at F.1.b (Sheet 27)	KCC
	4-10		All G.S. wagons of "A" Echelon moved to forward camp at A.5.d. (Sheet 28)	KCC
			for the purpose of collecting & carting materials to gun positions	
			A Echelon engaged in the supply of ammn. to gun positions as follows	
			78th Bde U.28.d (Sheet 20) 79th Bde C.4.a. (Sheet 28) during the night	
	5-10		4-5/10/17 – During the operation No. 94948 Driver G. CLARK No 2 Section	
			was wounded 1 horse was killed & 2 were wounded.	KCC
			Ammunition & material Dumps were established in C.4.a and U.25.d	
	6-10		During the night 5-6 Oct 1917 A Echelon assisted by animals of B Echelon	KCC
			continued to take ammunition to gun positions. The following casualties	

2353 Wt. W2544/1454 700,000 5/15 D. D. & L. A.D.S.S./Forms/C. 2118.

Instructions regarding War Diaries and Intelligence Summaries are contained in F. S. Regs., Part II. and the Staff Manual respectively. Title pages will be prepared in manuscript.

WAR DIARY
or
INTELLIGENCE SUMMARY.
(*Erase heading not required.*)

Army Form C. 2118.

Place	Date	Hour	Summary of Events and Information	Remarks and references to Appendices
	6.10		occurred:-	
			One 4.5" How Amm wagon was destroyed through the explosion of a projectile inside it.	
			One 4.5" How Amm wagon & four 18pr. Amm wagons destroyed by shell fire	FC
			One 4.5" How Amm Limber sank in swamp & could not be recovered	
			One 18pr Amm wagon body damaged and had to be abandoned owing to heavy shell fire	
			No 12984 Dr A. SWITHENBANK G and No11430 Dr J. HUTTON [illegible] wounded	
			Four horses & 6 mules killed - 4 horses & 9 mules wounded	
			One horse lost during heavy shell fire.	
			SAA Section (No.3) moved camp to E.12.d.6.6 (Sheet 27)	
	7.10		A Echelon moved to A.7.d (28) B Echelon to E.12 d (Sheet 27)	FC
			No 36982 Gr A. GREEN killed	
			10986 Dr G. FORSYTH and 11319 Dr E HARDY wounded	
			5 horses killed 2 horses & 2 mules wounded	
			These casualties occurred whilst ammunition was being supplied to Batteries during the night 6-7 Oct 1917	
	8.10		2Lieut. L.M. WOODLAND posted to 11 D.A. & departed today	FC
			Captain D.A. NICOLL R.F.A. joined from attd. to R.F.C.	
			During the night 7-8 the following casualties occurred during the supply of ammunition to Batteries.	

Instructions regarding War Diaries and Intelligence Summaries are contained in F. S. Regs., Part II. and the Staff Manual respectively. Title pages will be prepared in manuscript.

WAR DIARY
or
INTELLIGENCE SUMMARY.

(Erase heading not required.)

Army Form C. 2118.

Place	Date 1917	Hour	Summary of Events and Information	Remarks and references to Appendices
	8-10		No 188598 Driver T. LIVESLEY wounded - at duty, 2 horses wounded & one 18 pr. Amm. wagon destroyed.	JCC
	9-10		Lieut H. CHERMSIDE rejoined from Hospital.	
			No 68176 Driver F RICE wounded - at duty.	JCC
			4 horses wounded & 2 GS wagons damaged by shell fire	
	10-10		No change in A. Echelon	JCC
			B Echelon moved camp to B21 b 4.7 (Sheet 28)	
	11-10		A Echelon moved to camp at B.18 a. 1.1 (sheet 28)	JCC
	12-10		No 68246 Dr. HAGERMAN Z D wounded and 1 horse killed	JCC
	13-10		2 horses were wounded during the night 12-13	JCC
	14-10		No 11319 Driver E. HARDY reported missing probably wounded died in hosp on 10-10-17 of wounds received in action	JCC
			No 192487 Dr. E. ATKINSON } wounded on pack work taking supplies	
			" 121650 " F WHITEMORE } to Inf. in front line	
			4 mules killed	
	15-10		Last night (14-15) the following casualties occurred whilst supplying ammunition to guns & Infantry in front line -	JCC
			No 68273 Driver C. FORKNER }	
			" 72043 " W. H. RICHARDS } wounded.	
			" 96037 Corpl F. G. SMITH }	
			2 mules were killed and 2 horses & 10 mules wounded	
	16-10		No 68236 Driver T. Ringe } wounded in action	JCC
			" 51056 " W. EVANS }	

Instructions regarding War Diaries and Intelligence Summaries are contained in F. S. Regs., Part II. and the Staff Manual respectively. Title pages will be prepared in manuscript.

WAR DIARY
or
INTELLIGENCE SUMMARY.
(*Erase heading not required.*)

Army Form C. 2118.

Place	Date	Hour	Summary of Events and Information	Remarks and references to Appendices
	1917 16-10		3 horses & 3 mules were wounded & one mule was killed.	
			5 Sergeants + 1 Gnr reinforcements joined from Base & were disposed of as follows:- 3 Sergt to 78 Bde RFA	
			2 " to 79 Bde RFA	FCC
			1 Gunr to 17th Divl. T. Mortars	
			2 Sergeants supernumerary to Estab. were posted to 78 Bde RFA & 1 Sergt supernumerary to 79th Bde RFA	
	17-10		Two ~~mules~~ (FCC) horses of No1 Sect. wounded by hostile shell fire when employed in the supply of ammunition	FCC
	18-10		No change -	FCC
	19-10		No 116450 Gnr J Latham killed whilst supplying amm. to 79 Bde RFA near IRONCROSS at C.3.b (sheet 28)	FCC
	20-10		3 horses & 1 mule killed by hostile shell fire	FCC
	21-10		Camp of No1 Sec shelled by enemy at 5.30 am and No 676671 Dr. C. PASHLER was wounded 1 horse & 2 mules wounded & 1 mule killed	FCC
			1 horse & 2 mules wounded whilst supplying amm. to 78 Bde RFA	FCC
	22-10		1 horse + 3 mules wounded during ammunition supply -	FCC
			45 O.R. reinforcements joined from Base -	
			1 O.R. posted to 78th Bde RFA	
			No. 8945 Pte. J. GRAHAM transferred to RFA + posted to 17 DAC	
	23-10		During the night 22-23 a bomb fell in the camp of No1 Sec and No. 6P232 Dr. J.T. RUDD was wounded.	FCC
			Whilst supplying ammunition to 78th Bde RFA the following casualties occurred	

2353 Wt. W2544/1454 700,000 5/15 D. D. & L. A.D.S.S./Forms/C. 2118.

Instructions regarding War Diaries and Intelligence Summaries are contained in F. S. Regs., Part II. and the Staff Manual respectively. Title pages will be prepared in manuscript.

WAR DIARY
or
INTELLIGENCE SUMMARY.
(Erase heading not required.)

Army Form C. 2118.

Place	Date 1917	Hour	Summary of Events and Information	Remarks and references to Appendices
	23-10		No. 72196 Dr T. W. STANNARD and No. 94229 Dr J. A. BUTCHER	F.C.
			2 mules were killed and 3 mules & 1 horse were wounded.	
			20 O.R. posted to 78th Bde RFA	
			84 O.R. posted to 79th Bde RFA	
	24-10		No change.	F.C.
	25-10		Sections 1 & 2 moved camp to B.17.d.8.7	
			The following casualties occurred during the night 24-25 whilst supplying Amn	F.C.
			No 67676 Corpl J. C. LAMBERT } wounded	
			75648 Dr. W. FOSTER }	
			91784 " W. LE VASSEUR }	
			22534 " W. C. EDMUNDS }	
			14092 " H. HARDWICK }	
			1 horse & 7 mules were wounded & 6 mules were killed.	
			A limber wagon Q.F. 4.5 was destroyed by shell fire	
	26-10		Lieut. H.J. BARTLET posted to B/78 Bde RFA as Second in Command	F.C.
			5 O.R. reinforcements joined from Base	
			2 mules were killed during Ammunition Supply	
	27-10		During the night 26-27 following casualties occurred at LANGEMARCK whilst supply ammunition:-	F.C.
			72052 Dr. W. VAUGHAN was wounded	
			3 horses & 1 mule killed.	

2353 Wt. W2544/1454 700,000 5/15 D. D. & L. A.D.S.S./Forms/C. 2118.

Instructions regarding War Diaries and Intelligence Summaries are contained in F. S. Regs., Part II. and the Staff Manual respectively. Title pages will be prepared in manuscript.

WAR DIARY
or
INTELLIGENCE SUMMARY.
(Erase heading not required.)

Army Form C. 2118.

Place	Date 1917	Hour	Summary of Events and Information	Remarks and references to Appendices
	27-10		At about 7 pm this same evening camp of No 1 Sec. was bombed and the following casualties occurred No 189985 Dr. H DAVIS } wounded " 204947 " F. GOODWIN } 1 mule killed 1 horse & 12 mules wounded 16 O.R. reinforcements joined from Base	[initials]
	28-10		6 O.R. posted to 78th Bde RFA 10 O.R. posted to 79th Bde RFA	[initials]
	29-10		No 140014 D. W. HADDRELL No 2 Section was wounded and 1 horse killed by a bomb from hostile aircraft –	[initials]
	30-10		No change –	[initials]
	31-10		During the night 30–31 the following casualties occurred during the supply of Ammunition at about C.3.b. (sheet 20) No 94948 D. G. Clark } were wounded & returned to duty – 72111 " G. Coladine } 7 horses were also wounded	[initials]

[signature]
LT. COL. R.F.A.
COMMANDING 17th DIV: AMM. COL

2353 Wt. W2544/1454 700,000 5/15 D. D. & L. A.D.S.S./Forms/C. 2118.

Instructions regarding War Diaries and Intelligence Summaries are contained in F. S. Regs., Part II. and the Staff Manual respectively. Title pages will be prepared in manuscript.

WAR DIARY
or
INTELLIGENCE SUMMARY.

(*Erase heading not required.*)

Army Form C. 2118.

Place	Date	Hour	Summary of Events and Information	Remarks and references to Appendices
			Casualties	
			Officers Sick Nil	
			Other Ranks Sick 9.	
			Officers Killed Nil Officers Wounded. Nil	
			Other Ranks Killed & Died of Wounds, 5	
			Other Ranks Wounded 27	
			Horses Killed 19. Mules Killed 28	
			Horses Wounded. 32 Mules Wounded 51	
			Horses Died Nil Mules Died 5	
			Horses Evacuated 9. Mules Evacuated 6	

R S [signature]
CAPTAIN. R.F.A.
ADJUTANT 17th DIV. AMM. COL.

31/10/17

2353 Wt. W2544/1454 700,000 5/15 D. D. & L. A.D.S.S./Forms/C. 2118.

Instructions regarding War Diaries and Intelligence Summaries are contained in F. S. Regs., Part II. and the Staff Manual respectively. Title pages will be prepared in manuscript.

WAR DIARY
or
~~INTELLIGENCE SUMMARY.~~
(Erase heading not required.)

Army Form C. 2118.

Vol 29

Place	Date	Hour	Summary of Events and Information	Remarks and references to Appendices
			Confidential	
			War Diary	
			of	
			17th Divisional Ammunition Column	
			from 1/11/17 to 30/11/17.	
			F. C. Collins Capt R.F.A. Adjt for LT. COL. R.F.A. COMMANDING 17TH DIV. AMM. COL.	
			30/11/17 Volume 29.	

2353 Wt. W2544/1454 700,000 5/15 D. D. & L. A.D.S.S./Forms/C. 2118.

Instructions regarding War Diaries and Intelligence Summaries are contained in F. S. Regs., Part II. and the Staff Manual respectively. Title pages will be prepared in manuscript.

WAR DIARY
or
~~INTELLIGENCE SUMMARY.~~
(Erase heading not required.)

Army Form C. 2118.

Place	Date 1917	Hour	Summary of Events and Information	Remarks and references to Appendices
	1-11		Unit camped as follows:-	
			H. Qrs. at B.18.a.1.1. } Sheet 28	FCC
			No 1 sec at B.17.d.8.7	
			" 2 " at B.17.d.7.5	
			" 3 " at B.21.b.4.7	
			1 horse & 1 mule wounded	FCC
	2-11		No change	FCC
	3-11		No change	FCC
	4-11		Lieut. B.M. HALLWARD R.F.A. posted to A/79 Bde R.F.A.	
			1 O.R. posted to 79 Bde R.F.A. 1 O.R. from 79 Bde R.F.A.	FCC
	5-11		No change	FCC
	6-11		No change	FCC
	7-11		No change	FCC
	8-11		"A" Echelon moved camp (en route to rest) to about F.13. (Sheet 27)	FCC
	9-11		"A" Echelon moved to following camps & billets	FCC
			H Qrs I.31.c.4.1 } Sheet 27	
			No 1 sec. H.36.b.4.3	
			No 2 sec. H.36.d.2.6	

Army Form C. 2118.

WAR DIARY
or
~~INTELLIGENCE SUMMARY.~~
(Erase heading not required.)

Instructions regarding War Diaries and Intelligence Summaries are contained in F. S. Regs., Part II. and the Staff Manual respectively. Title pages will be prepared in manuscript.

Place	Date	Hour	Summary of Events and Information	Remarks and references to Appendices
	1917			
	10-11		A Echelon no change	FCC
			B Echelon moved to FE.13.a 2 4 Sheet 27	
	11-11		A Echelon no change	FCC
			B Echelon moved to O.1.c.3.6 Sheet 27	
	12-11		No change - 35 mules received as remounts	FCC
	13-11		2 Lieut. O. CLOUDESLEY ~~[illegible]~~ to Hospital	FCC
	14-11		No change -	FCC
	15-11		No change -	FCC
	16-11		No change - 1 riding horse and 21 mules posted from C/179 Bde RFA	FCC
	17-11		No change - 2 mules from 78 Bde RFA	FCC
	18-11		No change -	FCC
	19-11		No change -	FCC
	20-11		Lt. E. LAMB and 2 Lt J J SHEEHAN joined as reinforcements from Base -	Fcc

Army Form C. 2118.

Instructions regarding War Diaries and Intelligence Summaries are contained in F. S. Regs., Part II. and the Staff Manual respectively. Title pages will be prepared in manuscript.

WAR DIARY
or
~~INTELLIGENCE SUMMARY.~~
(*Erase heading not required.*)

Place	Date 1917	Hour	Summary of Events and Information	Remarks and references to Appendices
	21-11		No change	JCC
	22-11		Lieut. A D EVANS posted to the Unit and employed as Ammunition Officer XIX Corps.	JCC
			20 L. D. horses posted to "C" Battery 76 Bde R F A	JCC
	23-11		No change	JCC
	24-11		Captain D A Nicoll R F A to hospital	JCC
	25-11		No change	JCC
	26-11		No change	JCC
	27-11		No change	JCC
	28-11		No change	JCC
	29-11		No change	JCC
	30-11		No change	JCC

J C Collins Capt RFA Adjt
for
LT. COL. R.F.A.
COMMANDING 17th DIV: AMM. COL.

2353 Wt. W2544/1454 700,000 5/15 D. D. & L. A.D.S.S./Forms/C. 2118.

Instructions regarding War Diaries and Intelligence Summaries are contained in F. S. Regs., Part II. and the Staff Manual respectively. Title pages will be prepared in manuscript.

WAR DIARY
or
INTELLIGENCE SUMMARY.
(Erase heading not required.)

Army Form C. 2118.

Place	Date	Hour	Summary of Events and Information	Remarks and references to Appendices
			Casualties	
			Officers Sick 2.	
			Other Ranks Sick 5	
			Officers Killed Nil Officers Wounded Nil	
			Other Ranks Killed & Died of Wounds Nil	
			Other Ranks Wounded Nil	
			Horses Killed Nil Mules Killed Nil	
			Horses Wounded Nil Mules Wounded Nil	
			Horses Died Nil Mules Died Nil	
			Horses Evacuated 6 Mules Evacuated 7.	
			Transferred to C/76 Bde 20 Horses.	
			30/10/17	
			F C Collins Capt Adjt for LT. COL. R.F.A. COMMANDING 17th DIV: AMM. COL	

2353 Wt. W2544/1454 700,000 5/15 D. D. & L. A.D.S.S./Forms/C. 2118.

Instructions regarding War Diaries and Intelligence Summaries are contained in F. S. Regs., Part II. and the Staff Manual respectively. Title pages will be prepared in manuscript.

WAR DIARY
or
INTELLIGENCE SUMMARY.
(Erase heading not required.)

Army Form C. 2118.

Place	Date	Hour	Summary of Events and Information	Remarks and references to Appendices
			Return of Strength	

	O	OR	Animals
Strength on 1-11-17	17	614	676
Joined	3	1	59
Total	20	615	735
Gone	1	11	22
Strength on 30/11/17	19	604	713

30/11/17

H C Collins Capt RFA Adjt
for LT. COL. R.F.A.
COMMANDING 17th DIV: AMM. COL

2353 Wt. W2544/1454 700,000 5/15 D. D. & L. A.D.S.S./Forms/C. 2118.

Instructions regarding War Diaries and Intelligence Summaries are contained in F. S. Regs., Part II. and the Staff Manual respectively. Title pages will be prepared in manuscript.

WAR DIARY
or
INTELLIGENCE SUMMARY.
(Erase heading not required.)

Army Form C. 2118.

Vol 30

Place	Date	Hour	Summary of Events and Information	Remarks and references to Appendices
			Confidential War Diary of 17th Divisional Ammunition Column from 1/12/17 to 30/12/17	
			31/12/17 Volume 30. R.S. Smith [signature] LT. COL. R.F.A. COMMANDING 17th DIV: AMM. COL.	

2353 Wt. W2544/1454 700,000 5/15 D. D. & L. A.D.S.S./Forms/C. 2118.

Instructions regarding War Diaries and Intelligence Summaries are contained in F. S. Regs., Part II. and the Staff Manual respectively. Title pages will be prepared in manuscript.

WAR DIARY
or
~~INTELLIGENCE SUMMARY.~~
(Erase heading not required.)

Army Form C. 2118.

Place	Date 1917	Hour	Summary of Events and Information	Remarks and references to Appendices
	1-12		Unit billetted as follows.	
			H. Qrs I. 31. C 4. 1 (sheet 27)	
			No1 Sec H. 36 b 4 3 (sheet 27)	J.C.C.
			"2" H. 36 d. 2. 6 (sheet 27)	
			"3" O. 1 C. 3. 6 (sheet 27)	
	2-12		No change.	J.C.C.
	3-12		No change -	J.C.C.
	4-12		No change -	J.C.C.
	5-12		No change -	J.C.C.
	6-12		Lt. A. G. McCLELLAN RFA to England to resume medical Studies	J.C.C.
				J.C.C.
	7-12		no change	
	8-12		One O.R. reinforcement joined from Base	J.C.C.

2353 Wt. W2544/1454 700,000 5/15 D. D. & L. A.D.S.S./Forms/C. 2118.

Instructions regarding War Diaries and Intelligence Summaries are contained in F. S. Regs., Part II. and the Staff Manual respectively. Title pages will be prepared in manuscript.

WAR DIARY
or
~~INTELLIGENCE SUMMARY.~~

(Erase heading not required.)

Army Form C. 2118.

Place	Date 1917	Hour	Summary of Events and Information	Remarks and references to Appendices
	9-12		no change	FCC
	10-12		no change	FCC
	11-12		no change	FCC
	12-12		8 O.R. reinforcements from Base	FCC
	13-12		no change	FCC
	14-12		no change	FCC
	15-12		no change	FCC
	16-12		Unit marched to HERBELLE	FCC
	17-12		Unit marched to VALHUON	FCC
	18-12		Unit remained at VALHUON	FCC
	19-12		Unit marched to ETREE-WAMIN	FCC
	20-12		At ETREE WAMIN	FCC
	21-12		Unit marched LATTRE St QUENTIN	FCC

2353 Wt. W2544/1454 700,000 5/15 D. D. & L. A.D.S.S./Forms/C. 2118.

Instructions regarding War Diaries and Intelligence Summaries are contained in F. S. Regs., Part II. and the Staff Manual respectively. Title pages will be prepared in manuscript.

WAR DIARY
or
~~INTELLIGENCE SUMMARY.~~
(Erase heading not required.)

Army Form C. 2118.

Place	Date 1917	Hour	Summary of Events and Information	Remarks and references to Appendices
	22.12		At LATTRE St QUINTEN	Hcc
	23.12		-do-	Hcc
	24-12		Unit marched to ACHIET-le-PETIT	Hcc
	25.12		Unit marched to BEAULENCOURT	Hcc
	26.12		Unit marched to MANACOURT and joined 17th Div. 5th Corps 3rd Army	Hcc
	27.12		Took over an Amm. Dump at P.12 d (Sheet 57c) 11 O.R. reinforcements joined from Base	Hcc
	28-12		4. O.R. reinforcements to 78 Bde RFA 4 O.R. reinforcements to 79 Bde	RHL
	29-12		No change	RHL
	30-12		No change	RHL
	31-12		No change.	RHL

[signature]
LT. COL. R.F.A.
COMMANDING 17th DIV: AMM. COL

2353 Wt. W2544/1454 700,000 5/15 D. D. & L. A.D.S.S./Forms/C. 2118.

Army Form C. 2118.

Instructions regarding War Diaries and Intelligence Summaries are contained in F. S. Regs., Part II. and the Staff Manual respectively. Title Pages will be prepared in manuscript.

WAR DIARY
or
INTELLIGENCE SUMMARY
(Erase heading not required.)

Vol 31

Place	Date	Hour	Summary of Events and Information	Remarks and references to Appendices
			Confidential War Diary of 17th. Divisional Ammunition Column from 1/1/18 to 31/1/18. F.C. Collins CAPTAIN. R.F.A. ADJUTANT 17th DIV. AMM. COL. 31/1/18. Volume 31	

2449 Wt. W14957/M90 750,000 1/16 J.B.C. & A. Forms/C.2118/12.

Instructions regarding War Diaries and Intelligence Summaries are contained in F. S. Regs., Part II. and the Staff Manual respectively. Title pages will be prepared in manuscript.

WAR DIARY
or
INTELLIGENCE SUMMARY.
(Erase heading not required.)

Army Form C. 2118.

Place	Date	Hour	Summary of Events and Information	Remarks and references to Appendices
In the Field	1/1/18		Unit billetted at MANANCOURT 2/Lt A. C. TOlhurst to hospital (Sick). 1 OR from 108th A.F.A joined & posted to H.Q. 17 DAC	FCC
do	2/1/18		No change	FCC
do	3/1/18.		No change.	FCC
do	4/1/18.		Lt. A. D. Evans posted to 1st D.A.C.	FCC
do	5/1/18		20 Gunners posted to 78th Bde R.F.A.	FCC
do	6/1/18		No change	FCC
do	7/1/18		No change	FCC
do	8/1/18.		Unit marched to DERNANCOURT. S of ALBERT	FCC
do	9/1/18		Unit marched to BEAUCOURT ~~SUR~~ SUR HALLUE N.E. of AMIENS	FCC
do	10/1/18		No change.	FCC
do	11/1/18		No change	FCC
do	12/1/18		No change	FCC
do	13/1/18		15 Gunners posted to 78 Bde RFA	FCC
do	14/1/18		no change	FCC
do	15/1/18		No change	FCC

2353 Wt. W2544/1454 700,000 5/15 D. D. & L. A.D.S.S./Forms/C. 2118.

Instructions regarding War Diaries and Intelligence Summaries are contained in F. S. Regs., Part II. and the Staff Manual respectively. Title pages will be prepared in manuscript.

Army Form C. 2118.

WAR DIARY
or
~~INTELLIGENCE SUMMARY.~~
(Erase heading not required.)

Place	Date 1918	Hour	Summary of Events and Information	Remarks and references to Appendices
	15.1		No change	FCC
	16.1		No change	FCC
	17.1		~~No~~ Lieut F. A. MARGRY joined from Base & was posted to No 3 Sec	FCC
	18.1		No change	FCC
	19.1		No change	FCC
	20.1		No change	FCC
	21.1		No change	FCC
	22.1		~~No~~ Lieut. F A MARGRY posted to 17th Dvl. T. Mortars	FCC
	23.1		14 O.R. posted to 17th Dvl. T. Mortars	FCC
	24.1		Lieut H.R. HEWETSON joined from Base & posted to No 3 Sec	FCC
	25.1		5 O.R. reinforcements joined from Base	FCC
	26.1		No change	FCC

Instructions regarding War Diaries and Intelligence Summaries are contained in F. S. Regs., Part II. and the Staff Manual respectively. Title pages will be prepared in manuscript.

WAR DIARY

or

~~INTELLIGENCE SUMMARY.~~

(Erase heading not required.)

Army Form C. 2118.

Place ~~1918~~	Date 1918	Hour	Summary of Events and Information	Remarks and references to Appendices
27-1-	27-1		2/Lieut. A.E. TOLHURST rejoined from Hospital	FCC
	28-1		Lieut. H.R. HEWETSON posted to 17th Div. T. Mortars	FCC
	29-1		15 O.R. reinforcements posted, but attached to 17th Div. T. Mortars	FCC
	30-1		No change	FCC
	31-1		No change	FCC

FC Collins

CAPTAIN, R.F.A.

ADJUTANT 17th ...

2353 Wt. W2544/1454 700,000 5/15 D. D. & L. A.D.S.S./Forms/C. 2118.

Army Form C. 2118.

Instructions regarding War Diaries and Intelligence Summaries are contained in F. S. Regs., Part II. and the Staff Manual respectively. Title Pages will be prepared in manuscript.

WAR DIARY
or
INTELLIGENCE SUMMARY
(Erase heading not required.)

Place	Date	Hour	Summary of Events and Information	Remarks and references to Appendices
			Casualties	
			Officers Sick Nil	
			Other Ranks Sick	
			Officers Killed Nil Officers Wounded Nil	
			Other Ranks Killed Nil Other Ranks Wounded Nil	
			Horses Killed Nil Mules Killed Nil	
			Horses Wounded Nil Mules Wounded Nil	
			Horses Died Nil Mules Died Nil	
			Horses Evacuated 1 Mules Evacuated 2	
			H C Allen CAPTAIN & ADJUTANT 17th DIV. AMM. COL.	
			1/31/18.	

2449 Wt. W14957/M90 750,000 1/16 J.B.C. & A. Forms/C.2118/12.

Instructions regarding War Diaries and Intelligence Summaries are contained in F. S. Regs., Part II. and the Staff Manual respectively. Title Pages will be prepared in manuscript.

WAR DIARY
or
INTELLIGENCE SUMMARY
(Erase heading not required.)

Army Form C. 2118.

Place	Date	Hour	Summary of Events and Information	Remarks and references to Appendices
			Return of Strength	

	O	OR	Animals
Strength on 31-12-17	19	620	707
Joined	3	30	
Total	22	650	
Gone	2	69	5
Strength on 31/1/18.	20	581	702

JD Collins

CAPTAIN R.F.A.
ADJUTANT 17th DIV. ARMY [illegible]

1/31/18.

2449 Wt. W14957/M90 750,000 1/16 J.B.C. & A. Forms/C.2118/12.

Instructions regarding War Diaries and Intelligence Summaries are contained in F. S. Regs., Part II. and the Staff Manual respectively. Title Pages will be prepared in manuscript.

WAR DIARY
or
INTELLIGENCE SUMMARY

(Erase heading not required.)

Army Form C. 2118.

Vol 32

Place	Date	Hour	Summary of Events and Information	Remarks and references to Appendices
			Confidential War Diary of 17th Divisional Ammunition Column from 1/2/18 to 28/2/18. 28/2/18. R.H.S. Dunn[?] LT. COL. R.F.A. COMMANDING 17th DIV: AMM. COL	

2449 Wt. W14957/M90 750,000 1/16 J.B.C. & A. Forms/C.2118/12.

Army Form C. 2118.

Instructions regarding War Diaries and Intelligence Summaries are contained in F. S. Regs., Part II. and the Staff Manual respectively. Title pages will be prepared in manuscript.

WAR DIARY
or
INTELLIGENCE SUMMARY.
(Erase heading not required.)

Place	Date	Hour	Summary of Events and Information	Remarks and references to Appendices
			Return of Strength	

	O	OR	Animals
Strength on 30/11/17	19	604	713
Joined	–	24	–
Total	19	628	713
Gone		8	6
Strength on 31/12/17	19	620	707

31/12/17.

[signature]
LT. COL. R.F.A.
COMMANDING 17th DIV: AMM. COL

Army Form C. 2118.

WAR DIARY
or
INTELLIGENCE SUMMARY.
(Erase heading not required.)

Instructions regarding War Diaries and Intelligence Summaries are contained in F. S. Regs., Part II. and the Staff Manual respectively. Title pages will be prepared in manuscript.

Place	Date	Hour	Summary of Events and Information	Remarks and references to Appendices
			Casualties	
			Officers Sick Nil	
			Other Ranks Sick 13	
			Officers Killed Nil Officers Wounded Nil	
			Other Ranks Killed Nil Other Ranks Wounded Nil	
			Horses Killed Nil Mules Killed Nil	
			Horses Wounded Nil Mules Wounded Nil	
			Horses Died Nil Mules Died Nil	
			Horses Evacuated 4 Mules Evacuated 2	
			R. S. Smyth LT. COL. R.F.A. COMMANDING 17th DIV: AMM. COL.	
			31/12/17	

2353 Wt. W2544/1454 700,000 5/15 D. D. & L. A.D.S.S./Forms/C. 2118.

Army Form C. 2118.

WAR DIARY
or
~~INTELLIGENCE SUMMARY~~
(Erase heading not required.)

Instructions regarding War Diaries and Intelligence Summaries are contained in F. S. Regs., Part II. and the Staff Manual respectively. Title Pages will be prepared in manuscript.

Place	Date 1918	Hour	Summary of Events and Information	Remarks and references to Appendices
BEAUCOURT SUR HALLUE	1-2.		Unit in billets at BEAUCOURT-SUR-HALLUE	FCC
	2.2.		no change.	FCC
			No 53758 Driver - Paid L/Bdr. A. SALTER died at 41st Stat. Hospl. as the result of an accident on duty. He was driving a pair of horses attached to a G.S. wagon when the horses suddenly jumped forward & he was pitched out onto the road.	FCC
	3-2.		No change.	FCC
	4.2.		No change.	FCC
	5.2.		No change.	FCC
	6-2		No change.	FCC
	7.2.		13 O.R. joined from Base as reinforcements and attached to Trench Mortars	FCC
	8-2		Captain A.R. FINN R.A.M.C. joined Unit and assumed duties as Medical Officer i/c of the Unit vice CAPTAIN W.A HISLOP R.A.M.C. posted to 53rd Field Ambulance for duty.	
	9.2		Lieut. M.P. TUTEUR R.G.A. appointed to assume temporarily the duties of Town Major VELU	FCC

2449 Wt. W14957/M90 750,000 1/16 J.B.C. & A. Forms/C.2118/12.

Army Form C. 2118.

Instructions regarding War Diaries and Intelligence Summaries are contained in F. S. Regs., Part II. and the Staff Manual respectively. Title Pages will be prepared in manuscript.

WAR DIARY
or
~~INTELLIGENCE SUMMARY~~
(Erase heading not required.)

Place	Date 1918	Hour	Summary of Events and Information	Remarks and references to Appendices
BEAUCOURT sur HALLUE	10-2		No change	JCC
	11-2		No change	JCC
	12-2		No change	JCC
	13-2		No change	JCC
	14-2		No change	JCC
	15-2		No change	JCC
	16-2		No change	JCC
	17-2		No change	JCC
	18-2		No change	JCC
	19-2		No change	JCC
	20-2		47 OR reinforcements posted from Base as reinforcements - 10 of these were attached to 78 Bde + 10 to 79 Bde R Fus.	

2449 Wt. W14957/M90 750,000 1/16 J.B.C. & A. Forms/C.2118/12.

Instructions regarding War Diaries and Intelligence Summaries are contained in F. S. Regs., Part II. and the Staff Manual respectively. Title Pages will be prepared in manuscript.

WAR DIARY
or
~~INTELLIGENCE SUMMARY~~

(Erase heading not required.)

Army Form C. 2118.

Place	Date 1918	Hour	Summary of Events and Information	Remarks and references to Appendices
BEAUCOURT sur HALLUE	21.2		No change	Fcc
	22-2		No change	Fcc
	23-2		Lieut. H. J. BARTLET R.F.A. joined on posting from 78 Bde. R.F.A.	Fcc
	24-2		No change	Fcc
	25-2		No change	Fcc
	26.2		No change	Fcc
	27-2		No change	Fcc
	28-2		No change	Fcc

2449 Wt. W14957/M90 750,000 1/16 J.B.C. & A. Forms/C.2118/12.

Army Form C. 2118.

Instructions regarding War Diaries and Intelligence Summaries are contained in F. S. Regs., Part II. and the Staff Manual respectively. Title Pages will be prepared in manuscript.

WAR DIARY
or
INTELLIGENCE SUMMARY
(Erase heading not required.)

Place	Date	Hour	Summary of Events and Information	Remarks and references to Appendices
			Casualties	

Officers Sick	Nil		
Other Ranks Sick			
Officers Killed	Nil	Officers Wounded	Nil
Other Ranks Killed	Nil	Other Ranks Wounded	Nil
Horses Killed	Nil	Mules Killed	Nil
Horses Wounded	Nil	Mules Wounded	Nil
Horses Died	Nil	Mules Died	Nil
Horses Evacuated	3.	Mules Evacuated	7

25/7/18

[illegible]
Lt. Col. R.F.A.
Commanding 17th Div. Amm. Col.

2449 Wt. W14957/M90 750,000 1/16 J.B.C. & A. Forms/C.2118/12.

Army Form C. 2118.

Instructions regarding War Diaries and Intelligence Summaries are contained in F. S. Regs., Part II. and the Staff Manual respectively. Title Pages will be prepared in manuscript.

WAR DIARY
or
INTELLIGENCE SUMMARY
(Erase heading not required.)

Place	Date	Hour	Summary of Events and Information	Remarks and references to Appendices
			Return of Strength	

	O	OR	Animals
Strength on 31/1/18	20	581	702
Joined	1	71	32
Total	21	652	734
Gone.	1	32	4
Strength on 28/2/18	20	620	727

28/2/18

[signature]
LT. COL. R.F.A.
COMMANDING 17th DIV: AMM. COL

2449 Wt. W14957/M90 750,000 1/16 J.B.C. & A. Forms/C.2118/12.

17th Div.

17th DIVISIONAL AMMUNITION COLUMN, R.F.A.

M A R C H

1 9 1 8

Instructions regarding War Diaries and Intelligence Summaries are contained in F. S. Regs., Part II. and the Staff Manual respectively. Title Pages will be prepared in manuscript.

or

INTELLIGENCE SUMMARY

(*Erase heading not required.*)

Vol 33

Place	Date	Hour	Summary of Events and Information	Remarks and references to Appendices
			Confidential War Diary of 17th Divisional Ammunition Column from 1/3/18 to 31/3/18 J C Crum Capt RFA Adj 17 DAC	

1875 Wt. W593/826 1,000,000 4/15 J.B.C. & A. A.D.S.S./Forms/C. 2118.

Army Form C. 2118.

Instructions regarding War Diaries and Intelligence Summaries are contained in F. S. Regs., Part II. and the Staff Manual respectively. Title Pages will be prepared in manuscript.

WAR DIARY
or
~~INTELLIGENCE SUMMARY~~
(Erase heading not required.)

Place	Date 1918	Hour	Summary of Events and Information	Remarks and references to Appendices
BERTINCOURT	21.3		9 O.R. joined from 78 Bde RFA } from attachment to these units 7 O.R. " " 79 " } 7 O.R. " " T Mortars	JCC
			At 6pm. Unit received urgent telephonic orders to march without delay to BEAULENCOURT area	
	22.3.		During the night following details were handed to Batteries etc 6 GS wagons with teams to H.Q. 17 D.A. 1 " " " to C/78 Bde RFA 2 - 18pr wagons & limbers to A/78 " 6 - 18pr — " — to B/78 " 10 " — " — to C/78 " 6 " limbers with teams to C/78 " 6 - 4.5 wagons & limbers to D/78 6 " " with teams to B/79 6 18pr wagons & limbers to A/79	JCC
	23.3		At 7pm owing to retirement of our troops Unit was ordered to move to near COURCELLETE - Move completed by 11pm. camped at M.25a (sheet 57c)	JCC
	24.3		Following details were sent as stated 6 wagons 18pr with limbers & teams to B/78	JCC

Instructions regarding War Diaries and Intelligence Summaries are contained in F. S. Regs., Part II. and the Staff Manual respectively. Title Pages will be prepared in manuscript.

WAR DIARY
or
INTELLIGENCE SUMMARY
(Erase heading not required.)

Army Form C. 2118

Place	Date	Hour	Summary of Events and Information	Remarks and references to Appendices
	24.3.		4 - 18pr. Wagons & limbers with teams to C/179 Bde RFA	JCC
			5 - 18pr. ——— " ——— to B/179 "	
			9 - 4.5" ——— " ——— to D/178 "	
			Received Orders at 1pm. to move to La BOISELLE - Completed move at 4 pm	
			Orders received at 5pm to move to HENNENCOURT - Completed move at 9 pm	
	25.3		Marched to CONTAY at 1pm.	JCC
	26.3		Orders received at 3.30pm to march with 17th Div. Transport to FORCEVILLE - arrived there at 10pm. Marched again at midnight to PUCHEVILLERS	JCC
	27.3.		At PUCHEVILLERS	JCC
	28.3		-do-	JCC
	29.3		Marched as follows H.Qrs to MIRVAUX Nos 1, 2 & 3 Sections to PIERREGOT	JCC
	30-3		H.Qrs and Nos. 1 & 2 Sections marched to VADENCOURT - Ordered to send details to Amm Ref. Point near CONTAY	JCC
	31-3		At VADENCOURT - No 3 Section at PIERREGOT	JCC

JC Collins Capt R.F.A.
adj 17 DAC

1875 Wt. W593/826 1,000,000 4/15 J.B.C. & A. A.D.S.S./Forms/C. 2118.

Army Form C. 2118

Instructions regarding War Diaries and Intelligence Summaries are contained in F. S. Regs., Part II. and the Staff Manual respectively. Title Pages will be prepared in manuscript.

WAR DIARY
or
INTELLIGENCE SUMMARY
(Erase heading not required.)

Place	Date	Hour	Summary of Events and Information	Remarks and references to Appendices
			Casualties	
			Officers Sick - Nil	
			O Ranks " - 8	
			Officers killed - nil	
			Other ranks - do - No 110114 Dr T. OGDEN, " 222994 " J BROOKE } in action	
			Officers wounded - Lieut A.J. Daintz (at duty)	
			Oth Ranks -"- No 87003 Dr H. L. WEBBER (at duty), 71778 " T.H GRINNETT	
			Horses {Killed, Wounded} nil	
			Mules killed in action 4	
			" wounded 2	
			Horses evacuated 6	
			Mules -"- 2.	
			31-3-18	
			J C Collins Capt RA, Adjt 17 DAC	

1875 Wt. W593/826 1,000,000 4/15 J.B.C. & A. A.D.S.S./Forms/C. 2118.

17th Divisional Artillery

WAR
DIARY

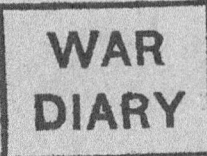

17th DIVISIONAL AMMUNITION COLUMN R.F.A.

APRIL 1918

Army Form C. 2118.

WAR DIARY

or

~~INTELLIGENCE SUMMARY.~~

(Erase heading not required.)

Instructions regarding War Diaries and Intelligence Summaries are contained in F. S. Regs., Part II. and the Staff Manual respectively. Title pages will be prepared in manuscript.

Vol 34

Place	Date	Hour	Summary of Events and Information	Remarks and references to Appendices
			Confidential War Diary of 17th Divisional Ammunition Column. from 1/4/18 to 30/4/18 [illegible] LT. COL. R.F.A. COMMANDING 17th DIV: AMM. COL	

A5834 Wt. W4973/M687 750,000 8/16 D. D. & L. Ltd. Forms/C.2118/13.

Army Form C. 2118.

Instructions regarding War Diaries and Intelligence Summaries are contained in F. S. Regs., Part II. and the Staff Manual respectively. Title pages will be prepared in manuscript.

WAR DIARY
or
~~INTELLIGENCE SUMMARY.~~

(*Erase heading not required.*)

Place	Date 1918	Hour	Summary of Events and Information	Remarks and references to Appendices
Ittlefield	1-4		Unit camped as follows:-	
			HQrs, Nos 1 & 2 sections at VADENCOURT } Sheet 11 (Lens)	JCC
			No 3 section at PIERREGOT }	
			employed in supply of Ammunition to guns of 78th & 79 Bde in action about V.11 & V.17 (Sheet 57d S.E) and 17th Div in line at W.16 & 22 (Sheet 57d)	
"	2-4		No change	JCC
"	3-4		No change 17th Div Infantry relief carried out & completed	JCC
"	4-4		17th Div Arty handed over to 12th D.A. ~~to~~ under whose orders this unit came at 12 Noon	JCC
"	5-4		No change - 78th Bde RFA began to come out of action on relief by 63rd Bde RFA	JCC
"	6-4		78th Bde RFA relief completed	JCC
"	7-4		No change - Lieut H J BARTLET appointed 2nd in Command D/79 & left this Unit accordingly.	JCC
"	8-4		No 1 section moved to PIERREGOT	JCC
"	9-4		No change	JCC
"	10-4		No change	JCC
			Lieut RW HARPER and 2Lt G.E.S LAMB attached ~~posted~~ to 79 Bde RFA	JCC
"	11-4		No change 2Lt O CLOUDESLEY to 79 Bde RFA (attached)	JCC
"	12-4		No change	JCC
			Captain A FINN RAMC was relieved by Capt H.L. REAZIN RAMC	
"	13-4		No change	JCC
			2Lt A E BOURNE (attached from C/79) to Hospital	
"	14-4		No change	JCC
"	15-4		No change	JCC
			Lieut M.J. TARRY RFA posted from 78 Bde RFA	JCC
"	16-4		No change	JCC

A5834 Wt. W4973/M687 750,000 8/16 D. D. & L. Ltd. Forms/C.2118/13.

Army Form C. 2118.

WAR DIARY
or
INTELLIGENCE SUMMARY.
(Erase heading not required.)

Instructions regarding War Diaries and Intelligence Summaries are contained in F. S. Regs., Part II. and the Staff Manual respectively. Title pages will be prepared in manuscript.

Place	Date 1918	Hour	Summary of Events and Information	Remarks and references to Appendices
	17.4		Units camped as follows:- HQrs, Nos 1 & 2 Sections at VADENCOURT (Sheet 11 Lens) No 3 Section at PIERREGOT (Sheet 11 Lens)	JCC
			No 3 Section moved to camp at O.23 d. 7.7 (Sheet 57d)	JCC
			57 O.R. reinforcements joined from Base. Capt. W.E GORMAN RAMC In medical charge was joined in relief of Capt REAZIN who left the same day.	
	18.4.		No change -	JCC
	19.4.		No 1 Section moved camp to O.11. central (Sheet 57d) 2 Smiths posted to 77 Field Army Bde.	JCC
	20.4.		HQrs. and No 2 Section moved camp, former to LEALVILLERS, latter to O.11 central camped near No 1 Section. Took over 17 A.R.P. at ACHEUX.	JCC
	21.4		No change - Units now as follows:- HQrs at LEALVILLERS; Nos 1 & 2 Sections at O.11 central; 3 Section at O.23 d. 7.7 } Sheet 57d)	JCC
	22.4		No change -	JCC
	23.4.		1 O.R. joined from 12th D.A.C. and posted to No 2 Section	JCC
	24.4		No change. 1 O.R. posted to D/78 Bde RFA, 1 O.R. posted 17 Div. Trn.	JCC JCC
	25.4.		No change. 5 O.R. reinforcements joined from Base	JCC

Army Form C. 2118.

Instructions regarding War Diaries and Intelligence Summaries are contained in F. S. Regs., Part II. and the Staff Manual respectively. Title pages will be prepared in manuscript.

WAR DIARY
or
~~INTELLIGENCE SUMMARY.~~

(Erase heading not required.)

Place	Date 1918	Hour	Summary of Events and Information	Remarks and references to Appendices
The field	26.4.		No change.	JCC
			Captain W.C. GORMAN RAMC In medical Charge of unit was relieved by Lt. R.S. PATERSON RAMC	JCC
	27.4		no change.	JCC
	28.4		No 3 Section moved, camp to O.22.d.1.9, otherwise no change	JCC
	29.4		14 O.R reinforcements arrived from Base	JCC
	30.4		5 O.R posted to 78 Bde RFA	JCC
			9 O.R posted to 79 — " —	

LT. COL. R.F.A.
COMMANDING 17th DIV: AMM. COL.

A5834 Wt. W4973/M687 750,000 8/16 D. D. & L. Ltd. Forms/C.2118/13.

Instructions regarding War Diaries and Intelligence Summaries are contained in F. S. Regs., Part II. and the Staff Manual respectively. Title pages will be prepared in manuscript.

WAR DIARY
or
INTELLIGENCE SUMMARY.
(Erase heading not required.)

Place	Date	Hour	Summary of Events and Information	Remarks and references to Appendices
			Casualties	
			Officers Sick - Nil	
			O. Ranks " - 19	
			Officers killed Nil	
			O Ranks " Nil	
			Officers Wounded Nil	
			O Ranks " 1 Wounded (Gassed) Attached 79 Bde RFA	
			Horses {Killed} Nil	
			Horses {Wounded} Nil	
			Mules Killed Nil	
			" Wounded Nil	
			Horses evacuated 5	
			Mules " 5	
			[signature]	
	30/4/18		LT. COL. R.F.A. COMMANDING 17th DIV: AMM. COL	

A5834 Wt. W4973/M687 750,000 8/16 D. D. & L. Ltd. Forms/C.2118/13.

Army Form C. 2118.

Instructions regarding War Diaries and Intelligence Summaries are contained in F. S. Regs., Part II. and the Staff Manual respectively. Title pages will be prepared in manuscript.

WAR DIARY
or
INTELLIGENCE SUMMARY.
(Erase heading not required.)

Place	Date	Hour	Summary of Events and Information				Remarks and references to Appendices
			Return of Strength				
				O.	O.R	Animals	
			Strength	17	582	710	
			Joined	2	76	10	
			Total	19	658	720	
			Gone	–	38	10	
			Strength on 30/4/18.	19.	620.	710	

30/4/18.

[signature]
LT. COL. R.F.A.
COMMANDING 17th DIV. AMN. COL.

A5834 Wt. W4973/M687 750,000 8/16 D. D. & L. Ltd. Forms/C.2118/13.

Instructions regarding War Diaries and Intelligence Summaries are contained in F. S. Regs., Part II. and the Staff Manual respectively. Title pages will be prepared in manuscript.

WAR DIARY
or
INTELLIGENCE SUMMARY.

(Erase heading not required.)

Army Form C. 2118.

D A Column

Vol 35

Place	Date	Hour	Summary of Events and Information	Remarks and references to Appendices
			Confidential	
			War Diary	
			of	
			17th Divisional Ammunition Column	
			from 1/5/18 to 31/5/18	
			R. H. S. Dunlop(?)	
			LT. COL. R.F.A. COMMANDING 17th DIV: AMM. COL.	

31/5/18

A5834 Wt. W4973/M687 750,000 8/16 D. D. & L. Ltd. Forms/C.2118/13.

Army Form C. 2118.

WAR DIARY
or
INTELLIGENCE SUMMARY.
(Erase heading not required.)

...arding War Diaries and Intelligence ...re contained in F. S. Regs., Part II. ...ff Manual respectively. Title pages will be prepared in manuscript.

Place	Date 1918	Hour	Summary of Events and Information	Remarks and references to Appendices
	1-5		Unit located as follows: Head Quarters - LEALVILLERS Nos 1 & 2 Sections - O. 11. Central } sheet 57 d. No 3 Section O. 22. d. 1. 9 } 1 O.R. posted from 79th Bde RFA 1 O.R. transferred to Signal Depot Royal Engineers.	JCC
	2-5		Inspection of Unit by Major General Robertson Comdg 17th Divn at which he presented Divisional Certificates of Gallantry to Lieut. A. J. DAINTY } No 3 Section Driver T. HUDSON } 17th D.A.C. as a recognition of their gallant conduct on 25th March when engaged in the delivery of ammunition to the Infantry at FRICOURT during the retirement 21-28 March, the convoy they were with came under heavy shell fire. One wagon was blown up, several casualties occurred but through the coolness of the Officer and gallantry of both Officer & man the ammunition was safely delivered. 150 Indian personnel joined the Unit from Adv. RA Indian Base Depot in connection with the impending transfer of the Unit to a new War Estab. This personnel consisted of following ranks: Clerks 1 Hav. Major 1 Hav. 4 — Cooks 3 Naiks 4 — also followers: Sweepers 3 L/Naiks 7 Grs 36 Drs 91	JCC

Army Form C. 2118.

WAR DIARY
or
INTELLIGENCE SUMMARY.
(Erase heading not required.)

Instructions regarding War Diaries and Intelligence Summaries are contained in F. S. Regs., Part II. and the Staff Manual respectively. Title pages will be prepared in manuscript.

Place	Date 1918	Hour	Summary of Events and Information	Remarks and references to Appendices
	3.5.		250R Reinforcements joined from the Base	
			Two remounts joined from Remount Depot	FCC
	4.5		11 O.R. posted to 78th Bde R.F.A.	FCC
			13 O.R. posted to 79th Bde R.F.A.	
	5.5		No Change	FCC
	6.5		1 mule joined from Remount Depot	FCC
	7.5		56 O.R. reinforcements joined from Base	FCC
	"		33 O.R. posted to 78 Bde R.F.A.	
			22 O.R. posted to 79 Bde R.F.A.	
	8.5		1 O.R. posted to 315 Bde R.F.A.	FCC
	9.5		No. 3 Section moved to N.21.d.5.7 (Sheet 57d)	FCC
			4 O.R. reinforcements joined from Base	
	10.5		1 O.R. posted to 78th Bde R.F.A.	FCC
			3 O.R. posted to 315 Bde R.F.A.	
	11.5		No Change	FCC
	12.5		Lieut O. CLOUDESLEY posted to 79th Bde R.F.A. from attached to that Bde	FCC
	13.5		No Change	FCC
	14.5		1 O.R. to Base under age.	FCC
	15.5		1 O.R. joined from Vety Hospl	FCC
	16.5		20 O.R. reinforcements joined from Base	FCC
	17.5		15 O.R. reinforcements joined from 39th Div Arty	FCC
	18.5		17 O.R. posted to 79th Bde R.F.A.	FCC
			1 O.R. posted to 78th Bde R.F.A.	FCC
	19.5		1 O.R. posted to 181st Bde R.F.A.	FCC
	20.5		10 O.R. reinforcements joined from V Corps reinforcement Camp	FCC
			Handed over A.R.P. at U.6.a (Sheet 57d) to 63rd D.A. - All Batteries went into V Corps Mobile Reserve.	

A5834 Wt. W4973/M687 750,000 8/16 D. D. & L. Ltd. Forms/C.2118/13.

Army Form C. 2118.

Instructions regarding War Diaries and Intelligence Summaries are contained in F. S. Regs., Part II. and the Staff Manual respectively. Title pages will be prepared in manuscript.

WAR DIARY
or
~~INTELLIGENCE SUMMARY~~.
(Erase heading not required.)

Place	Date	Hour	Summary of Events and Information	Remarks and references to Appendices
~~21.5.1~~	21.5.18		15 O.R. reinforcements posted to 17th Div. T. Mortars	JCC
			1 O.R. posted to 79th Bde R.F.A.	
			1 O.R. posted from 79th Bde R.F.A.	
	22.5.18		No Change	JCC
			No 79104 Serjeant F. J. LANGLEY late of No 1 Sec. (evacuated to Base wounded in Oct 17) mentioned in C in Chiefs despatches of 14-4-18.	
	23.5.18		10 O.R. posted to 79th Bde R.F.A.	JCC
	24.5.18		5 O.R. joined from V Corps reinforcement Camp	JCC
	25.5.18		5 O.R. posted to 78 Bde R.F.A.	JCC
			47 O.R. reinforcements joined from V Corps reinforcement Camp	
	26.5.18		Took over A.R.P. at P18 d (Sheet 57 D) from 12th Divl. Arty	JCC
			37 O.R. reinforcements joined from V Corps reinforcement Camp.	
	27.5.18		Following casualties occurred at Baths ACHEUX from shell fire:-	JCC
			No 43088 Driver T. BURDEN — Killed	
			73085 " A. E. NORWOOD } Wounded	
			120645 " E. RAVEN }	
	28.5.18		No 28 O.R. reinforcements posted to 79th Bde R.F.A.	JCC
			19 O.R. " " 78 "	
			No 3 Section moved to O.6.C.5.3 (Sheet 57D)	
	29.5.18		18 O.R. reinforcements posted to 79th Bde R.F.A.	JCC
			18 " " 78 "	
			1 " " 17th T.M.	

A5834 Wt. W4973/M687 750,000 8/16 D. D. & L. Ltd. Forms/C.2118/13.

Instructions regarding War Diaries and Intelligence Summaries are contained in F. S. Regs., Part II. and the Staff Manual respectively. Title pages will be prepared in manuscript.

WAR DIARY
or
~~INTELLIGENCE SUMMARY.~~
(Erase heading not required.)

Army Form C. 2118.

Place	Date 1918	Hour	Summary of Events and Information	Remarks and references to Appendices
	30 5		No change.	JCC
	31 5		No change. No 42659 Driver J. KEY, HQrs Staff wounded by shell fire	JCC

[signature]
LT. COL. R.F.A.
COMMANDING [illegible] DIV: AMM. COL

A5834 Wt. W4973/M687 750,000 8/16 D. D. & L. Ltd. Forms/C.2118/13.

Army Form C. 2118.

Instructions regarding War Diaries and Intelligence Summaries are contained in F. S. Regs., Part II. and the Staff Manual respectively. Title pages will be prepared in manuscript.

WAR DIARY
or
INTELLIGENCE SUMMARY.
(Erase heading not required.)

Place	Date	Hour	Summary of Events and Information	Remarks and references to Appendices
			Casualties	
			Officers Sick Nil	
			O. Ranks " 9	
			Officers Killed Nil	
			Officers Wounded Nil	
			Other Ranks Killed 1.	
			Other Ranks Wounded 3	
			Horses {Killed} Nil {Wounded} Nil	
			Mules {Killed} Nil {Wounded} Nil	
			Horses evacuated 5	
			Mules evacuated 1	
			31/8/18	
			[signature] LT. COL. [illegible] COMMANDING [illegible] AMM. COL.	

A5834 Wt. W4973/M687 750,000 8/16 D. D. & L. Ltd. Forms/C.2118/13.

Army Form C. 2118.

Instructions regarding War Diaries and Intelligence Summaries are contained in F. S. Regs., Part II. and the Staff Manual respectively. Title pages will be prepared in manuscript.

WAR DIARY
or
INTELLIGENCE SUMMARY.
(Erase heading not required.)

Place	Date	Hour	Summary of Events and Information				Remarks and references to Appendices
			Return of Strength.				
				O	OR	Animals	
			Strength	19	620	710	
			Gained	–	230	3	
			Total	19	850	713	
			Loss	1	230	–	
			Strength on 31/8/18	18	620	713	
			31/8/18				

[signature]
LT. COL. R.F.A.
[COMMA]NDING 17th DIV: AMM. COL.

A5834 Wt. W4973/M687 750,000 8/16 D. D. & L. Ltd. Forms/C.2118/13.

Instructions regarding War Diaries and Intelligence Summaries are contained in F. S. Regs., Part II. and the Staff Manual respectively. Title pages will be prepared in manuscript.

WAR DIARY
or
INTELLIGENCE SUMMARY.

(Erase heading not required.)

Army Form C. 2118.

Vol 36

Place	Date	Hour	Summary of Events and Information	Remarks and references to Appendices
			Confidential	
			War Diary	
			17 Divisional Ammunition Column	
			from 1/6/18 to 30/6/18	

M. P. Tucker Lt R.F.A.
for Lt. Col. R.F.A.
COMMANDING, 17th DIV: AMM. COL.

30/6/18.

A5834 Wt. W4973/M687 750,000 8/16 D. D. & L. Ltd. Forms/C.2118/13.

Instructions regarding War Diaries and Intelligence Summaries are contained in F. S. Regs., Part II. and the Staff Manual respectively. Title pages will be prepared in manuscript.

WAR DIARY
or
INTELLIGENCE SUMMARY.
(Erase heading not required.)

Army Form C. 2118.

Place	Date 1918	Hour	Summary of Events and Information	Remarks and references to Appendices
	1-6.		Lt. Col R W L Dunlop CB DSO went into hospital sick. Command of unit falls on Captain A. C. GRUNCELL. Unit located as follows:-	JCC
			Nos 1 & 2 sections O. 11. central (Sheet 57d)	
			" 3 " O. 23. d. 7 7	
	2.6.		Lieut R H G Wilson admitted to hospital	JCC
	3.6		No change -	JCC
	4.6		No change -	JCC
	5-6		No change -	JCC
	6-6		No change -	JCC
	7-6		No change	JCC
	8-6		No change	JCC
	9-6		No change	JCC

A5834 Wt. W4973/M687 750,000 8/16 D. D. & L. Ltd. Forms/C.2118/13.

Instructions regarding War Diaries and Intelligence Summaries are contained in F. S. Regs., Part II. and the Staff Manual respectively. Title pages will be prepared in manuscript.

WAR DIARY
or
~~INTELLIGENCE SUMMARY.~~
(*Erase heading not required.*)

Army Form C. 2118.

Place	Date 1918	Hour	Summary of Events and Information	Remarks and references to Appendices
	10.6.		No change –	FCC
	11-6		No change –	FCC
	12.6.		Captain A.C. Grimwell appointed to Command 35th D.A.C. –	FCC
			In consequence of this appointment following changes took place	M.P.T.
			Captain C.J. Henning from Comdg. No 3 Sec. to Command 17 D.A.C. (Temporarily)	M.P.T.
			" F.C. Collins from Adjutant to Command of No 2 Section	M.P.T.
			Lieut M.P. Tucker Acting Adjutant	M.P.T.
			" A.J. Dainty Commanding No 3 Section	M.P.T.
	13-6		No change	M.P.T.
	14-6		No change	M.P.T.
	15-6		2 Reinforcements joined & posted to 79 Bde	M.P.T.
	16-6		2 Reinforcements joined & posted to 78 Bde	M.P.T.
	17-6		No change	M.P.T.
	18-6		No change	M.P.T.
	19-6		No change	M.P.T.
	20-6		No change	M.P.T.
	21-6		13 O.Rs proceeded to join Third Army R.A. Reinforcement Camp	M.P.T.

Instructions regarding War Diaries and Intelligence Summaries are contained in F. S. Regs., Part II. and the Staff Manual respectively. Title pages will be prepared in manuscript.

WAR DIARY
or
INTELLIGENCE SUMMARY.
(Erase heading not required.)

Army Form C. 2118.

Place	Date	Hour	Summary of Events and Information	Remarks and references to Appendices
	22-6		No change	
	23-6		2/Lt. G. S. Gerry from Base posted to 78th Bde R.F.A.	M.P.T.
			Lt. R. H. G. Wilson evacuated to England	M.P.T.
	24-6		2/Lt. J. C. Hebbishaw from Base	M.P.T.
	25-6		2/Lt. J. C. Hebbishaw to Hos. (sick)	M.P.T.
			18 Drivers surplus to Establishment proceeded to join Third Army	M.P.T.
			R.A. Reinforcement Camp as reinforcements.	M.P.T.
			S.A.A. Section moved camp to T.5.d.7.5.	M.P.T.
	26-6		1 O.R. reinforcement from Base.	M.P.T.
			No. 25029 Driver B. Marston to hospital Wounded by Bombs	M.P.T.
			41051 Driver E. G. Wright " "	M.P.T.
			19752 Driver Debi Sahai (Indian) " "	M.P.T.
			1 L.D. 1 H.D. horses + 6 L.D. Mules killed by Bombs	M.P.T.
			9 L.D. horses + 23 L.D. Mules wounded by Bombs	M.P.T.
	27-6		No change.	M.P.T.
	28-6		No change.	M.P.T.
	29-6		No change. 1 O.R. reinforcement posted to 78th Bde.	M.P.T.
	30-6		No change.	

M. P. Turner Lt R.F.A.
for Captain
~~Lt. Col.~~ R.F.A.
COMMANDING 17th DIV: AMM. COL

A5834 Wt. W4973/M687 750,000 8/16 D. D. & L. Ltd. Forms/C.2118/13.

Instructions regarding War Diaries and Intelligence Summaries are contained in F. S. Regs., Part II. and the Staff Manual respectively. Title pages will be prepared in manuscript.

WAR DIARY
or
~~INTELLIGENCE~~ SUMMARY.
(Erase heading not required.)

Army Form C. 2118.

Place	Date	Hour	Summary of Events and Information				Remarks and references to Appendices
			Return of Strength				
				O	OR	Animals	
			Strength	18	630	713	
			Found	6	75		
			Total	24	695	713	
			Gone	10	111	48	
			Strength on 30/6/18	14	584	665	

M R Tudor Lt R.F.A.
for Captain
~~Lt. Col.~~ R.F.A.
COMMANDING 17th DIV: AMM. COL

30/6/18

A5834 Wt. W4973/M687 750,000 8/16 D. D. & L. Ltd. Forms/C.2118/13.

Instructions regarding War Diaries and Intelligence Summaries are contained in F. S. Regs., Part II. and the Staff Manual respectively. Title pages will be prepared in manuscript.

WAR DIARY
or
INTELLIGENCE SUMMARY.
(Erase heading not required.)

Army Form C. 2118.

Place	Date	Hour	Summary of Events and Information	Remarks and references to Appendices
	30/6/18		Casualties	
			Officers Sick ~~2~~ 3.	
			O. Ranks " 8	
			Officers Killed Nil	
			Officers Wounded Nil	
			Other Ranks Killed Nil	
			Other Ranks Wounded 3. (1 Native).	
			Horses { Killed } 7.	
			Horses { Wounded } 9.	
			Mules { Killed } 6.	
			Mules { Wounded } 23.	
			Horses Evacuated 7	
			Mules Evacuated 5	
			Horses Transferred to 3 78 Bde & 6 79 Bde to Y.A.	
			Mules Transferred to 3 78 Bde & 6 79 Bde to Y.A.	
			Horses Transferred to Base	
			Mules Transferred to Base 1	

M. P. Tucker W.O. R.A.
for Captain
~~Lt. Col.~~ R.F.A.
COMMANDING 17th DIV: AMM. COL.

A5834 Wt. W4973/M687 750,000 8/16 D. D. & L. Ltd. Forms/C.2118/13.

Instructions regarding War Diaries and Intelligence Summaries are contained in F. S. Regs., Part II. and the Staff Manual respectively. Title pages will be prepared in manuscript.

WAR DIARY
or
INTELLIGENCE SUMMARY.
(Erase heading not required.)

Army Form C. 2118.

Vol 37

Place	Date	Hour	Summary of Events and Information	Remarks and references to Appendices
			Confidential War Diary of 17th Divisional Ammunition Column from 1/7/18 to 31/7/18. M. G. Tudeur CAPTAIN R.F.A. ADJUTANT 17th DIV. AMM. COL.	
		31/7/18.		

Army Form C. 2118.

WAR DIARY
or
INTELLIGENCE SUMMARY.
(*Erase heading not required.*)

Instructions regarding War Diaries and Intelligence Summaries are contained in F. S. Regs., Part II. and the Staff Manual respectively. Title pages will be prepared in manuscript.

Place	Date 1918	Hour	Summary of Events and Information	Remarks and references to Appendices
	1-7.		Unit located as follows: No 1 & 2 Sections O.11. Central (Sheet 57d) No 3 T. 12c 7 7	M.R.S.
	2-7.		No change.	M.R.S.
	3-7		No change	M.R.S.
	4-7		No change. 1 O.R. from Base.	M.R.S.
	5-7		No change	M.R.S.
	6-7		No change.	M.R.S.
	7-7		1 Officer (Lt W.A. Carne) & 15 Reinforcements from Base 2/Lt G.E.S. Lamb posted to 3rd Balloon Wing.	M.R.S.
	8-7.		No change	M.R.S.
	9-7.		3. O.Ranks to 17 Div Trench Mortars. 70 LD Remounts from Fourth Army Remount Depot.	M.R.S.
	10-7.		4 Artificers from Base.	M.R.S.
	11-7		No change	M.R.S.
	12-7.		4 Artificers to 78 & 79 Bde RFA. 48 LD Remounts to 79 Bde & 17 LD Remounts to 78 Bde. 5 to DAC	M.R.S.
	13-7.		No change	M.R.S.
	14-7		No change	M.R.S.
	15-7.		39 Reinforcements from 3rd Army Reinforcement Camp. 2 Officers (2/Lt M.G. Heslop & 2/Lt D.G. Molton from 3rd Army Rein Camp).	M.R.S.
	16-7.		20 O.Ranks posted to 79 Bde & 18 posted to 78 Bde. 1 OR to 38 T Coy. 2/Lt M.G. Heslop & 2/Lt D.G. Molton to 78 Bde RFA.	M.R.S.
	17-7.		1 Officer (Lt Yealman) from Base & posted to 78 Bde RFA. 10 Other Ranks from 3rd Army Reinforcement Camp. 5 posted to 78 Bde & 5 posted to 79 Bde RFA.	M.R.S.

A5834 Wt. W4973/M687 750,000 8/16 D. D. & L. Ltd. Forms/C.2118/13.

Instructions regarding War Diaries and Intelligence Summaries are contained in F. S. Regs., Part II. and the Staff Manual respectively. Title pages will be prepared in manuscript.

WAR DIARY
or
INTELLIGENCE SUMMARY.
(Erase heading not required.)

Army Form C. 2118.

Place	Date	Hour	Summary of Events and Information	Remarks and references to Appendices
Field	18-7.		2 officers from 3rd Army Reinforcement Camp 2/Lt J M Playfair & 2/Lt A A K Bailey	M.R.S.
			2/Lt J M Playfair & 2/Lt A A K Bailey posted to Trench Mortars.	M.R.S.
	19-7		No change.	M.R.S.
	20-7.		No change.	M.R.S.
			12 Other Ranks Reinforcements from 3rd Army Reinforcement Camps.	M.R.S.
	21-7		6. Other Ranks posted to 78 Bde & 6 Other Ranks posted to 79 Bde.	M.R.S.
	22-7		3 artificers posted to Bdes. 2 to 78 Bde & 1 to 79 Bde R.F.A.	M.R.S.
	23-7.		2 Other Ranks posted from 17 D.A. & posted to No 3 Section.	M.R.S.
	24-7.		2/Lt G.J. Habbishaw from Reinforcement Camps	M.R.S.
			2/Lt G.J. Habbishaw posted to B/79 Bde R.F.A.	M.R.S.
	25/7.		17. Other Ranks from 3rd Army Reinforcements Camps. 1 O.Rank from 235 Bde. 1 O.R. posted to 235 Bde R.F.A.	M.R.S.
	26-7		No change.	M.R.S.
	27-7		16. Other Ranks posted to 79 Bde R.F.A. 1 O.R. posted to 78 Bde R.F.A.	M.R.S.
	28-7		14 Other Ranks posted from 3rd Army Reinforcement Camps.	M.R.S.
	29-7.		4 Other Ranks posted to 78 Bde. 9 Other Ranks to 79 Bde R.F.A.	M.R.S.
	30-7		No change.	M.R.S.
	31-7			M.R.S.
				M.R.S.
				M.R.S.
				M.R.S.
				M.R.S.
				M.R.S.
				M.R.S.

Army Form C. 2118.

WAR DIARY
or
INTELLIGENCE SUMMARY.
(Erase heading not required.)

Instructions regarding War Diaries and Intelligence Summaries are contained in F. S. Regs., Part II. and the Staff Manual respectively. Title pages will be prepared in manuscript.

Place	Date	Hour	Summary of Events and Information				Remarks and references to Appendices
			Return of Strength	O	OR	Animals	MPS
			Strength	14	584	665	MPS
			Joined	7	124	70	MPS
			Total	21	708	735	MPS
			Gone	8	124	75	MPS
			Strength on 31/7/18	13	584	660	MPS

31/7/18

CAPTAIN. R.F.A.
ADJUTANT 17th DIV. AMM. COL.

A5834 Wt. W4973/M687 750,000 8/16 D. D. & L. Ltd. Forms/C.2118/13.

Instructions regarding War Diaries and Intelligence Summaries are contained in F. S. Regs., Part II. and the Staff Manual respectively. Title pages will be prepared in manuscript.

WAR DIARY
or
INTELLIGENCE SUMMARY.
(Erase heading not required.)

Army Form C. 2118.

Place	Date	Hour	Summary of Events and Information	Remarks and references to Appendices
			Casualties	
			Officers Sick Nil	MF
			O. Ranks " 29	MF
			Officers Killed Nil	MF
			Officers Wounded Nil.	MF
			Other Ranks Killed Nil	MF
			Other Ranks Wounded 7	MF
			Horses { Killed Nil.	MF
			Horses { Wounded Nil	MF
			Mules { Killed Nil	MF
			Mules { Wounded 2.	MF
			Horses Evacuated 3	MF
			Mules Evacuated Nil	MF

31/7/18

CAPTAIN R.F.A.
ADJUTANT 17th DIV. AMM. COL.

A5834 Wt. W4973/M687 750,000 8/16 D. D. & L. Ltd. Forms/C.2118/13.

17th Divl.
Artillery

17th DIVISIONAL AMMUNITION COLUMN,

AUGUST 1918.

24

Instructions regarding War Diaries and Intelligence Summaries are contained in F. S. Regs., Part II. and the Staff Manual respectively. Title pages will be prepared in manuscript.

WAR DIARY
or
INTELLIGENCE SUMMARY.

(Erase heading not required.)

Army Form C. 2118.

Vol 38

Place	Date	Hour	Summary of Events and Information	Remarks and references to Appendices
			Confidential War Diary of 17th Divisional Ammunition Column from 1/8/18 to 31/8/18 Chs [illegible] Lt Col LT. COL. R.F.A. COMMANDING 17th DIV: AMM: COL. 31/8/18	

A5834 Wt. W4973/M687 750,000 8/16 D. D. & L. Ltd. Forms/C.2118/13.

Instructions regarding War Diaries and Intelligence Summaries are contained in F. S. Regs., Part II. and the Staff Manual respectively. Title pages will be prepared in manuscript.

WAR DIARY
or
INTELLIGENCE SUMMARY.
(Erase heading not required.)

Army Form C. 2118.

Place	Date	Hour	Summary of Events and Information	Remarks and references to Appendices
	1-8.		Unit located as follos.	M.A.T.
			HQ U.2.a.21 } Sheet 57d.	M.A.T.
			No 1 Sec U.6.a.21	M.A.T.
			No 2 Sec U.5.b.3.2.	M.A.T.
			No 3. T.12.d.10-20.	M.A.T.
			19 Reinforcements joined from 3rd Army Camp. 1 OR posted to HQ 17 D.A.	M.A.T.
	2.8.		Lt McStTarry to Hospital (Sick). 9 ORs posted to 78 Bde RFA, 9 O Ranks posted to 79 Bde RFA	M.A.T.
	3.8.		No change.	M.A.T.
	4.8.		Lt A. Watkins from Base & posted to Trench Mortars. 21 O Ranks joined from 3rd Army Rein. Camp	M.A.T.
			11 O Ranks posted to 79 Bde & 10 posted to 78 Bde RFA	M.A.T.
	5.8		No change	M.A.T.
	6.8		No change	M.A.T.
	7.8		No change	M.A.T.
	8.8		No change	M.A.T.
	9-8		7 O Ranks posted to 78 Bde & 1 OR to 79 Bde	M.A.T.
	9-8		Captain Morris Evans joined from 3rd Army Reinforcement Camp	M.A.T.
	9-8		Unit marched to Australian Corps and camped at GLISY	M.A.T.
	10-8		No change	M.A.T.
	11-8		Unit marched to VECQUEMONT	M.A.T.
	12-8		Unit marched to CERISY and camped as follows:-	M.A.T.
			HQ P.6.d.12 } 57D	M.A.T.
			No 1 Sec P.6.d.2.4	M.A.T.
			2. P.6.d.2.2	M.A.T.
			3. P.6.d.6.2	M.A.T.
			3. Other Ranks transferred to England for tour of home duty.	M.A.T.
			The following Ammunition Dumps from 3rd Australian D.A.C. were taken over	M.A.T.
			CERISY Dump	M.A.T.
			GAILLY X Roads	M.A.T.
			VAIRE Dump	M.A.T.

A5834 Wt. W4973/M687 750,000 8/16 D. D. & L. Ltd. Forms/C.2118/13.

[signature]
LT. COL. R.F.A.
COMMANDING 17th DIV: AMM. COL.

Instructions regarding War Diaries and Intelligence Summaries are contained in F. S. Regs., Part II. and the Staff Manual respectively. Title pages will be prepared in manuscript.

WAR DIARY
or
INTELLIGENCE SUMMARY.
(Erase heading not required.)

Army Form C. 2118.

Place	Date	Hour	Summary of Events and Information	Remarks and references to Appendices
	13. 8.		No change	MAT
	14. 8.		No change	MAT
	15. 8		The following ~~details~~ Surplus details ~~[illegible]~~ on Re-organization were posted to 3rd Army Reinforcement camp:-	MAT
			66 Drivers	MAT
			45 Gnrs	MAT
			3 Corporals	MAT
			1 Bombardier.	MAT
			Lt-Colonel R. W. L. [illegible] RGA assumed command & [illegible] RGA [illegible] from Base. Major [illegible] relinquishes [illegible] [illegible] Section [illegible] relinquishes rank & captain.	MAT
	16-8.		S.A.A. Section moved to VECQUEMONT on relief by 5th D.A.C. (S.A.A. Sec)	MAT
	17-8		HQ, No 1 & 2 Sections moved to DAOURS on relief [illegible] 5th Aus. D.A.C.	MAT
	18-8		No change	MAT
	19-8		Unit marched to TOUTENCOURT and camped as follows:-	MAT
			HQ. U. 3. d. 3. 2. }	MAT
			No 1 Sec O 32. b } Sheet 57 D	MAT
			2 O 32. d	MAT
			3 T. 12. c. 8. 8.	MAT
	20-8		No change 1 O. Ranks from 3rd Army Rein. Camp.	MAT
	21-8		No change	MAT
	22-8		No change	MAT
	23-8		Unit marched to FORCEVILLE Area and camped as follows:-	MAT
			HQ at O. 18 d 7. 2. }	MAT
			No 1 at O. 18 d 7. 2 } Sheet 57 D	MAT
			No 2 at O. 18 d 7. 2.	MAT
			3 at P. 8. c. 5. 8	MAT
			Ammunition Dump at P. 7 [illegible] 2. 2. commenced and Bdes supplied with Ammunition.	MAT

R. H. [illegible]
LT. COL.
ADJUTANT [illegible] DIV. AMM. COL.

A5834 Wt. W4973/M687 750,000 8/16 D. D. & L. Ltd. Forms/C.2118/13.

Instructions regarding War Diaries and Intelligence Summaries are contained in F. S. Regs., Part II. and the Staff Manual respectively. Title pages will be prepared in manuscript.

WAR DIARY
or
INTELLIGENCE SUMMARY.

(*Erase heading not required.*)

Army Form C. 2118.

Place	Date	Hour	Summary of Events and Information	Remarks and references to Appendices
	24/8		No change. 1 O.Rank posted from HQ 17 [illegible]	MAT
	25/8		Unit marched to MESNIL Area and camped as follows	MAT
			HQ Q 28 d 2 1 — 7 Officers & [illegible] Ranks Trench Mortar attached for duty	MAT
			No 1 Sec Q 29 a 4 2 — A.R.P. established at Q 29 4 1 and Bdes supplied with	MAT
			No 2 Sec Q 29 a 1 0 — Ammunition. 14431 Dvr BHOPAL; 30944 " RUDER; 26409 " ITWARI; 31229 " RAMRUP — accidentally injured by explosion of Bomb	MAT
	26/8		No change	MAT
	27/8		Unit marched to POZIERES Area and camped as follows	MAT
			HQ X 9 a 8 3 } — 31421 Dvr CHEDAMI Accidentally injured	MAT
			No 1 Sec X 9 a 1 1 } ALBERT [illegible]	MAT
			2 " X 9 a 8 2 }	MAT
			A.R.P. established at X 5 a 2 6 [illegible]	MAT
	28/8		No change	MAT
	29/8		No change	MAT
	30/8		No change	MAT
	31/8		Unit moved to camp at R 29 b 9 8 — ALBERT [illegible]	MAT

[illegible signature]
LT. COL. R.F.A.
COMMANDING 17th DIV: AMM: COL

A5834 Wt. W4973/M687 750,000 8/16 D. D. & L. Ltd. Forms/C.2118/13.

Army Form C. 2118.

WAR DIARY
or
INTELLIGENCE SUMMARY.
(*Erase heading not required.*)

Instructions regarding War Diaries and Intelligence Summaries are contained in F. S. Regs., Part II. and the Staff Manual respectively. Title pages will be prepared in manuscript.

Place	Date	Hour	Summary of Events and Information	Remarks and references to Appendices
			Casualties	
			Officers Sick 1	
			O. Ranks " 2	
			Officers Killed Nil	
			Officers Wounded Nil	
			Other Ranks Killed Nil	
			" " Wounded Nil	
			Accidentally Injured 1 Other Ranks	
			Horses Mules Killed Nil	
			Horses Mules Wounded Nil	
			Horses Evacuated 6	
			Mules " 11	
	31/8/18			

[signature] LT. COL. R.F.A.
COMMANDING 17th DIV. AMM. COL.
ADJUTANT 17th DIV. AMM. COLUMN.

A5834 Wt. W4973/M687 750,000 8/16 D. D. & L. Ltd. Forms/C.2118/13.

Instructions regarding War Diaries and Intelligence Summaries are contained in F. S. Regs., Part II. and the Staff Manual respectively. Title pages will be prepared in manuscript.

WAR DIARY
or
INTELLIGENCE SUMMARY.
(Erase heading not required.)

Army Form C. 2118.

Place	Date	Hour	Summary of Events and Information				Remarks and references to Appendices
				O	OR	Animals	
			Strength on 31/7/18	13	584	660	
			Joined	4	189	–	
			Total	17	773	660	
			[illegible]	1	176	25	
			Strength on 31/8/18	16	597	635	

P R [illegible]
LT. COL. R.F.A.
COMMANDING 17th DIV: AMM. COL.

31/8/18

A5834 Wt. W4973/M687 750,000 8/16 D. D. & L. Ltd. Forms/C.2118/13.

Instructions regarding War Diaries and Intelligence Summaries are contained in F. S. Regs., Part II. and the Staff Manual respectively. Title pages will be prepared in manuscript.

WAR DIARY
or
INTELLIGENCE SUMMARY.
(Erase heading not required.)

Army Form C. 2118.

WD 39

Place	Date	Hour	Summary of Events and Information	Remarks and references to Appendices
			Confidential.	
			War Diary	
			of	
			17th Divisional Ammunition Column	
			from 1/9/18 to 30/9/18	
			30/9/18	
			R. L. Dewhurst [signature] LT. COL. R.F.A. COMMANDING 17th DIV: AMM. COL.	

A5834 Wt. W4973/M687 750,000 8/16 D. D. & L. Ltd. Forms/C.2118/13.

Instructions regarding War Diaries and Intelligence Summaries are contained in F. S. Regs., Part II. and the Staff Manual respectively. Title pages will be prepared in manuscript.

WAR DIARY
or
INTELLIGENCE SUMMARY.
(*Erase heading not required.*)

Army Form C. 2118.

Place	Date	Hour	Summary of Events and Information	Remarks and references to Appendices
	1/9/18		Unit camped as follows. HQ R 29b.9.8 ⎫ Maps No1 R 29t.2.4 ⎬ ALBERT combined. 2 R.29t.2.1 ⎭	E/S
	2/9/18		No change. 1 OR posted to 79 Bde RFA	E/S
	3/9/18		Unit moved to camp as follows - HQ at O.31 a 5 5 No1 at O 31 a 2 1 No. 2 at O.31 a 9 3	E/S.
	4/9/18		22 Other ranks from Base. 1 O.R from Aus. Heavy Artillery Corps	E/S
	5/9/18		11 Other ranks to 78 Bde RFA. 11 Other Ranks to 79 Bde RFA	E/S
	6/9/18		No change	E/S
	7/9/18		1 O.R. from 3rd Army R.A. Rein. Camp. Lt J. A. OLD wounded to Hospital. Enemy aircraft bombed camps at 12.15 am. 4 bombs dropped. 1 LD Horse killed 2 LD Horse Wounded 1 HD Horse Wounded 4 Other Ranks from 3rd Army R.A. Rein Camp	E/S
	8/9/18		No change	E/S
	9/9/18		No change	E/S
	10/9/18		2/Lt J a Riley, 2/Lt J B Jackson, 2/Lt H Bingham 2/Lt T. Anderton, 2/Lt A Hollingworth from 3rd Army RA Reinforcement Camps: 1 OR posted to 78 Bde RFA.	E/S
	11/9/18		44 ORks reinforcements from 3rd Army Reinforcement Camps.	E/S

Instructions regarding War Diaries and Intelligence Summaries are contained in F. S. Regs., Part II. and the Staff Manual respectively. Title pages will be prepared in manuscript.

WAR DIARY or INTELLIGENCE SUMMARY.

(Erase heading not required.)

Army Form C. 2118.

Place	Date	Hour	Summary of Events and Information	Remarks and references to Appendices
	11.9.18		2/Lt J. A. Riley & 2/Lt A Hollingworth posted to 78 Bde RFA	
			2/Lt H. Bingham posted to 79 Bde RFA.	
			2/Lt T Anderton posted to No1 Sec 17 DAC	G/S
			2/Lt J.B Jackson posted to No 2 Sec 17 DAC.	G/S
	12/9/18		1 O Ranks from 3rd Army RA Reinforcement Camp.	
	13/9/18		Unit camped as follows:–	G/S
			HQ at P. V. 2 a 2. 3	
			No1 Sec " P. V 2. a 2. 3	
			2 " P. V. 2 a 2. 3	
			18 Reinforcements posted to 78 Bde RFA. 26 Reinforcements posted to 79 Bde RFA	
	14/9/18		Lt (a/Captain) G T Morris-Evans posted to RH & RFA Base Depot for Medical Inspection as Category.	G/S
			25 Other Ranks from 3rd Army RA Reinforcement Camp.	
	15/9/18		Enemy Aircraft bombed camp at V 2 a 2. 3. Number of bombs dropped 4.	G/S
			No 71667 Dvr J Booth wounded. 2 Horses Killed 1 wounded.	G/S
	16/9/18		22 Other Ranks from 3rd Army Reinforcement Camp	G/S
	17/9/18		No change.	G/S
	18/9/18		No change	G/S
	19/9/18		No change	

A5834 Wt. W4973/M687 750,000 8/16 D. D. & L. Ltd. Forms/C.2118/13.

Instructions regarding War Diaries and Intelligence Summaries are contained in F. S. Regs., Part II. and the Staff Manual respectively. Title pages will be prepared in manuscript.

WAR DIARY
or
INTELLIGENCE SUMMARY.
(Erase heading not required.)

Army Form C. 2118.

Place	Date	Hour	Summary of Events and Information	Remarks and references to Appendices
	20/9/18		16 Other Ranks reinforcements joined from 3rd Army RA Rein Camp	S/B
	21/9/18		2/Lt ANDERTON T posted to TMs. 2/Lt FA MARGRY posted from TMs to No1 Sec A.R.P. at VALLUART WOOD P.32 taken over from 38th D.A. 1 OR from T.Ms	S/B
	22/9/18		No change	S/B
	23/9/18		6 Other Ranks posted to 78 Bde. 7 to 79 Bde. 1 to 17 Div M.T. Coy. 2 to DAC Enemy shelled camp at V.1.a. 2 Mules killed & 6 Mules wounded	S/B
	24/9/18		No change	S/B
	25/9/18		No change	S/B
	26/9/18		18 Other Ranks Reinforcements from Base. 1 ORs to TMs. 30611 Havildar Hoshiaia Ram wounded in action 1 animal killed	S/B
	27/9/18		No change. 35009 Gnr ANGAD killed in action. 8 artificers from Base.	S/B
	28/9/18		10 Other Ranks Reinforcements posted to 78 Bde & 8 posted to 79 Bde RFA.	S/B
	29/9/18		3 Artificers posted as follows:- 2 artificers 78 Bde & 1 to 79 Bde RFA	S/B
	30/9/18		No change	

[signature]
Lt. Col.
Commanding 17th Div Art.

Instructions regarding War Diaries and Intelligence Summaries are contained in F. S. Regs., Part II. and the Staff Manual respectively. Title pages will be prepared in manuscript.

WAR DIARY
or
INTELLIGENCE SUMMARY.
(Erase heading not required.)

Army Form C. 2118.

Place	Date	Hour	Summary of Events and Information	Remarks and references to Appendices
			Casualties.	
			Officers Sick Nil	
			O. Ranks " 3	
			Officers Killed Nil	
			Officers Wounded. 1 (Lt J.A. OLD).	
			Other Ranks Killed 1. 3500 Gnr ANGAD	
			Other Ranks Wounded 1. 20611 Hav. HOSHNIA RAM.	
			Horses Killed 2	
			Mules Killed 15	
			Horses Wounded -	
			Mules Wounded. 10	
			Horses Evacuated 5	
			Mules Evacuated. 7.	

9/30/18.

R.H.S. [signature]
LT. COL. R.F.A.
COMMANDING 17th DIV: AMM. COL.

A5834 Wt. W4973/M687 750,000 8/16 D. D. & L. Ltd. Forms/C.2118/13

WAR DIARY
or
INTELLIGENCE SUMMARY.
(Erase heading not required.)

Army Form C. 2118.

Instructions regarding War Diaries and Intelligence Summaries are contained in F. S. Regs., Part II. and the Staff Manual respectively. Title pages will be prepared in manuscript.

Place	Date	Hour	Summary of Events and Information	Remarks and references to Appendices
			Strength Return	

	O	OR	Animals
Strength on 31/8/18	16	597	665
Joined	7	166	44
Total	23	763	679
Gone	6	164	48
Strength on 30/9/18.	17	599	631

30/9/18.

[illegible signature]
LT. COL. R.F.A.
COMMANDING 17th DIV: AMM. COL.

A5834 Wt. W4973/M687 750,000 8/16 D. D. & L. Ltd. Forms/C.2118/13.

16

Instructions regarding War Diaries and Intelligence Summaries are contained in F. S. Regs., Part II. and the Staff Manual respectively. Title pages will be prepared in manuscript.

WAR DIARY
or
INTELLIGENCE SUMMARY.
(Erase heading not required.)

Army Form C. 2118.

Vol 40

Place	Date	Hour	Summary of Events and Information	Remarks and references to Appendices
			Confidential War Diary of 17th Divisional Ammunition Column from 1/10/18 to 31/10/18 R W Smith Lt. Col. LT. COL. R.F.A. COMMANDING 17th DIV: AMM. COL. 31/10/18	

A5834 Wt. W4973/M687 750,000 8/16 D. D. & L. Ltd. Forms/C.2118/13.

Army Form C. 2118.

Instructions regarding War Diaries and Intelligence Summaries are contained in F. S. Regs., Part II. and the Staff Manual respectively. Title pages will be prepared in manuscript.

WAR DIARY
or
INTELLIGENCE SUMMARY.
(Erase heading not required.)

Place	Date	Hour	Summary of Events and Information	Remarks and references to Appendices
	1/10/18		Unit moved to camps in W.2.b.8.2 (Sheet 57b)	M.A.T.
	2/10/18		Lt R.S. Paterson (RAMC) posted to 78 Bde R.F.A	M.A.T.
	3/10/18		No change	M.A.T.
	4/10/18		No change	M.A.T.
	5/10/18		No change	M.A.T.
	6/10/18		1 L.D. Mule wounded.	M.A.T.
	7/10/18		Unit moved to camps in R.25.d.2.5 (Sheet 57B).	M.A.T.
			No. 34334 Gr. DEVI Accidentally injured.	M.A.T.
	8/10/18		No. 30823 Dr. HMRAI killed in action.	M.A.T.
			Wounded: 3056 Havildar ALLA DITTA KHAN	M.A.T.
			12886 Gunner CHETA	M.A.T.
			19538 Driver PHADRI PERSHAD	M.A.T.
			19794 Driver DEO. KARAN	M.A.T.
			27904 Driver KANAH	M.A.T.
			33272 Gunner NEGASIYA.	M.A.T.
			24 L.D. Animals Killed. 13 L.D. Animals Wounded. Camp of S.A.A. Section bombed on evening of 7/10/18 by enemy aircraft, at R.35.b.0.5. (Sheet 57b).	M.A.T.
	9/10/18		No change	M.A.T.
	10/10/18		Unit moved to camps at O.11.d.2.8 (Sheet 57b).	M.A.T.
			5 L.D. Remounts joined from Base.	M.A.T.

A5834 Wt. W4973/M687 750,000 8/16 D. D. & L. Ltd. Forms/C.2118/13.

Instructions regarding War Diaries and Intelligence Summaries are contained in F. S. Regs., Part II. and the Staff Manual respectively. Title pages will be prepared in manuscript.

WAR DIARY
or
INTELLIGENCE SUMMARY.
(*Erase heading not required.*)

Army Form C. 2118.

Place	Date	Hour	Summary of Events and Information	Remarks and references to Appendices
	11/10/18.		Unit moved to Camps in J 20 d 8. 2. (Sheet 57b)	M.A.T.
			Lt. E J BARRATT posted to 6/79 + appointed A/ Captain second in command.	M.A.T.
	12/10/18.		39 L.D. Remounts joined from Base. 45 Reinforcements joined from Base.	M.A.T.
	13/10/18.		16 L.D. Remounts posted to 79 Bde R.F.A.	M.A.T.
			17 L.D. Remounts posted to 78 Bde R.F.A.	M.A.T.
			6 L.D. Remounts posted to 17 D.A.C.	M.A.T.
	14/10/18		19 Reinforcements posted to 78th Bde R.F.A.	M.A.T.
			17 Reinforcements posted to 79th Bde R.F.A.	M.A.T.
	15/10/18		No change	M.A.T.
	16/10/18		No change	M.A.T.
	17/10/18		No change	M.A.T.
	18/10/18		No change	M.A.T.
	19/10/18		30. O.R.s Reinforcements from Base + 1 Officer (Lt. H. CHERMSIDE).	M.A.T.
	20/10/18.		20 O.R.s Reinforcements from Base.	M.A.T.
	21/10/18		3 O.R.s Reinforcements joined. 24 O.R.s posted to 79 Bde R.F.A. 5 O.R.s to 78 Bde R.F.A.	M.A.T.
	22/10/18.		11 O.R.s Reinforcements posted to 79 Bde R.F.A. 4 O.R.s posted to 78 Bde R.F.A.	M.A.T.
	23/10/18		2 O.R.s posted to 78 Bde R.F.A. + 1 O.R. posted to 79 Bde R.F.A. Unit moved to Camp in E 23 d 8. 2 (Sheet 57b)	M.A.T.
	24/10/18		Captain G. C. Henning to Hospital (Sick)	M.A.T.

A5834 Wt. W4973/M687 750,000 8/16 D. D. & L. Ltd. Forms/C.2118/13.

Army Form C. 2118.

Instructions regarding War Diaries and Intelligence Summaries are contained in F. S. Regs., Part II. and the Staff Manual respectively. Title pages will be prepared in manuscript.

WAR DIARY
or
INTELLIGENCE SUMMARY.
(Erase heading not required.)

Place	Date	Hour	Summary of Events and Information	Remarks and references to Appendices
	25/10/18		No change Lt. A.J. DAINTY appointed as O.C. S.A.A. Section vice Capt. C.C. Henning to Hospital 24/10/18	M.A.T.
	26/10/18		No change	M.A.T.
	27/10/18		No change. 38 O.R's Reinforcements from Base	M.A.T.
	28/10/18.		26. O.R's posted to 78 Bde.	M.A.T.
	29/10/18.		No 84151 A/L/Bdr (Dvr) G.E. LILLEY wounded (at duty).	M.A.T.
	30/10/18		Lt. J.E. JACKSON from Base & posted to No 2 Section	M.A.T.
	31/10/18		No change.	M.A.T.

LT. COL. R.F.A.
COMMANDING 17th DIV! AMM. COL.

A5834 Wt. W4973/M687 750,000 8/16 D. D. & L. Ltd. Forms/C.2118/13

Instructions regarding War Diaries and Intelligence Summaries are contained in F. S. Regs., Part II. and the Staff Manual respectively. Title pages will be prepared in manuscript.

WAR DIARY
or
INTELLIGENCE SUMMARY.
(Erase heading not required.)

Army Form C. 2118.

Place	Date	Hour	Summary of Events and Information	Remarks and references to Appendices
			Casualties.	
			Officer Sick . Captain C.J. Henning. R.F.A.	
			O. Rank. " 32.	
			Officers Killed. Nil	
			Officers Wounded Nil	
			Other Ranks Killed Nil	
			Other Ranks Wounded 1. OR.	
			Horses Killed 5	
			Mules Killed 20	
			Horses Wounded 2	
			Mules Wounded 13	
			Horses Evacuated 3	
			Mules Evacuated 2	
	31/10/18			

[signature]
LT. COL. R.F.A.
COMMANDING 17th DIV: AMM. COL

A5834 Wt. W4973/M687 750,000 8/16 D. D. & L. Ltd. Forms/C.2118/13.

Army Form C. 2118.

WAR DIARY
or
INTELLIGENCE SUMMARY.

(Erase heading not required.)

Instructions regarding War Diaries and Intelligence Summaries are contained in F. S. Regs., Part II. and the Staff Manual respectively. Title pages will be prepared in manuscript.

Place	Date	Hour	Summary of Events and Information	Remarks and references to Appendices
			Strength Return	

	O	O.R.	Animals
Strength on 30/9/18.	17	597	635
Joined	2	138	51
Total	19	735	686
Gone	2	156	51
Strength on 01/9/18.	17	579	635

31/10/18.

[signature]
LT. COL. R.F.A.
COMMANDING 17th DIV. [illegible]

A5834 Wt. W4973/M687 750,000 8/16 D. D. & L. Ltd. Forms/C.2118/13.

Instructions regarding War Diaries and Intelligence Summaries are contained in F. S. Regs., Part II. and the Staff Manual respectively. Title pages will be prepared in manuscript.

WAR DIARY
or
INTELLIGENCE SUMMARY.
(Erase heading not required.)

Army Form C. 2118.

Vol 41

Place	Date	Hour	Summary of Events and Information	Remarks and references to Appendices
			Confidential War Diary of 17th Divisional Ammunition Column from 1/11/18 to 30/11/18 30/11/18 R.A. Smith LT. COL. R.F.A. COMMANDING 17th DIV: AMM. COL.	

A5834 Wt. W4973/M687 750,000 8/16 D. D. & L. Ltd. Forms/C.2118/13.

Instructions regarding War Diaries and Intelligence Summaries are contained in F. S. Regs., Part II. and the Staff Manual respectively. Title pages will be prepared in manuscript.

WAR DIARY
or
INTELLIGENCE SUMMARY.
(Erase heading not required.)

Army Form C. 2118.

Place	Date November	Hour	Summary of Events and Information	Remarks and references to Appendices
In the Field	1st		94844 Dr Harris F Wounded	M.A.S.
	1		2nd Lt Elliott & 2nd Lt Wheeler G.R joined	M.A.S.
	2nd		25 O.R. Reinforcements joined from 3rd Army R.A Reinforcement Camp.	M.A.S.
	3rd		14 O.R. Posted 48th Bde. 11 O.R. posted 49th Bde 2Lts Elliot & Wheeler to 49th Bde.	M.A.S.
	4th		6 mules Killed. 1 Indian arrived from Base.	M.A.S.
	5th		Unit moved to F.8.a.0.1 (Sheet 57 B).	M.A.S.
	6th		Unit moved to X.24.d.9.3. (Sheet 51 a)	M.A.S.
	7th		Unit moved to T.19.b (Sheet 51 a)	M.A.S.
	8th		No 43286 Gr Brockwell wounded.	M.A.S.
	9th		54 O.R. Reinforcements joined	M.A.S.
	10th		3 O.R. Reinforcements joined	M.A.S.
	11th		24 O.R posted to 48th Bde. 30 O.R. posted to 49th Bde	M.A.S.
	12th		No change.	M.A.S.
	13th		Unit moved to VENDEGIES	M.A.S.
	14th		Unit moved to CLARY 6 O.R. Reinforcements joined.	M.A.S.
	15th		Unit moved to ESNES. 1 OR posted 48th Bde. 5 O.R. posted 49th Bde	M.A.S.
	16th		No change.	M.A.S.
	17th		No change.	M.A.S.
	18th		No change.	M.A.S.
	19th		No change.	M.A.S.
	20th		No change.	M.A.S.
	21st		No change.	M.A.S.
	22nd		No change.	M.A.S.
	23rd		No change.	M.A.S.
	24th		No change.	M.A.S.
	25th		2 O.R. posted to 49th Bde.	M.A.S.

A5834 Wt. W4973/M687 750,000 8/16 D. D. & L. Ltd. Forms/C.2118/13.

Instructions regarding War Diaries and Intelligence Summaries are contained in F. S. Regs., Part II. and the Staff Manual respectively. Title pages will be prepared in manuscript.

WAR DIARY
or
INTELLIGENCE SUMMARY.
(Erase heading not required.)

Army Form C. 2118.

Place	Date	Hour	Summary of Events and Information	Remarks and references to Appendices
	25-11-18		137. OR's joined from Base.	
	26-11-18		No change	
	27-11-18		61 OR's posted to 78 Bde RFA. 54 OR's posted to 79 Bde RFA	
	28-11-18		No change	
	29-11-18		6 OR's released for duty at home (Miners)	
	29-11-18		20 OR's joined from Base	
	30-11-18		8 OR's to 78 Bde, 7 OR's to 79 Bde RFA,	

R. W. A. Dunlop
LT. COL. R.F.A.
COMMANDING 17th DIV: AMM. COL.

A5834 Wt. W4973/M687 750,000 8/16 D. D. & L. Ltd. Forms/C.2118/13.

Instructions regarding War Diaries and Intelligence Summaries are contained in F. S. Regs., Part II. and the Staff Manual respectively. Title pages will be prepared in manuscript.

WAR DIARY
or
INTELLIGENCE SUMMARY.
(*Erase heading not required.*)

Army Form C. 2118.

Place	Date	Hour	Summary of Events and Information	Remarks and references to Appendices

	O	OR	Animals
Strength on 31 10/18	14	519	646
Joined	2	253	19
Total	19	832	665
Gone.	2	306	11
Strength on 30 10/18.	17	526	654

30/11/18

[signature]
LT. COL. R.F.A.
COMMANDING ... COL.

Instructions regarding War Diaries and Intelligence Summaries are contained in F. S. Regs., Part II. and the Staff Manual respectively. Title pages will be prepared in manuscript.

WAR DIARY
or
INTELLIGENCE SUMMARY.
(Erase heading not required.)

Army Form C. 2118.

Place	Date	Hour	Summary of Events and Information	Remarks and references to Appendices
			Casualties	
			Officers Nil } Killed. O.Ranks. Nil. }	
			Officers. Nil } Wounded. O.Ranks. 2. }	
			Horses 1 } Killed. Mules. 8 }	
			Horses Nil } Wounded. Mules 4 }	
			Horses Nil } Evacuated. Mules 2 }	
			Officers Nil } Sick. O.Ranks 18 }	
			R... [signature] LT. COL. R.F.A. COMMANDING 17th DIV: AMM. COL.	
	30/11/18			

A5834 Wt. W4973/M687 750,000 8/16 D. D. & L. Ltd. Forms/C.2118/13.

Instructions regarding War Diaries and Intelligence Summaries are contained in F. S. Regs., Part II. and the Staff Manual respectively. Title pages will be prepared in manuscript.

WAR DIARY
or
INTELLIGENCE SUMMARY.
(Erase heading not required.)

Army Form C. 2118.

1842

Place	Date	Hour	Summary of Events and Information	Remarks and references to Appendices
			Confidential	
			War Diary of	
			17th Divisional Ammunition Column	
			From 1/12/18 to 31/12/18	
			M. B. [illegible] Capt. RFA for Lt. Col. R.F.A. Commanding 17th Div. Amm. Col.	
			31/12/18	

A5834 Wt. W4973/M687 750,000 8/16 D. D. & L. Ltd. Forms/C.2118/13.

Instructions regarding War Diaries and Intelligence Summaries are contained in F. S. Regs., Part II. and the Staff Manual respectively. Title pages will be prepared in manuscript.

WAR DIARY
or
INTELLIGENCE SUMMARY.
(Erase heading not required.)

Army Form C. 2118.

Place	Date	Hour	Summary of Events and Information	Remarks and references to Appendices
	1/12/18		Unit camped at ESNES	M.A.T.
	2/12/18		29 O.Rs released for Coal-Mining. Captain Henning R.F.A. from hospital.	M.A.T.
	3/12/18		Chaplain C Andrews & servant joined from 49 Bde R.F.A.	M.A.T.
	4/12/18		12 O.Rs reinforcements from Base	M.A.T.
	5/12/18		1 O.R from 78 Bde R.F.A	M.A.T.
	6/12/18		12 O.R Released for Mining.	M.A.T.
	7/12/18		No change	M.A.T.
	8/12/18		Unit moved to ETRICOURT	M.A.T.
	9/12/18		Unit moved to MEAULTE	M.A.T.
	10/12/18		Unit moved to ALLONVILLE	M.A.T.
	11/12/18		Unit moved to BETTENCOURT. 1 O.R joined from Base	M.A.T.
	12/12/18		No change	M.A.T.
	13/12/18		646124 Dvr. R ATKINSON from DOULLENS.	M.A.T.
	14/12/18		112 O.Rs joined from Base	M.A.T.
	15/12/18		No change	M.A.T.
	16/12/18		1 officer 2 O.Rs reinforcements joined from Base. 65 O.Rs to 78 Bde. 41 O.Rs to 49 Bde RFA	M.A.T.
	17/12/18		2 O.Rs to 46 Bde RFA.	M.A.T.
	18/12/18		3 O.Rs released for Mining	M.A.T.
	19/12/18		No change	M.A.T.
	20/12/18		No change	M.A.T.
	21/12/18		No change	M.A.T.
	22/12/18		No change	M.A.T.
	23/12/18		No change	M.A.T.
	24/12/18		No change Captain E C RIDOUT RFA to hospital (sick)	M.A.T.

A5834 Wt. W4973/M687 750,000 8/16 D. D. & L. Ltd. Forms/C.2118/13

Instructions regarding War Diaries and Intelligence Summaries are contained in F. S. Regs., Part II. and the Staff Manual respectively. Title pages will be prepared in manuscript.

WAR DIARY
or
INTELLIGENCE SUMMARY.
(Erase heading not required.)

Army Form C. 2118.

Place	Date	Hour	Summary of Events and Information	Remarks and references to Appendices
✓	25/12/18		Lt. C. T. Morris Evans R.F.A. from Base.	M.R.
	26/12/18		No Change	M.R.
	27/12/18		4 Other Ranks Reinforcements from Base	M.R.
	28/12/18		4 Other Ranks " " "	M.R.
	29/12/18		No change	M.R.
	30/12/18		5 Other Ranks posted to 78 Bde R.F.A. 1 O.R. to 79 Bde R.F.A. + 1 O.R. to 155 A.F.A. Bde	M.R.
	31/12/18		No Change.	M.R.

M. R. [illegible] Capt R.F.A.
for
LT. COL. R.F.A.
COMMANDING 17th DIV: AMM. COL

A5834 Wt. W4973/M687 750,000 8/16 D. D. & L. Ltd. Forms/C.2118/13.

Instructions regarding War Diaries and Intelligence Summaries are contained in F. S. Regs., Part II. and the Staff Manual respectively. Title pages will be prepared in manuscript.

WAR DIARY
or
INTELLIGENCE SUMMARY.
(*Erase heading not required.*)

Army Form C. 2118.

Place	Date	Hour	Summary of Events and Information	Remarks and references to Appendices
			Casualties	
			Officers } Killed Nil Other Ranks }	
			Officers } Wounded Nil. Other Ranks }	
			Officers . Sick . 1 Captain E. C. RIDOUT. R.F.A.	
			Other Ranks Sick .	
			Horse } Killed Nil Mule }	
			Horse } Wounded Nil Mule }	
			Horse Evacuated. 6	
			Mule Evacuated. –	
			[illegible] Capt. R.F.A for LT. COL. R.F.A. COMMANDING 17th DIV: AMM. COL	
	31/12/16			

Instructions regarding War Diaries and Intelligence Summaries are contained in F. S. Regs., Part II. and the Staff Manual respectively. Title pages will be prepared in manuscript.

WAR DIARY
or
INTELLIGENCE SUMMARY.

(*Erase heading not required.*)

Army Form C. 2118.

Place	Date	Hour	Summary of Events and Information	Remarks and references to Appendices
			Strength Return	

	O	O.R.	Animals
Strength on 30/11/18	17	526	654
Joined	2	135	—
Total	19	661	654
Gone	1	203	6
Strength on 31/12/18	18	458	648

M. [illegible] Capt R.F.A.

LT. COL. R.F.A.
COMMANDING 17th DIV. AMM. [illegible]

31/12/18

A5834 Wt. W4973/M687 750,000 8/16 D. D. & L. Ltd. Forms/C.2118/13.

Instructions regarding War Diaries and Intelligence Summaries are contained in F. S. Regs., Part II. and the Staff Manual respectively. Title pages will be prepared in manuscript.

WAR DIARY
or
INTELLIGENCE SUMMARY.
(Erase heading not required.)

Army Form C. 2118.

V 8 ~~17~~ 43

Place	Date	Hour	Summary of Events and Information	Remarks and references to Appendices
			Confidential	
			War Diary of 17 Divisional Ammunition Column from 1/1/19 to 31/1/19	
			31/1/19	
			M. P. Fideur Capt. for LT. COL. R.F.A. COMMANDING 17th DIV: AMM. COL.	

(A7092). Wt W12839/M1293 750,000 1/17. D. D. & L., Ltd. Forms/C.2118/14.

Army Form C. 2118.

Instructions regarding War Diaries and Intelligence Summaries are contained in F. S. Regs., Part II. and the Staff Manual respectively. Title pages will be prepared in manuscript.

WAR DIARY
or
INTELLIGENCE SUMMARY.

(*Erase heading not required.*)

Place	Date	Hour	Summary of Events and Information				Remarks and references to Appendices
			Strength Return.				
				O	O.R.	Animals	
			Strength on 31 12/18	18	458	648	
			Joined.	1	21	—	
			Total	19	479	648	
			Gone	5	46	327	
			Strength on 31 1/19	14	408	321	
				M. P. Drew			
				CAPTAIN R.F.A. ADJUTANT 17th DIV. AMM. COLUMN			
	31/1/19						

(A7092). Wt W12839/M1293 750,000. 1/17. D. D. & L., Ltd. Forms/C.2118/14.

Instructions regarding War Diaries and Intelligence Summaries are contained in F. S. Regs., Part II. and the Staff Manual respectively. Title pages will be prepared in manuscript.

WAR DIARY
or
INTELLIGENCE SUMMARY.
(*Erase heading not required.*)

Army Form C. 2118.

Place	Date	Hour	Summary of Events and Information	Remarks and references to Appendices
			Casualties	
			Officers } Killed Nil.	
			Other Ranks }	
			Officers } Wounded Nil.	
			Other Rank }	
			Officers } Accidentally injured. Other Ranks 3 (1 British 2 Indians)	
			Other Ranks }	
			Officers Sick 2	
			Other Ranks Sick 16	
			Horses } Killed & Wounded Nil	
			Mules }	
			Horses Evacuated 20	
			Mules " 2	
			Horses Transferred 50	
			Mules 252	

M. P. [illegible]
CAPTAIN R.F.A.
ADJUTANT 17th DIV. AMM. COLUMN

(A7092). Wt W12839/M1293 75,0.0. 1/17. D. D. & L., Ltd. Forms/C.2118/14.

Instructions regarding War Diaries and Intelligence Summaries are contained in F. S. Regs., Part II. and the Staff Manual respectively. Title pages will be prepared in manuscript.

WAR DIARY
or
INTELLIGENCE SUMMARY.
(Erase heading not required.)

Army Form C. 2118.

Place	Date	Hour	Summary of Events and Information	Remarks and references to Appendices
	18/1/19		No change.	M.F.
	19/1/19		5 CZ Horses to 29 M.V.S. 7 CZ Horse & 11 CZ Mules to B/79 Bde RFA. 3 CZ Mules to C/79 Bde RFA 4 CZ " to 29 MVS [illegible]	M.F.
	20/1/19		4 CZ Mules to C/155 Bde. RFA 18 CZ Mules to D/155 Bde RFA 18 CZ Mules to A/155 " " 1 CZ Horse & 29 CZ Mules to B/155 Bde RFA 2 CZ Horse to A/155 " " 6 CZ Horses to C/155 Bde RFA	M.F.
	21/1/19		2 CZ Horses to 29 M.V.S	M.F.
	22/1/19		2 AY. 3 C-Y. 1 BY Horses to Corps Horse Camp.	M.F.
	23/1/19		1 C-Z Horse to 29 M.V.S.	M.F.
	24/1/19		No change. 1 LD to 29 M.V.S (BZ)	M.F.
	25/1/19		No change. No 74823 Dr R.J. EARL died of injuries	M.F.
	26/1/19		9 LD to B/155 Bde. 7 LD to C/155 Bde, 8 Mules to C/155 Bde, 10 Mules to B/155 Bde 1 Rider, 4 LD Horses, 11 Mules to C/155 Bde to [illegible] [illegible]	M.F.
	27/1/19		No change	M.F.
	28/1/19		6 O Ranks Demobilized	M.F.
	29/1/19		135 CZ Mules to TOURNAI. 2 LD Horses (AZ. CZ) to 29 M.V.S.	M.F.
	30/1/19		1 O.R. for Repatriation	M.F.
	31/1/19		No change.	M.F.

(A7092). Wt W12839/M1293 75,0:0. 1/17. D. D. & L., Ltd. Forms/C.2118/14.

Instructions regarding War Diaries and Intelligence Summaries are contained in F. S. Regs., Part II. and the Staff Manual respectively. Title pages will be prepared in manuscript.

WAR DIARY

or

~~INTELLIGENCE SUMMARY.~~

(Erase heading not required.)

Army Form C. 2118.

Place	Date	Hour	Summary of Events and Information	Remarks and references to Appendices
	1/1/19		Unit camped at BETTENCOURT-RIVIERE.	MAF
	2/1/19		No change	MAF
	3/1/19		Lt. H. CHERMSIDE R.F.A. to hospital (Sick)	MAF
			10 O.R. Reinforcements from Base. Lt. J.E. JONES RFA. posted to A/79 Bde. RFA	MAF
	4/1/19		No change.	MAF
	5/1/19		1 O.R from Base.	MAF
	6/1/19		1. O.R. to Div. Reception Camp for Demobilization	MAF
	7/1/19		7. O.R. to 79 Bde R.F.A. 1 O.R. to 78 Bde R.F.A. 2. O.R. to 155. Army Bde RFA.	MAF
			Lt. C.T. MORRIS-EVANS to hospital.	MAF
	8/1/19		No change	MAF
	9/1/19		No change	MAF
	10/1/19		No. 74823 Dr. R.J. EARL accidentally injured (to hospital)	MAF
	11/1/19		No change	MAF
	12/1/19		No change	MAF
	13/1/19		No change.	MAF
	14/1/19		1 Officer & 29 Other Ranks to Div Reception Camp for Demobilization.	MAF
			6 OR reinforcements joined.	MAF
	15/1/19		No change	MAF
	16/1/19		Corps Horse Camp commenced at BOURDON. 2 AY, 2 BY & 2 CY Horses to Corps	MAF
			Horse Camp. Lt C.T. MORRIS EVANS RFA from hospital. [illegible] from Trench Mortar	MAF
	17/1/19		2 AY & 1 BY Horses to Corps Horse Camp.	MAF

(A7092). Wt W12839/M1293 750,000. 1/17. D. D. & L., Ltd. Forms/C.2118/14.

Instructions regarding War Diaries and Intelligence Summaries are contained in F. S. Regs., Part II. and the Staff Manual respectively. Title pages will be prepared in manuscript.

WAR DIARY
or
INTELLIGENCE SUMMARY.
(Erase heading not required.)

Army Form C. 2118.

Place	Date	Hour	Summary of Events and Information	Remarks and references to Appendices
			No 44 Confidential War Diary of 17th Divisional Ammunition Column from 2/1/19 to 28/2/19 28/2/19 R. H. Dunlop [signature] LT. COL. R.F.A. COMMANDING 17th DIV: AMM. COL.	

D. D. & L., London, E.C.
(A10266) Wt W5300/P713 750,000 2/18 Sch. 52 Forms/C2118/16

Instructions regarding War Diaries and Intelligence Summaries are contained in F. S. Regs., Part II. and the Staff Manual respectively. Title pages will be prepared in manuscript.

WAR DIARY
or
INTELLIGENCE SUMMARY.
(Erase heading not required.)

Army Form C. 2118.

Place	Date	Hour	Summary of Events and Information	Remarks and references to Appendices
✓	1/2/19		Unit Billetted at BETTENCOURT-RIVIERE	
			26 Other Ranks demobilized	
	2/2/19		1 Officer & 52 Other Ranks posted from Trench Mortars.	
	3/2/19		No change	
	4/2/19		"	
	5/2/19		57 other Ranks to 17 Div Rec Camp for Demobilization	
	6/2/19		No change	
	7/2/19		"	
	8/2/19		15 other Ranks to 17 Div Rec Camp for Demobilization	
	9/2/19		No change	
	10/2/19		"	
	11/2/19		1 OR posted to RA Section 3rd Echelon	
	12/2/19		No change	
	13/2/19		"	
	14/2/19		"	
	15/2/19		"	
	16/2/19		"	
	17/2/19		"	
	18/2/19		"	
	19/2/19		"	
	20/2/19		"	
	21/2/19		1 O.R. to 17 Div Rec Camp for Demobilization	
	22/2/19		No change	

D. D. & L., London, E.C.
(A10266) Wt W5300/P713 750,000 2/18 Sch. 52 Forms/C2118/16

Army Form C. 2118.

Instructions regarding War Diaries and Intelligence Summaries are contained in F. S. Regs., Part II. and the Staff Manual respectively. Title pages will be prepared in manuscript.

WAR DIARY
or
INTELLIGENCE SUMMARY.
(Erase heading not required.)

Place	Date	Hour	Summary of Events and Information	Remarks and references to Appendices
BETTENCOURT	23/2/19		No Change	
	24/2/19		No change	
	25/2/19		50. Z. Mules for Sale at AIRAINES	
	26/2/19		No change	
	27/2/19		6 .Z. Horses for Sale at AIRAINES	
	28/2/19		58. Z. Mules for Sale at FORGES-LES-EAUX	

D. D. & L., London, E.C.
(A10266) Wt W5300/P713 750,000 2/15 Sch. 52 Forms/C2118/16

Army Form C. 2118.

WAR DIARY
or
INTELLIGENCE SUMMARY.
(Erase heading not required.)

Instructions regarding War Diaries and Intelligence Summaries are contained in F. S. Regs., Part II. and the Staff Manual respectively. Title pages will be prepared in manuscript.

Place	Date	Hour	Summary of Events and Information	Remarks and references to Appendices
			Strength Return	

	O.	OR	Animals
Strength on 3/1/19	14	403	321
Joined	5	-	-
Total	19	-	-
Gone	-	142	128
Strength on 28/2/19	19	261	193

28/2/19

[signature]
LT. COL. R.F.A.
COMMANDING 17th DIV: AMM. COL.

D. D. & L., London, E.C.
(A10266) Wt W5300/P713 750,000 2/18 Sch. 52 Forms/C2118/16

Instructions regarding War Diaries and Intelligence Summaries are contained in F. S. Regs., Part II. and the Staff Manual respectively. Title pages will be prepared in manuscript.

WAR DIARY
or
INTELLIGENCE SUMMARY.
(Erase heading not required.)

Army Form C. 2118.

Place	Date	Hour	Summary of Events and Information	Remarks and references to Appendices
			Casualties	
			Officers / Other Ranks } Killed Nil	
			Officers / Other Ranks } Wounded Nil	
			Officers Sick Nil	
			Other Ranks Sick 14	
			Horses & Mules Killed & Wounded - Nil	
			Horses Evacuated 6	
			Mules " 7	
			Horses Transferred 6	
			Mules " 108	
			28/7/19	
			R. Smith [signature] LT. COL. R.F.A. COMMANDING 17th DIV: ARTY.	

D. D. & L., London, E.C.
(A10266) Wt W5300/P713 750,000 2/18 Sch. 52 Forms/C2118/16

Instructions regarding War Diaries and Intelligence Summaries are contained in F. S. Regs., Part II. and the Staff Manual respectively. Title pages will be prepared in manuscript.

WAR DIARY
or
INTELLIGENCE SUMMARY.
(Erase heading not required.)

Army Form C. 2118.

WR 45

Place	Date	Hour	Summary of Events and Information	Remarks and references to Appendices
			Confidential War Diary of 17 Divisional Ammunition Column from 1/3/19 to 31/3/19 [illegible signature]	

31/3/19

D. D. & L., London, E.C.
(A10266) Wt W5300/P713 750,000 2/18 Sch. 52 Forms/C2118/16

Instructions regarding War Diaries and Intelligence Summaries are contained in F. S. Regs., Part II. and the Staff Manual respectively. Title pages will be prepared in manuscript.

WAR DIARY
or
INTELLIGENCE SUMMARY.
(Erase heading not required.)

Army Form C. 2118.

Place	Date	Hour	Summary of Events and Information	Remarks and references to Appendices
BETTENCOURT	1/3/19		Unit billetted at BETTENCOURT-RIVIERE	
	2/3/19		No change	
	3/3/19		30 X Mules to COLOGNE	
	4/3/19		1 Officer + 3 O.R.s to 2nd Army COLOGNE. 40 Z Horses to FORGES LES EAUX. 20 Z Horses to 59 M.V.S. for Sale	
	5/3/19		3 O.R.s to Div Rec Camp for Demobilization	
	6/3/19		No change	
	7/3/19		No change	
	8/3/19		No change	
	9/3/19		Lt T. MORRIS-EVANS R.F.A. to Army of Occupation	
	10/3/19		No change. 13 X Horses to BERDIN Horse Camp	
	11/3/19		No change	
	12/3/19		1 O. Rank to Div Rec Camp for Demobilization	
	13/3/19		No change. 2 Z Horses for Sale AMIENS	
	14/3/19		"	
	15/3/19		"	
	16/3/19		"	
	17/3/19		"	
	18/3/19		"	
	19/3/19		1 O. Rank to Div Rec Camp for Demobilization	
	20/3/19		No change	
	21/3/19		"	
	22/3/19		Captain A.W.J. Davies R.F.A. to Div Rec Camp for Demobilization. 4 Mules to BERDIN	
	23/3/19		No change	

D. D. & L., London, E.C.
(A10266) Wt W5300/P713 750,000 2/18 Sch. 52 Forms/C2118/16

Army Form C. 2118.

WAR DIARY
or
INTELLIGENCE SUMMARY.
(Erase heading not required.)

Instructions regarding War Diaries and Intelligence Summaries are contained in F. S. Regs., Part II. and the Staff Manual respectively. Title pages will be prepared in manuscript.

Place	Date	Hour	Summary of Events and Information	Remarks and references to Appendices
BETTENCOURT	24/3/19		9 O. Ranks posted to 3rd [illegible]	
	25/3/19		No Change	
	26/3/19			
	27/3/19		Lt R W Harper & Lt L S Tabor to Dis. Rec. Camp for Demobilization	
	28/3/19		No Change	
	29/3/19			
	30/3/19			
	31/3/19		2 L.D. Riders to No 4 Remount Squadron ABBEVILLE	

[illegible signature]
LT COL. R.F.A.
COMMANDING 17TH DIV. AMM. COL.

D. D. & L., London, E.C.
(A10266) Wt W5300/P713 750,000 2/18 Sch. 52 Forms/C2118/16

Army Form C. 2118.

Instructions regarding War Diaries and Intelligence Summaries are contained in F. S. Regs., Part II. and the Staff Manual respectively. Title pages will be prepared in manuscript.

WAR DIARY
or
INTELLIGENCE SUMMARY.
(Erase heading not required.)

Place	Date	Hour	Summary of Events and Information	Remarks and references to Appendices
			Casualties	
			Officers } Killed Nil	
			O Ranks }	
			Officers } Wounded Nil	
			O Ranks }	
			Officers Sick Nil	
			O Ranks Sick 6	
			Horses Mules Killed & Wounded Nil	
			Horses Evacuated 2	
			Mules 3	
			Horses Transferred 78	
			Mules 34	
			LT. COL. R.F.A. COMMANDING 17th DIV. AMM. COL.	
			3[illegible]/1/1[illegible]	

A5834 Wt. W4973/M687 750,000 8/16 D. D. & L. Ltd. Forms/C.2118/13.

Instructions regarding War Diaries and Intelligence Summaries are contained in F. S. Regs., Part II. and the Staff Manual respectively. Title pages will be prepared in manuscript.

WAR DIARY
or
INTELLIGENCE SUMMARY.
(Erase heading not required.)

Army Form C. 2118.

Place	Date	Hour	Summary of Events and Information	Remarks and references to Appendices
			Strength Return	

	O	OR	Animals
Strength 28/2/19	19	257	193
Joined		2	
Total	19	259	193
Gone	4	27	139
Strength on 31/3/19	15	232	54

31/3/19

[illegible]
LT. COL. R.F.A.
COMMANDING 17th [illegible]

D. D. & L., London, E.C.
(A10266) Wt W5300/P713 750,000 2/18 Sch. 52 Forms/C2118/16

Army Form C. 2118.

Instructions regarding War Diaries and Intelligence Summaries are contained in F. S. Regs., Part II. and the Staff Manual respectively. Title pages will be prepared in manuscript.

WAR DIARY
or
INTELLIGENCE SUMMARY.
(Erase heading not required.)

Vol 46

Place	Date	Hour	Summary of Events and Information	Remarks and references to Appendices
			Confidential.	
			War Diary of 17th Divisional Ammunition Column from 1/4/19 to 30/4/19	
			30/4/19	
			[illegible] Captain Commanding 17th Div. Amm. Col.	

D. D. & L., London, E.C.
(A10266) Wt W5300/P713 750,000 2/18 Sch. 52 Forms/C2118/16

Army Form C. 2118.

WAR DIARY
or
INTELLIGENCE SUMMARY.
(Erase heading not required.)

Instructions regarding War Diaries and Intelligence Summaries are contained in F. S. Regs., Part II. and the Staff Manual respectively. Title pages will be prepared in manuscript.

Place	Date	Hour	Summary of Events and Information	Remarks and references to Appendices
			Strength Return	

	O	OR	Animals
Strength 31/3/19	15	232	54
Joined	1	13	20
Total	16	245	74
Gone	4	58	25
Strength on 30/4/19	10	187	49

30/4/19

J C [illegible] Captain
Commanding [illegible] Amm. Col.

D. D. & L., London, E.C.
(A10266) Wt W5300/P713 750,000 2/18 Sch. 52 Forms/C2118/16

Instructions regarding War Diaries and Intelligence Summaries are contained in F. S. Regs., Part II. and the Staff Manual respectively. Title pages will be prepared in manuscript.

WAR DIARY
or
INTELLIGENCE SUMMARY.
(Erase heading not required.)

Army Form C. 2118.

Place	Date	Hour	Summary of Events and Information	Remarks and references to Appendices
			Casualties	
			Officers Sick — O.Rs. Sick 7	
			Officers Killed — O.Rs. Killed —	
			Officer Wounded — O.Rs. Wounded —	
			O.Rs. Accidentally Injured 1.	
			Horses & Mules Killed & Wounded Nil	
			Horse Evacuated 2	
			Mules " 3	
			Horse Transferred 4	
			Mules " 18	
			Horse Joined 20	
			Mules " 2	
			FCC[illegible] Capt.	
			COMMANDING 17th DIV. AMM. COL.	
			30/1/19.	

D. D. & L., London, E.C.
(A10266) Wt W5300/P713 750,000 2/15 Sch. 52 Forms/C2118/16

Instructions regarding War Diaries and Intelligence Summaries are contained in F. S. Regs., Part II. and the Staff Manual respectively. Title pages will be prepared in manuscript.

WAR DIARY
or
INTELLIGENCE SUMMARY.
(Erase heading not required.)

Army Form C. 2118.

Place	Date	Hour	Summary of Events and Information	Remarks and references to Appendices
BETTENCOURT	1/4/19		Captain R.T. Manley (T.F.) from Base.	M
	2/4/19		No change	M
	3/4/19		1 O.R. from HQ 17. D.A.	
	4/4/19		No change	
	5/4/19		5 O.Rs to 17 Div. Reception Camp for Demobilization	
	6/4/19		No change	
	7/4/19		No change	
	8/4/19		No change	
	9/4/19		Lt Colonel R.O.L. Dunlop [?] C.M.G. DSO. R.F.A. posted to Command Western Divisional Ammunition Column. 2 O.Rs + 2 Riding Horses posted to Western D.A.C. Lt T.E. Jackson [?] + 1 O.R. posted to Western D.A.	
	10/4/19		No change	
	11/4/19		No change	
	12/4/19		2 O.R. to 17 Div Reception Camp for Demobilization.	
	13/4/19		No change	
	14/4/19		Captain G.D. Parlow [?] M.C. R.F.A. Captain H.H. Paul + 2 O.Rs posted to "Z" Horse Depot ST. SAVEUSE [?] 20 HD. L. Horses posted to Unit from Mobile [?] A.S.C. 62 Indians posted to "Z" Horse Depot ST SAVEUSE [?]	
	15/4/19		50 O.Rs posted to 2nd Army R.A. Reinforcement Camp COLOGNE	
	16/4/19		No change	
	17/4/19		"	
	18/4/19		"	
	19/4/19		"	
	20/4/19		"	
	21/4/19		"	
	22/4/19		"	
	23/4/19		"	
	24/4/19		"	
	25/4/19		"	
	26/4/19		"	
	27/4/19		"	
	28/4/19		"	
	29/4/19		"	
	30/4/19		"	

J.C. Allin [?]

Captain ~~LT/COL~~ R.F.A.
COMMANDING 17th DIV: AMM. COL.

A5834 Wt. W4973/M687 750,000 8/16 D. D. & L. Ltd. Forms/C.2118/13

Instructions regarding War Diaries and Intelligence Summaries are contained in F. S. Regs., Part II. and the Staff Manual respectively. Title pages will be prepared in manuscript.

WAR DIARY
or
INTELLIGENCE SUMMARY.
(Erase heading not required.)

Army Form C. 2118.

Place	Date	Hour	Summary of Events and Information	Remarks and references to Appendices
BETTENCOURT	1/5/19		Unit billeted at BETTENCOURT-RIVIERE	
"	2/5/19		No change	
"	3/5/19		No change	
"	4/5/19		6 ORs to Corps Concentration Camp for Demob.	
"	5/5/19		No change	
"	6/5/19		12 LD Mules to Army Animal Collecting Camp CANDAS.	
"	7/5/19		No change	
"	8/5/19		8 ORs from 79 Bde RFA. 18 Mules & 2 LD Horses from 79 Bde.	
"	9/5/19		18 Mules & 2 LD Horses to Bourdon Horse Camp.	
"	10/5/19		9 ORs from 79 Bde RFA	
"	11/5/19		1 OR to Hospital (sick)	
"	12/5/19		No change	
"	13/5/19		1 OR to Corps Concentration Camp for Demob.	
"	14/5/19		1 OR to Hospital (sick)	
"	15/5/19		No change	
"	16/5/19		2/Lt J.P. Sheehan, Lt W. Ainsworth & 3 ORs to Corps Concentration Camp for Demob.	
"	17/5/19		Captain C.P. Henning to England (on duty)	
"	18/5/19		No change	
"	19/5/19		No change	
"	20/5/19		No change	
"	21/5/19		No change	
"	22/5/19		No change	
"	23/5/19		No change	
"	24/5/19		Captain R.T. Manley, 2/Lt [illegible] Elliott & 10 ORs posted to 155 Bde RFA. Unit entrained at LONGPRE to proceed home as Cadre Unit.	
"	25/5/19		Arrived at HAVRE	
"	26/5/19		Proceeded to ENGLAND destination SHOREHAM	

[illegible] Capt RFA
[illegible]

D. D. & L., London, E.C.
(A10266) Wt W5300/P713 750,000 2/18 Sch. 52 Forms/C2118/16

Instructions regarding War Diaries and Intelligence Summaries are contained in F. S. Regs., Part II. and the Staff Manual respectively. Title pages will be prepared in manuscript.

WAR DIARY
or
INTELLIGENCE SUMMARY.
(Erase heading not required.)

Army Form C. 2118.

Place	Date	Hour	Summary of Events and Information	Remarks and references to Appendices
			Strength Return	

	O.	O.R.	Animals
Strength 30/4/19.	10	187	49
Joined	1	17	20
Total	11	204	69
Gone	6	45	69
Strength on 26/5/19	5	159	–

26/5/19

[illegible signature]

D. D. & L., London, E.C.
(A10266) Wt W5300/P713 750,000 2/18 Sch. 52 Forms/C2118/16

Instructions regarding War Diaries and Intelligence Summaries are contained in F. S. Regs., Part II. and the Staff Manual respectively. Title pages will be prepared in manuscript.

WAR DIARY
or
INTELLIGENCE SUMMARY.
(*Erase heading not required.*)

Army Form C. 2118.

Place	Date	Hour	Summary of Events and Information	Remarks and references to Appendices
			Casualties	
			Officers Sick — O.R.s Sick 4	
			Officers Killed — O.R.s Killed —	
			Officers Wounded — O.R.s Wounded —	
			Horses & Mules Killed & Wounded Nil	
			Horses Evacuated Nil	
			Mules " Nil	
			Horses Transferred 53	
			Mules " 30	
			Horses Joined 2	
			Mules " 18	
			M. [illegible] Capt. [illegible]	
			26/1/19	

D. D. & L., London, E.C.
(A10266) Wt W5300/P713 750,000 2/15 Sch. 52 Forms/C2118/16

Instructions regarding War Diaries and Intelligence Summaries are contained in F. S. Regs., Part II. and the Staff Manual respectively. Title pages will be prepared in manuscript.

WAR DIARY
or
INTELLIGENCE SUMMARY.
(Erase heading not required.)

Army Form C. 2118. 17

VIII 47

Place	Date	Hour	Summary of Events and Information	Remarks and references to Appendices
			Confidential.	Ceased
			War Diary of 17th Divisional Ammunition Column from 1/5/19 to 26/5/19.	
			26/5/19	
			M. P. [illegible] Capt. R.F.A. Adjt 17th D.A.C.	

D. D. & L., London, E.C.
(A10266) Wt W5300/P713 750,000 2/18 Sch. 52 Forms/C2118/16

17 DIV

32

TRENCH MORTAR BTY

1915 AUG TO 1916 FEB

7 X VII

WAR DIARY
or
INTELLIGENCE SUMMARY
(Erase heading not required.)

Instructions regarding War Diaries and Intelligence Summaries are contained in F. S. Regs., Part II. and the Staff Manual respectively. Title Pages will be prepared in manuscript.

Army Form C. 2118

32nd T.H. By

Place	Date	Hour	Summary of Events and Information	Remarks and references to Appendices
	2.8/15		Battery at rest. OC. on leave. Lt Forsythe took command and reconnoitred positions in R3 and Q1, and received orders to relieve 24 T.H.B. by 10 p.m. on the 3rd. Arranged with the B.M. 50 Bde. to attach battery to R.E.s for rations.	
	3.8/15		The battery returned to its old position after one full day's rest. Two 1½ inch of 24 By. were attached to this battery for use against the mound and the crater.	
	4		One gun in action in Q1 and one 1½" in R1. Fired ~~three~~ four rounds from Q1 at supposed enemy mortar emplacement. Men slept with guns.	
	5		The 1½" was laid on O.2.d.3.5. — enemy mortar's firing position — N.C.O. to fire if opportunity offered. 2Lt R.W. Mignonget Antrim R.G.A. S.R. joined the battery.	
	6.		2Lt Forsyth visited O.C. 8 Lancs & G.O.C. 50th Brigade. Stood by the guns as before. One 1½" returned to 24 Battery.	Gr Brown reported sick and went to hospital
	7		Infantry rather battered by enemy fire so battery remained quiet. Laid out lines of fire for Sunday 3.15 AM. 2Lt J Williams returned from leave.	
	8		Fired six at a sniper post in the crater east of the mound. First four rounds effective. Fifth unobserved but detonated. Sixth effective. Target was indicated by Major Burk. Lt Forsyth left the battery.	Gunner Wilkie Hospital (sick)

J Williams 2/Lt RGA
OC. 32 T.H. Battery

10/8/15

1875 Wt. W593/826 1,000,000 4/15 J.B.C. & A. A.D.S.S./Forms/C. 2118.

Army Form C. 2118

WAR DIARY
or
INTELLIGENCE SUMMARY
(Erase heading not required.)

Instructions regarding War Diaries and Intelligence Summaries are contained in F. S. Regs., Part II. and the Staff Manual respectively. Title Pages will be prepared in manuscript.

32nd J. H. Bty

Place	Date	Hour	Summary of Events and Information	Remarks and references to Appendices
[illegible]	9.8.15		The day was spent in examining the enemy trenches in front of the sector. A machine gun was reported in front of 24 and an enemy working party in front of 26. Gun and detachment were taken to 26 but although the B.C. remained with the infantry through the night in an attempt to locate these targets no success was obtained and no firing took place.	
[illegible]	10.		The damage done to the enemy trenches by our bombardment was inspected and the intention was to annoy enemy ~~repairing~~ parties. The infantry in our trenches had large parties on repair work following the earlier enemy bombardment so firing except in very special circumstances has at present been rendered inadvisable.	
	11.		Two 18 pr. bombs were fired at a snipers dugout east of the mound. The gun in 26 was manned by the request of one company of the E. Yorks but no firing was done at the request of the incoming company.	
	12.		A gun ~~was placed~~ position chosen in R 7 reserve trench. Another attempt was made to locate the enemy machine gun in front of 24, without success.	
	13		Four rounds of 3.7" were fired at the mound-and-trench in front of 26. Three rounds 18 pr. were fired at the trenches in front of R. at the time of the artillery bombardment. One 3.7" was placed in R 7 and dugout prepared for ammunition. The second 1.575" was brought up from 50th Bde Headquarters.	
	14		Two 18 pr. were fired from 232 old trench at a sandbag mound on right front. Six rounds were fired from a 3.7" in R 2 at the snipers loophole plates in the enemy trenches during the night.	Gr Summers, Gr Waghorn } [illegible]
	15		Six rounds were fired from R 2. A large enemy working party in front of 25 ~~was~~ worried	

J Williams 2nd Lt RGA
OC. 32 J.H. Battery

1875 Wt. W593/826 1,000,000 4/15 J.B.C. & A. A.D.S.S./Forms/C. 2118.

Instructions regarding War Diaries and Intelligence Summaries are contained in F. S. Regs., Part II. and the Staff Manual respectively. Title Pages will be prepared in manuscript.

WAR DIARY
or
INTELLIGENCE SUMMARY
(Erase heading not required.)

Army Form C. 2118

32nd Trench How. Bty.

Place	Date	Hour	Summary of Events and Information	Remarks and references to Appendices
	16		The infantry in the trenches did not feel settled and seemed unwilling for the battery to fire so the battery did not fire.	
	17		An enemy working party was detected at the foot of the mound. Four bombs were fired, two fell short two fell in the trench. The infantry stated that the enemy could be observed to scatter. A sniper had established himself in front of R_2-T, about 95 yards from our line. Six bombs were fired in an attempt to hit his loophole plate. Four detonated and the sniper ceased work leaving his periscope behind. Three bombs were fired from 23a at an enemy redoubt. All detonated. An enemy working party was detected in front of 25, protected by snipers. Ten bombs were fired at the spot of which one did not detonate.	
	18		Enemy party at foot of mound was again busy. Four bombs were dropped about the spot. at 23; eight rounds were fired at the enemy working party and four from 25. The enemy working parties are very bold and well protected by snipers on either flank.	
	19		Two light 1½ bombs were fired at the party in front of 25. A party of two Cpls and ten Ptes. reported to the battery and Cpl Shipp and Gnrs Sullivan, Collins, Wandle, Dooney, [illegible] and Rush left the battery for [illegible].	Gr Wilber returned from Hospital
	20.		Four heavy bombs were fired at the working party in front of R_3-T_1 and six rounds at the enemy trenches in front of 24. While Lt McGonigal was examining the gun and targets from T_2 our own artillery dropped shell between the trenches. The head and shoulders of one of an enemy party of seven immediately showed above the grass. The uniform was blue-grey and the cap band red. This performance was repeated as a second shell dropped. The party scattered before our snipers or howitzers could get to work effectively.	K 28/4/15

Instructions regarding War Diaries and Intelligence Summaries are contained in F. S. Regs., Part II. and the Staff Manual respectively. Title Pages will be prepared in manuscript.

WAR DIARY
or
INTELLIGENCE SUMMARY
(Erase heading not required.)

Army Form C. 2118

32nd Trench How. Bty

Place	Date	Hour	Summary of Events and Information	Remarks and references to Appendices
	21.		Three heavy bombs were fired at a party in front of T_3. This party has never been seen but the gradual progress of its work has been noticed. One bomb did not detonate. Six 3.7" bombs were fired at a party in the old trench where the enemy were discovered by our shell yesterday. The enemy replied later by bombing the same spot. Then enemy exploded a mine in front of Q_1. Lt McGonigal promptly manned the gun in Q_1.	
	22		Two large bombs were fired at the spot indicated by OC T_1. The crater was investigated from the infantry listening post by O.C. 27 T.H. Battery and O.C. 32 T.H. Battery. An enemy sniper was discovered to have dug himself in to the left of the old post. It was decided that the work done in front of this section warranted Captain Pratt (OC 27) in bringing at 2 inch trench howitzer to command this sector — mound to crater in front of T_1 — the ground mentioned in a request by the G.O.C. 17th Division to this battery, ~~[illegible]~~ as worthy of attention.	
			J William 2nd Lt OC 32 T.H. Battery.	

1875 Wt. W593/826 1,000,000 4/15 J.B.C. & A. A.D.S.S./Forms/C. 2118.

Instructions regarding War Diaries and Intelligence Summaries are contained in F. S. Regs., Part II. and the Staff Manual respectively. Title Pages will be prepared in manuscript.

WAR DIARY
or
INTELLIGENCE SUMMARY
(Erase heading not required.)

Army Form C. 2118

32nd T. H. Bty

Place	Date	Hour	Summary of Events and Information	Remarks and references to Appendices
	28		The crater was worried throughout the night — with the exception of the time allowed for the infantry relief. ~~Forty~~ four rounds in all were fired. The trenches at the foot of the mound and east and west were also worried with twenty eight rounds. This was to prevent the damage done by our artillery being repaired. A strong erection in front of Q1 suspected to be an enemy machine gun emplacement was examined during our bombardment which examination seemed to verify the fact. Only sixty rounds of ammunition left. Wired to Divisional Artillery	The dates in this diary are in accordance with the daily report 12 noon — 12 noon. This has only just been noticed and will be remedied in future.
	29		An attempt was made to find a position from which the crater could be effectively enfiladed. The crater was found to be more or less circular. It was thought better to move the gun from T1 so a position was taken up on the left of Q1. Fifty seven rounds were fired in bursts of ten or so at irregular intervals. At each burst the enemy fired a burst of whizz-bangs. Cl Shingle and Pte. Atkinson did not cease to serve their gun, and it was almost funny to hear the whizz-bangs burst and at the same instant to see the trail of sparks from our mortar start from apparently the same spot. The enemy also crumped this neighbourhood but they have done so fairly often before during the week. Only three rounds now left.	

J Williams 2nd Lt RGA
OC 32 T.H. Battery.

2/9/15

1875 Wt. W593/826 1,000,000 4/15 J.B.C. & A. A.D.S.S./Forms/C. 2118.

Instructions regarding War Diaries and Intelligence Summaries are contained in F. S. Regs., Part II. and the Staff Manual respectively. Title Pages will be prepared in manuscript.

WAR DIARY
or
INTELLIGENCE SUMMARY
(Erase heading not required.)

Army Form C. 2118

32nd Trench Mortar Bty

Place	Date	Hour	Summary of Events and Information	Remarks and references to Appendices
4	4		Thirty seven rounds were fired in all. In each case the object was to quieten enemy mortars and our fire was kept up till this object had been obtained. Fourteen were fired from U25. fourteen from Q1, six from R1 and three from S1.	
	5.		Two rounds were fired from U25 at an enemy M.G. This gun (or emplacement) has not since been used by the enemy but one further right still annoys our trenches. Three rounds were fired at this other today. Two rounds were fired from each of Q1 and R1 in reply to enemy fire. Our mortars were lying in wait and the enemy did not fire after our first two rounds which were fired together.	Infantry attached rejoined their units on departure of 17th Div.
	6		Twenty six rounds were fired from U25. Five in reply to enemy M.G. fire, twelve at an enemy M.G. emplacement and nine in reply to enemy trench mortar fire.	
	7 } 8 }		Battery did not fire. The enemy shelled the neighbourhood of our old position in U24 with heavy shell for a considerable period last night.	
	9		Twenty four rounds were fired from U25 in reply to enemy fire (grenade and trench mortar) at different times. The enemy shelled this position with heavy shell this afternoon making a large breach in the parapet on the left of the gun covering gun and position with debris.	
	10		Nine rounds were fired from U25 in reply to enemy fire and nine rounds from Q1 at a snipers dugout. The enemy again shelled the U25 position making another good-	

1875 Wt. W593/826 1,000,000 4/15 J.B.C. & A. A.D.S.S./Forms/C. 2118.

Instructions regarding War Diaries and Intelligence Summaries are contained in F. S. Regs., Part II. and the Staff Manual respectively. Title pages will be prepared in manuscript.

WAR DIARY
or
INTELLIGENCE SUMMARY.
(Erase heading not required.)

Army Form C. 2118.

32nd Trench Mortar Bty

Place	Date	Hour	Summary of Events and Information	Remarks and references to Appendices
	Oct. 11		Nine rounds were fired at a sniper's dugout in front of Q1.B. The enemy had damaged our periscopes and our infantry from this post but ceased to do so after being bombed. Nine rounds were also fired from U25 to quieten enemy grenade fire. The enemy mortar has not been used since it was last bombed from this trench.	
	12.		Four rounds were fired from U25 ~~to quieten~~ in retaliation to enemy grenade fire, at request of infantry and three rounds from Q1 in reply to enemy mortar fire.	
	13.		Five rounds were fired from T3 at an enemy mortar, eight from U25 to quieten enemy grenade fire and two, at the request of O.C. Cornwalls, which were reported by the bombing officer to fall one on each side of an enemy party repairing a gap.	
	14		Fifteen rounds were fired from U25, eight of which were fired during the bombardment and the remainder in reply to enemy fire. Seven rounds were fired at an enemy M.G. emplacement where a working party was observed by the infantry. Twenty two were fired at an observation post used by snipers on the mound. Three were fired from Q1 during the feint attack.	
	15		Two rounds were fired from Q1 at an enemy trench mortar. Three rounds from T3 at an enemy M.G. emplacement. Nine rounds were fired from U25 in retaliation	
	16		Two rounds were fired from Q1 at an enemy working party and two at an enemy mortar. Three rounds were fired from T3 at the same target as yesterday. Five of the enemy were observed in front of U25 with blacked faces and without equipment. They had apparently been out all night but were not observed till 3 pm. when rapid fire was opened on them	

2353 Wt. W2544/1454 700,000 5/15 D. D. & L. A.D.S.S./Forms/C. 2118.

Instructions regarding War Diaries and Intelligence Summaries are contained in F. S. Regs., Part II. and the Staff Manual respectively. Title pages will be prepared in manuscript.

WAR DIARY
or
INTELLIGENCE SUMMARY.
(Erase heading not required.)

Army Form C. 2118.

Place	Date	Hour	Summary of Events and Information	Remarks and references to Appendices
			by the trench mortar in U25. Three of the enemy succeeded in regaining their own trench. The enemy again shelled the neighbourhood of this mortar without effect. Some rounds were also fired from U25 in reply to enemy fire, thirteen rounds in all being fired.	
	17		The enemy apparently are not so industrious along this front as they have been the last few weeks. A pattern of trench mortar bomb new to this sector was dropped in our trenches in front of the mound. It weighs about 35 lbs. Nine rounds were fired in all from Q1, T3 and U25. — all to quieten enemy grenade and bomb fire.	

[signature] /16

2353 Wt. W2544/1454 700,000 5/15 D. D. & L. A.D.S.S./Forms/C. 2118.

Instructions regarding War Diaries and Intelligence Summaries are contained in F. S. Regs., Part II. and the Staff Manual respectively. Title Pages will be prepared in manuscript.

WAR DIARY
or
INTELLIGENCE SUMMARY
(Erase heading not required.)

Army Form C. 2118

Place	Date	Hour	Summary of Events and Information	Remarks and references to Appendices
			sised gap on the right of the gun and craters all round the position. Gr O Toole was in charge of the gun in each ~~occasion~~ case and did not leave his ~~gun~~ position until after the parapet had gone in one case and just before in the other. In each case he took his gun with him when he moved."	
			J Williams 2nd Lt RGA OC. 325 H Battery.	17/10/15

Instructions regarding War Diaries and Intelligence Summaries are contained in F. S. Regs., Part II. and the Staff Manual respectively. Title Pages will be prepared in manuscript.

WAR DIARY
or
INTELLIGENCE SUMMARY
(Erase heading not required.)

Army Form C. 21[illegible]

32nd Trench Mortar Bty

Place	Date	Hour	Summary of Events and Information	Remarks and references to Appendices
	30		Only two rounds being available the day was spent in building dugouts for the wet weather.	
	31		A large enemy party was working in the new crater so the remaining damaged rounds were fired. Work with the dugouts proceeded.	
	1		50 rounds without gas checks received, but useless. ~~forty~~ good rounds arrived.	
	2		The new crater made by the enemy last night was examined as soon as it was light but is near our trench that it is not likely to be of use to the enemy. In the old crater one of the enemy was detected at work with a maul. He was bombed and apparently ceased work. The enemy have done more work on the forward edge and one was detected smoking. He was bombed. The enemy have left a gap in the parapet on this forward edge and a loophole plate is near by.	
	3		10 Rounds were fired at a party in the same crater. One of the enemy could be seen watching the bombs to dodge them. Later the enemy could be seen returning but almost double. The bombs were spread over this interval and economy of ammunition studied. 2/Lt Price & Cpl McAlvin were both (not seriously) wounded by the detonation of a fuse brought to the O.C. by an infantry officer and placed in the O.C.'s hut pending examination. The hut was also destroyed.	
	4.		Twenty one rounds were fired from R3 and Q. The enemy were detected working on an old crater in front of Q. Five rounds did not detonate and four	X

1875 Wt. W593/826 1,000,000 4/15 J.B.C. & A. A.D.S.S./Forms/C. 2118.

Army Form C. 2118

Instructions regarding War Diaries and Intelligence Summaries are contained in F. S. Regs., Part II. and the Staff Manual respectively. Title Pages will be prepared in manuscript.

WAR DIARY
or
INTELLIGENCE SUMMARY

(Erase heading not required.)

Place	Date	Hour	Summary of Events and Information	Remarks and references to Appendices
			only just left the gun. The first of these Lt McGonigal immediately picked up and threw over the parapet. The guns were examined and it was found that the chambers of these two were enlarged minimising the effect of the gas check. They are still useful.	A
	5		Twenty ~~two~~ rounds were fired at the same targets.	
			J Williams 2Lt RGA OC 32 Trench Howitzer Battery	

1875 Wt. W593/826 1,000,000 4/15 J.B.C. & A. A.D.S.S./Forms/C. 2118.

Instructions regarding War Diaries and Intelligence Summaries are contained in F. S. Regs., Part II. and the Staff Manual respectively. Title Pages will be prepared in manuscript.

WAR DIARY
or
INTELLIGENCE SUMMARY
(Erase heading not required.)

Army Form C. 2118

32nd Trench Mortar Bty

Place	Date	Hour	Summary of Events and Information	Remarks and references to Appendices
	6		10 Rounds were fired at the crater in front of R3 and 10 at the work round the mound. The enemy replied with a mortar similar to ours. The work at the crater in front of R3 appears to have finished.	
	7		Ten rounds were fired at the crater in front of R3, ten from 24 and fifteen from 25. The trenches in front of the E. Yorks sector were examined for targets and two mortars placed, one in 24 and one in 25, which will be manned until wanted more particularly elsewhere. The enemy have built strong erections in front of these trenches. They have also built a T trench opposite T2 using the old communication trench as a basis. This has been well loopholed by them, as is usual with most of their work in this sector.	
	8		Sixteen bombs were fired at the various targets of the week. Pte Bailey and Masters went to hospital.	
	9		Twenty ~~two~~ rounds were fired from the three guns, one of which is now laid on a spot where an enemy party has been detected.	
	10		A sharp lookout was kept for enemy wiring parties but none were detected. Just after stand down one of the enemy could ~~been~~ seen ~~digging~~ to be at work at the foot of the mound. One bomb was fired and fell straight in the trench. The smoke blew underground and came out a few yards to the right. The enemy replied with two bombs but the mortar could not be located. The enemy party was not again seen but at 6 A.M. a mine was seen to explode behind the mound — blown by the enemy. An enemy party in front of 24-5 was seen dragging a tree. Six bombs were fired and the enemy left the tree.	

Army Form C. 2118

Instructions regarding War Diaries and Intelligence Summaries are contained in F. S. Regs., Part II. and the Staff Manual respectively. Title Pages will be prepared in manuscript.

WAR DIARY
or
INTELLIGENCE SUMMARY
(Erase heading not required.)

Place	Date	Hour	Summary of Events and Information	Remarks and references to Appendices
	11.		Five rounds were fired from 26 at the trenches in front during a bombardment. One round was fired from 24 at a target in front and its detonation was followed by a large explosion while a box or heavy timber was lifted in the air. Nine rounds were fired at an enemy erection [supposed M.G. emplacement] in front of Q1 right. The enemy immediately replied with trench mortar bombs and later ~~with~~ whiz bangs and crumps fell for half an hour in this neighbourhood. Eight rounds were dropped ~~on~~ and round the mound where parties have been detected. The enemy again exploded a mine behind the brickstack. The ~~[illegible]~~ shock was much greater than that of yesterday. Time was 4.10 AM	
	12.		Three rounds were fired from 26 at a mound in the enemy line and two at a working party which apparently ceased work. Five rounds were fired at a working party from 24 and sixteen at different ~~other~~ targets, including a sniper. The enemy were again detected in the R3 crater and also to have been at some time in that in front of F1. They have brought up a new pattern of mortar to this sector and apparently have plenty of ammunition. The bomb is made of cast iron and has a greater destructive power than either of his other light bombs.	[illegible] 20/11/15
			J Williams 2nd RGA OC. 32 T.M. Battery.	

1875 Wt. W593/826 1,000,000 4/15 J.B.C. & A. A.D.S.S./Forms/C. 2118.

Instructions regarding War Diaries and Intelligence Summaries are contained in F. S. Regs., Part II. and the Staff Manual respectively. Title Pages will be prepared in manuscript.

WAR DIARY
or
INTELLIGENCE SUMMARY
(Erase heading not required.)

Army Form C. 2118

32nd T.M. Bty

Place	Date	Hour	Summary of Events and Information	Remarks and references to Appendices
	13.		Five rounds were fired at an enemy party working east of the brickstacks. The men in the trenches reported that they saw a carrying and working party about the position where the enemy exploded the mines on the 10th + 11th. Three rounds were fired from 25 at the portion of the enemy trench from which the enemy fired their rifle grenades. Four rounds were fired from 24 at the trenches opposite one round causing a large explosion as though a bomb store had been blown up. The enemy in this sector have taken to using a large periscope easily seen and sometimes taken for a wooden cross. This is a new idea of his for this area.	The works of the battery noted in 5th Corps Extracts of Information No 130, 131 Dated 12th + 13th
	14		Ten rounds were fired at an erection in front of 25. It was covered with corrugated iron and tarred felt strips — apparently temporarily placed —. Two bombs caused a double explosion and the smoke lasted about half an hour. Apparently in reply to this fire the enemy sent over a volley of rifle grenades to which we replied with thirteen rounds from 24. An irregular fire was kept up throughout the night on that point at which the mines were noted. The enemy replied with three rounds rapid from their mortar in reply to our first three. Later in reply to our next single shot he kept up a prolonged fire and in reply to each of the other odd rounds replied with five or six. The infantry did not detect this party at stand-to this morning as they have done during the first two mornings. The enemy were again detected in 38 Crater and were bombed. The enemy replied — as soon as possible it seemed — with trench mortar fire.	K 23/9/15
	15		The enemy bombarded 24 trench and the C.T. with rifle grenades. This was replied to with a heavy fire from our mortar which sprayed the enemy trench opposite. The rifle grenade fire ceased and things quieted down generally till the enemy put a	

1875 Wt. W593/826 1,000,000 4/15 J.B.C. & A. A.D.S.S./Forms/C. 2118.

Army Form C. 2118

Instructions regarding War Diaries and Intelligence Summaries are contained in F. S. Regs., Part II. and the Staff Manual respectively. Title Pages will be prepared in manuscript.

WAR DIARY
or
INTELLIGENCE SUMMARY
(Erase heading not required.)

Place	Date	Hour	Summary of Events and Information	Remarks and references to Appendices
			single 5·9 shell about two yards from our position. The mortar and ammunition and detachment were covered in dirt but no harm was done. A portion of the C.T. parapet was destroyed. Four rounds were fired at the same target east of the brickstack.	
	16.		The enemy working party was again seen east of the mound and six rounds were fired at this target. Eight rounds were fired in reply to enemy rifle grenade fire from 25 and six from 23 B for the same purpose. The mounds reported in front of the U sector can be seen from Q1 and strong woodworks can be detected in their makeup. A light railway truck can also be seen near these mounds but always occupies the same position by day.	
	17		Five rounds were fired from 24 in reply to hostile fire and seven from 23 B. Fourteen were fired from Q1. Four at the request of General Pelcher and ten for the purpose of worrying the enemy working party and in an attempt to put an enemy mortar out of action. The enemy mortar ceased fire.	
	18		The enemy have brought up a trench mortar to the U sector. Ten rounds were fired at this mortar in reply to fire from the enemy. Twelve were also fired later. Fourteen rounds were fired at the target east of the brickstack and the enemy replied with whizz-bangs. They seem very touchy on this spot.	
	19		A machine gun position was located in front of 24-25 and was bombed from 25 trench. About five or six yards of enemy parapet was demolished and the left portion	

Instructions regarding War Diaries and Intelligence Summaries are contained in F. S. Regs., Part II. and the Staff Manual respectively. Title Pages will be prepared in manuscript.

WAR DIARY
or
INTELLIGENCE SUMMARY
(Erase heading not required.)

Army Form C. 2118

Place	Date	Hour	Summary of Events and Information	Remarks and references to Appendices
			of the emplacement. Timber and biscuit tins (?) were thrown in the air. Sixteen rounds in all were fired. Four rounds were fired at a loopholed position in front of 26 trench. The enemy appeared to have a dummy figure moving up and down in front of 24. This was watched and later men were seen, apparently on the look-out, about twelve yards to the right. These were bombed with five rounds, the last falling apparently a direct hit on the spot. Eight other rounds were fired at the enemy trenches from this gun. Fifteen rounds were fired at the crater in front of [illegible] where an enemy party has been reported. Three rounds were fired from 21 in an attempt to put out an enemy mortar.	
			J Williams 2nd Lt RGA OC. 32 TM Battery.	

1875 Wt. W593/826 1,000,000 4/15 J.B.C. & A. A.D.S.S./Forms/C. 2118.

Instructions regarding War Diaries and Intelligence Summaries are contained in F. S. Regs., Part II. and the Staff Manual respectively. Title Pages will be prepared in manuscript.

WAR DIARY
or
INTELLIGENCE SUMMARY
(Erase heading not required.)

Army Form C. 2118

32nd Trench Mortar Bty

Place	Date	Hour	Summary of Events and Information	Remarks and references to Appendices
	20		Twenty nine rounds were fired from U 24 at the enemy trenches and five from U 25. Three rounds were fired at an enemy working party in front of U 25. Enemy ceased work. Five rounds were fired in the neighbourhood of an enemy machine gun	
	21		Thirty eight rounds were fired. Two rounds were fired from U 16 and Two from U 24 at the request of the General. Twelve were fired from U 26 at strong points on the enemy line. Ten rounds were fired from T1 at the working party reported to be behind the crater and were spread over the area.	
	22		Fifteen rounds were fired at the enemy trench in front of U 24 and eight rounds at an enemy machine gun. Five rounds were fired from another position in this trench at a suspicious point in the enemy line and took away a portion of the enemy work scattering a quantity of timber. One round was fired from T1 attempting to hit an enemy working party and three from 23 B at the same target with more success. Two rounds were fired from Q1 at an enemy mortar. Ten rounds were fired from R3 at the old target between the brickstacks and the mound. Three rounds were fired at a work located by the infantry and thought to be a sap head by the RE officer. Three rounds were fired ranging on a new sandbag erection on the crest of crater 38.	
	23.		Six rounds were fired from Q1 at the last mentioned target and six rounds from R3 at the sap head. Nine rounds were fired from U 25 at the enemy trenches.	25/7/15

1875 Wt. W593/826 1,000,000 4/15 J.B.C. & A. A.D.S.S./Forms/C. 2118.

Instructions regarding War Diaries and Intelligence Summaries are contained in F. S. Regs., Part II. and the Staff Manual respectively. Title Pages will be prepared in manuscript.

WAR DIARY
or
INTELLIGENCE SUMMARY
(Erase heading not required.)

Army Form C. 2118

Place	Date	Hour	Summary of Events and Information	Remarks and references to Appendices
			Fire rounds were fired at the enemy trenches from U 24 and four rounds at a working party which ceased work. Eight rounds were fired from R 3 in an attempt to drop some on two curious structures with roofs of plaited brushwood and split saplings. The enemy replied with fire rounds. The enemy were seen in their new T trench opposite T 2 and fire bombs were dropped in this neighbourhood. A good lookout was kept for enemy working parties repairing the damage done by our bombardment and as soon as it was dark the largest party ever seen by the O.C. was detected working quite boldly in front of 23 B. The party was promptly bombed and an irregular fire kept up on this point during the night. Thirty one rounds were fired in all. The enemy had not repaired the break this morning.	
	24		Twenty six rounds were fired at the last mentioned target through the night. It was too misty to detect the enemy working but the breach is not yet repaired. One rounds was fired at the mound in front of 23 B from which an M.G. flash was seen to come. The M.G. has not fired since. Twenty two rounds were fired at the enemy trenches in front of U 24 and ten from U 25. Two of the latter lifted an unusually large amount of debris. The enemy were heard in front of B sap in Q 1 just before our bombardment.	
	25		Eight rounds were fired at fresh sandbagging (loophole plates) in front of U 24 and six fell in the trench and two just over. Twelve rounds were fired at the enemy trenches from U 25. Eleven rounds were fired from R 1 at an enemy working party. Nine rounds were fired at the saphead mentioned above and two rounds were fired at the crater 38 in front of R 3. One round that detonated was followed by a cloud of green smoke. Eight rounds	

Army Form C. 2118

Instructions regarding War Diaries and Intelligence Summaries are contained in F. S. Regs., Part II. and the Staff Manual respectively. Title Pages will be prepared in manuscript.

WAR DIARY
or
INTELLIGENCE SUMMARY
(Erase heading not required.)

Place	Date	Hour	Summary of Events and Information	Remarks and references to Appendices
			Eight rounds were fired at the portion of the enemy parapet damaged by yesterdays bombardment. Six rounds were fired at an enemy M.G. emplacement, in front of R_1. Two rounds were fired from 23 B picking up the old breach in the parapet which does not yet seem to be repaired. The enemy immediately retaliated. The enemy seems to be very busy along the whole sector. One man was seen working in the open for quite a considerable time. He wore a white ~~blazer~~ sweater and black or dark trousers. A party was also seen working quite carelessly at their parapet,	
	26.		Twelve rounds were fired from U 24 at an enemy working party with effect. Thirteen were fired from 23 B at the gap and nine at a listening post. About twenty were fired from R_1 at new works in front and the enemy retaliated, commencing with soon after the battery and firing for some hours. The position of his gun was located and ten rounds rapid (3 bombs in the air at once) was given to this spot at which a man had been seen apparently correcting enemy fire. The enemy ceased fire. During his fire the enemy used both patterns of his 3·5" trench mortar bomb. An enemy machine gun had previously been located at this point. Eleven rounds were fired at crater 38. Seven from R_3 and four from R_2. Eleven rounds were fired from U 24 at an enemy working party. The enemy were seen carrying timber to their works in front of Q1A.	
			J Williams 2/Lt RGA. OC. 32 T.M. Battery.	

1875 Wt. W593/826 1,000,000 4/15 J.B.C. & A. A.D.S.S./Forms/C. 2118.

Instructions regarding War Diaries and Intelligence Summaries are contained in F. S. Regs., Part II. and the Staff Manual respectively. Title Pages will be prepared in manuscript.

WAR DIARY
or
INTELLIGENCE SUMMARY
(Erase heading not required.)

32nd Trench Mortar Bty.

Army Form C. 2118

Place	Date	Hour	Summary of Events and Information	Remarks and references to Appendices
	27		Eighteen rounds were fired from 23 c in reply to an enemy trench mortar and rifle grenade fire. "Bt" Meakin, N.C.O in charge, in his keenness to obtain a rapid rate of fire was wounded by one of our bombs as it left the mortar. Eleven rounds were fired later when the enemy reopened. He ceased fire. Eleven rounds were fired from U24 at an enemy work, supposed to be an M.G. emplacement. Thirty six rounds were fired at the crater at irregular intervals. The enemy are again using periscopes.	
	28		Twenty one rounds were fired into the crater at odd intervals. Thirty eight rounds were fired from U24 in reply to enemy fire and at targets along the front. Twenty one rounds were fired at an enemy mortar which was worrying R1. The enemy ceased fire. The enemy have brought more mortars to this sector. The gun in U24 went out of action	
	29		Eleven rounds were fired from U24 in reply to enemy fire. The gun in R1 was manned through the night but the enemy did not reopen fire. The gun from U24 was examined but no damage could be discovered. It will be sent to the brigade for examination.	
	30		Fifteen rounds were fired from a gun in Q1 at enemy works in front of Q1 B. Ten rounds were fired from R2 into the crater. Twenty rounds were fired at a working party at the foot of the mound. The enemy blew a whistle after our explosion.	
	1		Twenty three rounds were fired at enemy in front of 24 at request of O.C. Trench during the bombardment. Nine rounds were fired from R2 into the crater. Two rounds were fired from R2. Three from Q2 and one from Q1, in an attempt to put an enemy mortar out of action. Enemy ceased fire.	

Instructions regarding War Diaries and Intelligence Summaries are contained in F. S. Regs., Part II. and the Staff Manual respectively. Title Pages will be prepared in manuscript.

WAR DIARY
or
INTELLIGENCE SUMMARY
(Erase heading not required.)

Army Form C. 2118

Place	Date	Hour	Summary of Events and Information	Remarks and references to Appendices
	2		Six rounds were fired at an enemy working party in front of U 24. A wheel was tossed up by the explosion of one bomb. Work in crater 38 seems to be at a standstill.	
	3.		Enemy mortar worried 24–26 last night, one mortar was located and ceased fire when five bombs were dropped in its locality. Other mortar ceased before it could be located.	
			J Williams McKell.	
			OC. 3 23. H. Battery.	

1875 Wt. W593/826 1,000,000 4/15 J.B.C. & A. A.D.S.S./Forms/C. 2118.

Instructions regarding War Diaries and Intelligence Summaries are contained in F. S. Regs., Part II. and the Staff Manual respectively. Title pages will be prepared in manuscript.

WAR DIARY
or
~~INTELLIGENCE SUMMARY.~~ 32nd Trench Mortar Battery

(Erase heading not required.)

Army Form C. 2118.

Place	Date	Hour	Summary of Events and Information	Remarks and references to Appendices
Map Square J.19.a.4.3	Nov 6	6.45 AM.	Thirty two rounds were fired in conjunction with Artillery & Machine Guns from Secret Orders received from Infantry. 17 rounds of 2 inch (at 450, 400 & 390 yards) at the enemy Support Trenches and the "Bird Cage". 9 rounds of 4 inch (at 400 & 450 yards) at the same targets, and 7 rounds 18 pdr 1½ inch to enfilade front line of enemy trenches. I observed the fire from the 2" & 4" gun and the effect was considerable.	
	7	1.45 PM.	At request of Infantry fired 2 rounds from 2" gun in retaliation for enemy trench mortar bombs. This number was sufficient to silence the fire.	
		3.0 PM.	Enemy firing mac' Minenwerfers and H.E shells. One 2 inch and 4 1½" bombs fired in retaliation. This was sufficient to check the enemy's fire. An enemy trench mortar observed to be firing from near Point 45 on Trench Map – range unknown. I searched for it with 1½" gun, shooting at 300 yards with 20° left traverse, gradually reducing the traverse.	
	8	10 AM.	Fired in conjunction with our Artillery & Machine Guns without orders. I fired both 1½ inch guns getting off 7 bombs before the positions were located by the enemy & shelled. I searched again for the enemy trench mortar and did considerable damage to the German parapets. Fired 2 four inch shells.	
	9	10.30 AM.	Enemy shelled 1½ inch positions at the same time as yesterday morning and one of the men wounded slightly in the arm. I suspect that the 1½ inch guns have been accurately located, and advise the immediate use of new positions.	

Hugh H. T. Davies 2nd Lieut.
O.C. 32nd T.M.B.

2353 Wt. W2544/1454 700,000 5/15 D. D. & L. A.D.S.S./Forms/C. 2118.

Instructions regarding War Diaries and Intelligence Summaries are contained in F. S. Regs., Part II. and the Staff Manual respectively. Title pages will be prepared in manuscript.

WAR DIARY
or
INTELLIGENCE SUMMARY.
(Erase heading not required.)

Army Form C. 2118.

32nd Trench Mortar Battery

Place	Date	Hour	Summary of Events and Information	Remarks and references to Appendices
I. 11 a.	Nov 10		Getting two 2 inch gun emplacements ready, and dugouts etc. built for ammunition. Rain greatly delayed the work. No rounds fired.	
	11			
	12			
	13			
	14			

25/11

Hugh H. Davies 2nd Lieut
32nd. T. M. B.

2353 Wt. W2544/1454 700,000 5/15 D. D. & L. A.D.S.S./Forms/C. 2118.

Instructions regarding War Diaries and Intelligence Summaries are contained in F. S. Regs., Part II. and the Staff Manual respectively. Title pages will be prepared in manuscript.

WAR DIARY
or
INTELLIGENCE SUMMARY. 32nd Trench Mortar Battery

(Erase heading not required.)

Army Form C. 2118.

Place	Date	Hour	Summary of Events and Information	Remarks and references to Appendices
	14		Relieved 2Lt Davies and continued to work on right gun emplacement and dug out. Manned right gun in unfinished emplacement.	
	15		Observed enemy working in crater opposite H 20. Finished right emplacement and commenced left emplacement to engage enemy working parties. Ground very swampy.	
	16		Levelled ~~left~~ ground ~~round~~ for left position and continued work on parapet and dugout.	
	17.		Built in two beams 10' × 9" × 3" underneath parapets for gun bed to rest in and finished gun position and dugout. Laid telephone wire for ranging. Examined crater and found enemy work~~ing at a~~ to be similar to our sap heads with large working party and large piles of sandbags filled with blue clay.	
	18		Ranged on enemy crater. Bed smashed across transversely at fifth round. Ceased fire.	
	19		Removed broken bed and replaced with new bed which came up this evening.	
	20		Fired 10 rounds at enemy crater of which 8 detonated and 6 apparently fell in crater. One threw up a tremendous amount of wood debris and a ~~part~~ piece returned to the gun position at 290". Gun shooting very steadily. Traversing gear and forecarriage bent. 2Lt Davies relieved O.C.	

J Williams 2Lt RGA
O.C. 32 T.M. Battery

1577 Wt. W10791/1773 500,000 1/15 D. D. & L. A.D.S.S./Forms/C. 2118.

Instructions regarding War Diaries and Intelligence Summaries are contained in F. S. Regs., Part II. and the Staff Manual respectively. Title pages will be prepared in manuscript.

WAR DIARY
or
INTELLIGENCE SUMMARY.
(Erase heading not required.)

Army Form C. 2118.

KK 15/12

Place	Date	Hour	Summary of Events and Information	Remarks and references to Appendices
RAILWAY WOOD	Dec. 5.	6 PM 6.30	Took over from 2nd Lieut. Williams R.G.A.	
L.T.M. Group.	6.		A quiet day. A new officers' dugout was completed and a dugout for the men commenced.	
	7.		Gunner Conway R.G.A. reported sick and was evacuated to hospital with Trench feet.	
		3.0 PM.	I was with Br. Moore near No 10. Sap repairing the telephone wire when he was shot through the left arm by a sniper.	
			The day was spent in working on improving the gun positions and the dugout.	
			I selected an emergency emplacement for a 3.7" howitzer.	
	8	1.15 PM.	In retaliation for enemy Minenwerfer attack, we fired 9 3.7 howitzer bombs at the enemy front line and immediately in rear of our points 24 – 42 (I 12 A.)	
	9	3.45 AM	I located an enemy working party at I 12 A $\frac{3}{4}$, 4. It was dispersed by 6 rounds from the 3.7" howitzer. They did no more work that morning.	
		12 noon	Gough was hit in the eye ~~from~~ by dirt following the explosion of an enemy Trench Mortar bomb and was evacuated to hospital.	
		1.0 PM	The rest of the day was wet, but good progress was made with the work in hand.	
	10.		Very wet. Little could be done. 2nd Lieut Smart 3rd Dorsets joined me.	
			During the night, I located the direction of an enemy machine gun by the flash from the end of a listening post in H 20. the bearing was 133° Magnetic. I was unable to get a second bearing though I stayed up until 3.0 AM.	

2353 Wt. W2544/1454 700,000 5/15 D. D. & L. A.D.S.S./Forms/C. 2118.

Instructions regarding War Diaries and Intelligence Summaries are contained in F. S. Regs., Part II. and the Staff Manual respectively. Title pages will be prepared in manuscript.

WAR DIARY
or
INTELLIGENCE SUMMARY.
(Erase heading not required.)

Vk 15/14

Army Form C. 2118.

Place	Date	Hour	Summary of Events and Information	Remarks and references to Appendices
RAILWAY WOOD	Dec 11	A.M. 4.15	A message received from the Brigade stating the possibility of the attack. I set all the men to carry ammunition to the guns and the [illegible] was possessed was on the guns. No attack, however, developed.	
		A.M. 11.30	The enemy shelled H 19 with Trench Mortars (one Minenwerfer and one 10 lb gun.)	
			I replied with 20 rounds of 3.7 howitzer at points 24–47 (I 17 A) and immediately to rear. During the observation I distinctly saw the shell leave their Minenwerfer and attempted to knock it out with 9 rounds from the 2" gun. Considerable damage was done by us. I cannot be certain of the exact range of the enemy Minenwerfer, but as near as I could judge it is at	
			I 17 A 16 3/4, 45.	
		5.0 PM	I left 2nd Lieut. Smart in charge of the guns, having instructed him in his various duties.	
			Hugh H. T. Davis 2nd Lieut. 8th Camerons 32nd T.M.B.	

2353 Wt. W2544/1454 700,000 5/15 D. D. & L. A.D.S.S./Forms/C. 2118.

Army Form C. 2118.

Instructions regarding War Diaries and Intelligence Summaries are contained in F. S. Regs., Part II. and the Staff Manual respectively. Title pages will be prepared in manuscript.

WAR DIARY
or
INTELLIGENCE SUMMARY.
(Erase heading not required.)

32nd Trench Mortar Battery

Place	Date	Hour	Summary of Events and Information	Remarks and references to Appendices
RAILWAY WOOD. A.T.M Group.	Dec. 14th	6 PM	Took over from 2nd Lieut. Smart who reported that one 3.7 in howitzer was missing since the enemy bombardment of that day.	
		9 P.M	Corporal Millett accidentally wounded by a bayonet protruding from a heap of débris over which he had to climb to reach the gun position. On account of an enemy mine blown at 8.0 P.M. I patrolled the front during the night, but everything was quiet.	
	15th		The bombardment of the previous day had done considerable damage so that there was a great deal of work to be done. A search was made for the missing 3.7 in howitzer which had been knocked out by a direct hit from a shell but no trace of it was found. During the night the parapet at the end of H19 was built up, and an attempt made to drain the trench leading to the B 2 inch gun.	
	16th	3.30 PM	The Infantry asked for retaliation for enemy shells falling in ~~Cambridge Rd.~~ CAMBRIDGE RD. I fired four 2 inch bombs at the enemy trench (I 12 A 3/4, 5 3/7) Considerable damage appeared to be done, and the enemy battery did not reply. Some time during the afternoon an enemy shell hit the dugout of the A 2 inch gun. The gun was slightly damaged the firecarriage being broken in one place, and the barrel dented in two places.	
	17th		The work of rebuilding the A 2 inch position was started.	

Instructions regarding War Diaries and Intelligence Summaries are contained in F. S. Regs., Part II. and the Staff Manual respectively. Title pages will be prepared in manuscript.

WAR DIARY
or
INTELLIGENCE SUMMARY.
(Erase heading not required.)

Army Form C. 2118.

Place	Date	Hour	Summary of Events and Information	Remarks and references to Appendices
1	17th		Lt Eden and his servant Gr Driscoll joined the Brigade and were posted to 32 Trench Howitzer Battery. He visited the trenches and gun positions of the left group with 2Lt J. Williams and relieves Lt Davies tomorrow.	
			J. Williams 2Lt RGA OC 32 T.H. Battery.	

2353 Wt. W2544/1454 700,000 5/15 D. D. & L. A.D.S.S./Forms/C. 2118.

Army Form C. 2118.

Instructions regarding War Diaries and Intelligence Summaries are contained in F. S. Regs., Part II. and the Staff Manual respectively. Title pages will be prepared in manuscript.

WAR DIARY
or
INTELLIGENCE SUMMARY.
(Erase heading not required.)

Place	Date	Hour	Summary of Events and Information	Remarks and references to Appendices
RAILWAY WOOD L.T.M. Group	Dec 17th	P.M. 3.30	One enemy Minnenwerfer bomb was fired. This was the first of its kind for 6 days so that it appears likely that the gun which I had located, had been knocked out. Two 2 inch bombs were fired in retaliation along the Trench from the enemy crater to point I 11 A ¾ 5¾. The Infantry bombers, who were in a good position to view reported that at least 20 yards of the enemy front line parapet had been levelled by the two rounds.	
	18	12 noon	During a bombardment by our artillery two enemy Minnenwerfer bombs were fired. Five 3.7 in howitzer rounds were fired in retaliation on the enemy trench between points 24 - 40.	
		P.M. 5.30	2nd Lieut. Edes took over.	

Hugh H. E. Davies 2nd Lieut.
32nd T.M.B.

Instructions regarding War Diaries and Intelligence Summaries are contained in F. S. Regs., Part II. and the Staff Manual respectively. Title pages will be prepared in manuscript.

WAR DIARY
or
INTELLIGENCE SUMMARY.
(Erase heading not required.)

Army Form C. 2118.

Place	Date	Hour	Summary of Events and Information	Remarks and references to Appendices
Railway Wood	Dec 18th	5.30pm	Took over from Lt Davies	
LTM Group	19th	5.30am	Bombardment commenced on both sides, caused by a gas attack North of our position. Fired 12 Rounds 3.7" into enemy trench all of which were effective.	
		9.am	Cleaning guns, repairing trenches and gun Position that were damaged during bombardment, and found 3.7" gun, that had been blown away in a previous bombardment.	
		1.30pm	Bombardment started by enemy, I dident fire as I had received orders from Infantry Bde to reserve my Ammunition for the following morning, when an attack was expected.	
			During the afternoon bombardment the enemy secured a a direct hit on my A Gun 2" emplacement, and no sign of the gun can be found. 29 bombs were at this position, some of which I think must have exploded, as the crater is about 20 ft across, and about 12 ft deep.	
	20th	9.0am	Cleaning guns, digging drain from our dug-outs, and searching round the crater where A Gun 2" had been, but found no parts of gun, and	

Army Form C. 2118.

Instructions regarding War Diaries and Intelligence Summaries are contained in F. S. Regs., Part II. and the Staff Manual respectively. Title pages will be prepared in manuscript.

WAR DIARY
or
INTELLIGENCE SUMMARY.
(Erase heading not required.)

Place	Date	Hour	Summary of Events and Information	Remarks and references to Appendices
	Dec 20th		only three Bombs, all of which had socket for tail blown off rendering them useless.	
		3.0pm	Fired 5 2" Bombs, 3 of which did much damage to enemy parapet, the remainder fell in his trench.	
		5pm	Commenced making new 2" emplacement in Crater where A gun was blown up, and brought up dugout material from dump.	
	21st		Cleaning guns, duck boarding drain from dugouts, and working on new 2" Emplacement	
	22nd		Very quiet, work carried on as the day before. Found six bombs in crater where A Gun 2" was blown up.	
		6.0pm	Handed over to Lt Davies.	

A J Ede Lt. RGA
32nd T M Bty.

C

17 Div

32 Trench Mortar Batty

Jan

Vol II

Army Form C. 2118.

Instructions regarding War Diaries and Intelligence Summaries are contained in F. S. Regs., Part II. and the Staff Manual respectively. Title pages will be prepared in manuscript.

WAR DIARY
or
~~INTELLIGENCE SUMMARY.~~

(Erase heading not required.)

Place	Date	Hour	Summary of Events and Information	Remarks and references to Appendices
17th Div. Rest Area. France	7		The battery came out of action and left the rest billets at [28] H.18.A.6.6. for the Divisional Rest Area, where the training laid down in Div. Orders will be carried out.	The dates omitted in this and other months have been those days when nothing worthy of note except the ordinary drill routine has occurred or when the battery has been in rest billets in the active area.
	16		The artillery personnel was posted to the medium batteries of the division and the infantry from these batteries posted to this battery. The battery was then divided into three 32 A, B & C, the infantry of each brigade being allotted to the battery which will be attached to that Brigade. The officers will remain with the Battery for the present pending the arrival of infantry officers.	
	23.		Thirty nine N.C.O's and men arrived from the 17th Division to make up the three "sub" batteries to war strength [23] About three of these were volunteers, the remainder being detailed for the work.	
	24		The award of a Military Cross to 2Lt McGonigal for gallantry when with this battery is notified in today's Times.	[August 20th]

G Williams Lt R.C.A.
O.C. 32 T.M. Battery.

Instructions regarding War Diaries and Intelligence Summaries are contained in F. S. Regs., Part II. and the Staff Manual respectively. Title pages will be prepared in manuscript.

WAR DIARY
or
INTELLIGENCE SUMMARY.
(Erase heading not required.)

172

Army Form C. 2118.

Place	Date	Hour	Summary of Events and Information	Remarks and references to Appendices
RESERVE WOOD, THE BLUFF	Feb. 9th	2.30 PM	Took over from 2nd Lieut. Backhouse of the Left Trench Mortar Group of the 3rd. Division.	
			There were two 2 inch and two 1½" guns in action, ~~but~~ all in good condition and in strong positions. The ammunition taken over comprised 9 rounds 2 inch and 13 rounds 1½ inch. The charges, Tubes etc were old and damp so that they were of little use.	
	10		Reconnoitred the trenches and wired for more ammunition.	
		7.0 PM	Fired at a sniper's post with 3 1½ inch bombs opposite Trench 31. One bomb exploded in the enemy front line, but it was impossible to tell if the post was knocked out.	
	11	11.0 AM	Registered the other three guns on the enemy communication trenches and did considerable damage. Fired 6 two inch and 3 1½ inch bombs. The regist~~ration~~ was done in conjunction with a H.A.R. show.	
	12		No ammunition was available so little could be done. A reserve position was however made, and a shell bed installed at the foot of THE BLUFF at the junction of KING ST and ANGLE TRENCH.	
	13		I visited Brigade Hq. and the two Battalion Hq. whose front I covered, and informed them of the position of the guns. They are as follows:–	

Instructions regarding War Diaries and Intelligence Summaries are contained in F. S. Regs., Part II. and the Staff Manual respectively. Title pages will be prepared in manuscript.

WAR DIARY
or
INTELLIGENCE SUMMARY.
(Erase heading not required.)

Army Form C. 2118.

Place	Date	Hour	Summary of Events and Information	Remarks and references to Appendices
RESERVE WOOD, THE BLUFF	FEB 13		"A" gun (1½ inch) between ~~[illegible]~~ WOOD ST. and HEDGE ROW — 150 yards from ~~the~~ our firing line.	
			"B" gun (2 inch) in LOVERS LANE — 200 yards from our firing line.	
			"C" gun (1½ inch) in DEANSGATE — 100 yards — — — —.	
			"D" gun (2 inch) between 36 Trench and 36 S Trench — 50 yards from our firing line.	
	14	1.30 PM	I went over to SPOIL BANK and met 2nd Lieut Higgins. We went up to the trenches to choose positions for two 2 inch and two 1½ inch	
		3.0 PM	A fierce bombardment by the enemy. Pte Steel was killed and Corporal Poland wounded by the shelling. None of the guns were hit.	
	15	5.0 PM	Acting on instructions from the Brigade Major I sent two guides to Hq. to bring a party carrying ammunition. Both guides and men carrying 4 bombs got back but the rest of the party never arrived, though I had two men out searching for them. Fired 10 rounds from the two 2 inch guns — all the ammunition available, enfilading trenches 30 and 31 which had been captured by the enemy.	

1577 Wt. W10791/1773 500,000 1/15 D. D. & L. A.D.S.S./Forms/C. 2118.

Instructions regarding War Diaries and Intelligence Summaries are contained in F. S. Regs., Part II. and the Staff Manual respectively. Title pages will be prepared in manuscript.

WAR DIARY
or
INTELLIGENCE SUMMARY.
(*Erase heading not required.*)

Army Form C. 2118.

Place	Date	Hour	Summary of Events and Information	Remarks and references to Appendices
RESERVE WOOD, THE BLUFF	Feb. 15		Corporal Skillen and Gunner Gorst wounded by shell fire.	
	16		Collected the 2 inch bombs left by the carrying party of the previous evening. One dug out ("C" gun) had been knocked in. Otherwise all the positions were untouched.	
		5.0 PM	Relieved by 2nd Lieut. Hamilton. I left him in possession of explicit instructions as to what had been done, & how the guns were laid etc.	
			Hugh H. Davies 2nd Lieut. O.C. 32 A Trench Mortar Battery.	

Instructions regarding War Diaries and Intelligence Summaries are contained in F. S. Regs., Part II. and the Staff Manual respectively. Title pages will be prepared in manuscript.

WAR DIARY
or
INTELLIGENCE SUMMARY.
(Erase heading not required.)

Army Form C. 2118.

Place	Date	Hour	Summary of Events and Information	Remarks and references to Appendices
Reserve Wood The Bluff	Feb 18th		to headquarters of the 76th I.B. to see the Brigadier who wanted to fire on two saps in trench 32 & 31 recently captured by the Germans. I received a visit from two Engineer officers in the evening in connection with this, and it was eventually decided to do nothing for the present	
	19th		Another attempt was made to dig out 'C' Gun and this time it proved successful - the elevating gear was damaged but otherwise the gun was alright - it was sent behind the lines for repairs. Men were on working on transporting ammunition	
	20th		I handed over the Reserve Wood - The Bluff sector to Lt Duncan of the 3rd Division but remained in the sector with the Battery helping Lt Duncan with emplacements and carrying ammunition from Chateau Lankoff	
	21st		The men of the battery spent the day in carrying ammunition to the 3 guns. I left the trenches with the Battery at 11 P.M.	

C. E. Hamilton 2/Lt.
O.C. 32 B. Trench Mortar Battery

1577 Wt. W10791/1773 500,000 1/15 D. D. & L. A.D.S.S./Forms/C. 2118.

17TH DIVISION

TRENCH MORTAR BATTERIES

~~JAN 1916~~ - DEC 1918

FEB 1917 to

Instructions regarding War Diaries and Intelligence Summaries are contained in F. S. Regs., Part II. and the Staff Manual respectively. Title Pages will be prepared in manuscript.

WAR DIARY
or
~~INTELLIGENCE~~ SUMMARY
(Erase heading not required.)

Army Form C. 2118

17th Divl Trench Mortars
Vol 2

Place	Date	Hour	Summary of Events and Information	Remarks and references to Appendices
	1917 Feb. 1		Trench Mortar H.Q. at COMBLES (Sheet 57c SW 4. T28c 37)	
			Battle H.Q. at SAILLY.SAILLISEL (" " " U14a 31)	
			V/17 heavy T.M.B. one gun position under construction at (U14a31)	
			Y/17 medium " 3 " " " (U14b25 - U14b16) Y/17	
			X/17 " " 3 " " " (U14d37 - U14d39) X/17	
			Z/17 " " reserve battery at COMBLES (Sheet 57c SW 3. T27d)	
			Work was carried on on all gun positions, 40 pioneers and 10 sappers were attached to the medium T.M.Bs from 5.30 pm until 11 pm. - 40 pioneers were attached from 11.30 pm until 5 a.m. daily until 7.2.17.	
			The personnel of Z/17 battery were employed in carrying material from COMBLES - SAILLY.SAILLISEL.	J
	Feb 2		V/17 Work continued on gun position.	
			X/17 do do do do.	
			Y/17 do do do do	
			Z/17. Employed as carrying party between COMBLES and SAILLY SAILLISEL	
	3		V/17 Work continued on gun position. One 9.45" TM taken to gun position	J
			X/17 do do do do	
			Y/17 do do do do	
			Z/17 Carried timber and other material to "battle H.Q." A carrying party of 98 infantry carried material to "battle H.Q."	J

Instructions regarding War Diaries and Intelligence Summaries are contained in F. S. Regs., Part II. and the Staff Manual respectively. Title Pages will be prepared in manuscript.

WAR DIARY
or
~~INTELLIGENCE SUMMARY~~
(Erase heading not required.)

Army Form C. 2118

Place	Date	Hour	Summary of Events and Information	Remarks and references to Appendices
	1917 Feb 4.		V/17 Work continued on gun position, bomb-stores and dugouts begun.	
			X/17 do do do do do do	
			Y/17 do do do do do do.	
			Z/17 Carried 6 2" TM's complete and revetting material to "battle HQ". Laid wire from TM H.Q at COMBLES to [illegible] Inf Bde HQ in the catacombs at COMBLES.	
			Carried 300 2" bombs from COMBLES dump (T 22 d 2.3) to dump at Fregicourt (U 19 b 2.7)	
			2nd Lieut W.P.A. Tulloch reported for duty. Posted to X/17 Batty.	
	5		V/17 Work on gun position &c. continued. 40 heavy bombs carried from COMBLES dump (T 28 b 6.8) to dump at Fregicourt (U 19 b 2.7)	
			X/17 Work on gun positions &c continued, gun-beds laid in the emplacements.	
			Y/17 Work on gun positions &c continued, gun beds laid in the emplacements, Wire laid from "battle HQ" to battalion HQ at SAILLY.SAILLISEL (U 14 a 0.7)	
			Z/17 With a carrying party of 94 infantry, carried 100 2" bombs to X/17 & Y/17 gun positions. Carried timber from Fregicourt dump to "battle HQ".	
			2nd Lieut E W Harford posted to "O" battery A.A.	

1875 Wt. W593/826 1,000,000 4/15 J.B.C. & A. A.D.S.S./Forms/C. 2118.

Instructions regarding War Diaries and Intelligence Summaries are contained in F. S. Regs., Part II. and the Staff Manual respectively. Title Pages will be prepared in manuscript.

WAR DIARY
or
~~INTELLIGENCE SUMMARY~~
(Erase heading not required.)

Army Form C. 2118

Place	Date	Hour	Summary of Events and Information	Remarks and references to Appendices
	1917 Feb 6.		V/17. Work on position &c continued.	
			X/17 do do do. Wire laid from "battle HQ" to gun position (U 14 d 3 8).	
			Y/17 Work on position &c continued. Wire laid from "battle HQ" to gun position (U 14 b 1 6).	
			Z/17 carried material from COMBLES to "battle HQ." & with a carrying party of 94 infantry carried 2" bombs from the dump at FREGICOURT to X/17 and Y/17 gun positions.	J
	7		V/17 Work on position &c continued. One 9·45" T.M. placed in position	
			X/17 do do do. 3 guns were placed in position.	
			2nd Lieut A J E Hawks posted to B 78 Battery RFA.	
			Y/17 Work ~~on~~ position ~~s~~ &c continued do do do	
			~~During the night of 7/8th Y/17 fired 38 rounds on earthworks at (U 8 d 1½ ½) & (U 14 b 7 9)~~	
			Z/17 Carried material from the dump at FREGICOURT to "battle HQ" A carrying party of 100 infantry carried 20 (9·45") bombs (152 lbs each) and the remainder of the 2" bombs + component parts from the dump at FREGICOURT to "battle HQ"	
			D.T.M.O moved up to "battle HQ".	J

1875 Wt. W593/826 1,000,000 4/15 J.B.C. & A. A.D.S.S./Forms/C. 2118.

Instructions regarding War Diaries and Intelligence Summaries are contained in F. S. Regs., Part II. and the Staff Manual respectively. Title Pages will be prepared in manuscript.

WAR DIARY
or
~~INTELLIGENCE SUMMARY~~
(Erase heading not required.)

Army Form C. 2118

Place	Date	Hour	Summary of Events and Information	Remarks and references to Appendices
	1917 Feb 8.		On the morning of the 8th Feby our infantry attacked the German lines in SAILLISEL. The T.M. Batteries did not fire with the exception of Y/17 noted above. They were held in reserve for the purpose of defeating an enemy counter attack if one should have been made.	
			V/17 Position was improved & construction of dugouts continued.	
			X/17 2 guns were put out of action on the night of the 7/8th and the emplacements damaged. These emplacements were repaired	
			Y/17 At 7.30 am – 9.0 am Y/17 batty fired 38 rounds on sapheads at (U 8 d 4½ ½) and (U 14 b 7.9) Positions were improved and dugouts strengthened	
			Z/17 Employed as carrying party and runners	
			All telephone communication was cut repeatedly and all messages had to be sent by runner.	
	9		V/17 Work done on improving position to give a wider zone of fire and material carried from FREGICOURT dump to gun position	
			X/17 Work done on position	
			Y/17 Work done on position 7 rounds fired by No 1 gun on supposed enemy TM at (U 9 c 0 2)	
			Z/17 Carried material to FREGICOURT dump. A carrying party of 80 infantry with personnel of T.M.B carried 14 bombs (192 lbs each)	

1875 Wt. W593/826 1,000,000 4/15 J.B.C. & A. A.D.S.S./Forms/C. 2118.

Instructions regarding War Diaries and Intelligence Summaries are contained in F. S. Regs., Part II. and the Staff Manual respectively. Title Pages will be prepared in manuscript.

WAR DIARY
or
~~INTELLIGENCE SUMMARY~~
(Erase heading not required.)

Army Form C. 2118

Place	Date	Hour	Summary of Events and Information	Remarks and references to Appendices
	1917 Feb 9		from FREGICOURT dump to V/17 gun position.	
	10		V/17 Continued work on gun position &c	
			X/17 do do do	
			Y/17 do do do.	
			Z/17 Carried material from COMBLES to SAILLY SAILLISEL. – carried 6 bombs (192 lbs each) from FREGICOURT dump to V/17 position	J
	11.		V/17 Relieved by V/29. moved to camp at CARNOY.	
			X/17 work on gun position &c	
			Y/17 do do one emplacement to be converted to a new zone.	
			Z/17 carried material from COMBLES to "battle HQ"	J
	12		V/17 Moved to 4th Army T.M. School.	
			X/17 Work done on gun pits and dugouts. 20 pioneers attached	
			Y/17 do do do do	
			Z/17 with a carrying party of infantry carried timber from COMBLES to "battle HQ"	J

1875 Wt. W593/826 1,000,000 4/15 J.B.C. & A. A.D.S.S./Forms/C. 2118.

Instructions regarding War Diaries and Intelligence Summaries are contained in F. S. Regs., Part II. and the Staff Manual respectively. Title Pages will be prepared in manuscript.

WAR DIARY
or
~~INTELLIGENCE SUMMARY~~
(Erase heading not required.)

Army Form C. 2118

Place	Date	Hour	Summary of Events and Information	Remarks and references to Appendices
	1917 Feb 13.		V/17 At 4th Army T.M. school	
			X/17 Continued improving positions - pioneer assistance	
			Y/17 do do and altering zone do	
			Z/17 Supplied carrying parties, guides, orderlies.	C.J.
	Feb 14		V/17 At 4th Army School.	
			X/17 Improving positions. pioneer assistance	
			Y/17 do do and altering zone with pioneer assistance	
			Z/17 Carrying parties, &c.	
			2nd Lieut H G Hutchstep reported for duty. Posted to X/17 T.M.B.	C.J.
	15		V/17 At 4th Army T.M. School	
			X/17 Improving positions	
			Y/17 do do and altering zone, with pioneer assistance	
			Z/17 Carrying parties & fatigues. Infantry carrying party carried material from FREGICOURT dump to "battle HQ" Working party of pioneers was provided to assist Y/17 in their work	C.J.
	16		V/17 At 4th Army T.M. School	
			X/17 Work on positions. Pioneers were attached for the work	
			Y/17 do do do do	
			Z/17 Fatigues	C.J.

1875 Wt. W593/826 1,000,000 4/15 J.B.C. & A. A.D.S.S./Forms/C. 2118.

Instructions regarding War Diaries and Intelligence Summaries are contained in F. S. Regs., Part II. and the Staff Manual respectively. Title Pages will be prepared in manuscript.

WAR DIARY
or
~~INTELLIGENCE SUMMARY~~
(Erase heading not required.)

Army Form C. 2118

Place	Date	Hour	Summary of Events and Information	Remarks and references to Appendices
	1917 Feb 17		V/17 At 4th Army T.M. School	
			X/17 Work on positions. with pioneer assistance	
			Y/17 do do do do	
			Z/17 Fatigues. With a carrying party of 50 infantry carried timber & revetting material to "battle HQ"	J.
	18.		V/17 At 4th Army T.M. School	
			X/17 Work done on positions with pioneer assistance	
			Y/17 do do do do	
			Z/17 Fatigues	
			The medium T.M. batteries handed over their position and guns in action to the 29th Division – Personnel of these batteries were withdrawn to Combles. D.T.M.O. left "battle HQ"	J.
	19		V/17 At 4th Army T.M. School	
			X/17 Moved to camp at ~~Carr~~ CARNOY (~~A~~ 13 b 3,0)	
			Y/17 do do do	
			Z/17 do do do	J.

Army Form C. 2118

Instructions regarding War Diaries and Intelligence Summaries are contained in F. S. Regs., Part II. and the Staff Manual respectively. Title Pages will be prepared in manuscript.

WAR DIARY
or
~~INTELLIGENCE SUMMARY~~
(Erase heading not required.)

Place	Date	Hour	Summary of Events and Information	Remarks and references to Appendices
	1917 Feb 20		V/17 At 4th Army T.M. School	
			X/17 Cleaning guns and stores. Pay. at CARNOY camp.	
			Y/17 do do do do	
			Z/17 do do do do	J.
	Feb 21		V/17 At 4th Army T.M. School	
			X/17 At Carnoy Camp (A 13 b, 3.0).	
			Y/17 do	
			Z/17 do	J.
	22		V/17 At 4th Army T M School	
			X/17 At Carnoy Camp. Baths.	
			Y/17 do do Kit Inspection	
			Z/17 do do	J.
	23.		V/17 At 4th Army T.M. School	
			X/17 At Carnoy Camp. Gas helmet inspection and issue of new box respirators	
			Y/17 do do do	
			Z/17 do do do	J.

1875 Wt. W593/826 1,000,000 4/15 J.B.C. & A. A.D.S.S./Forms/C. 2118.

Instructions regarding War Diaries and Intelligence Summaries are contained in F. S. Regs., Part II. and the Staff Manual respectively. Title Pages will be prepared in manuscript.

WAR DIARY
or
~~INTELLIGENCE SUMMARY~~
(Erase heading not required.)

Army Form C. 2118

Place	Date	Hour	Summary of Events and Information		Remarks and references to Appendices
	1917 Feb 24	2	V/17 At 4th Army T.M. School		
			X/17 At Carnoy Camp.	Kit inspection	
			Y/17 do		
			Z/17 do	Kit inspection	C.J.
	25		V/17 Returned from 4th Army T.M. School CARNOY.		
			X/17 At CARNOY camp	Fatigues	
			Y/17 do	do	
			Z/17 do	do	C.J.
	26		V/17 At CARNOY camp.	Instructional parade	
			X/17 do	do	
			Y/17 do	do	
			Z/17 do	do	C.J.
	27		V/17 At CARNOY camp.	do	
			X/17 do	do	
			Y/17 do	do	
			Z/17 do	do	C.J.

Instructions regarding War Diaries and Intelligence Summaries are contained in F. S. Regs., Part II. and the Staff Manual respectively. Title Pages will be prepared in manuscript.

WAR DIARY
or
INTELLIGENCE SUMMARY
(Erase heading not required.)

Army Form C. 2118

Trench Mortars 17th Divn

Vol 3

Place	Date	Hour	Summary of Events and Information	Remarks and references to Appendices
	1917 Feb 28		V/17 X/17 Y/17 Z/17 } At CARNOY. Instructional parades Gas drill	C.J.
	Mar 1		V/17 X/17 Y/17 Z/17 } do do Pay	C.J.
	2		V/17 X/17 Y/17 Z/17 } do	C.J.
	3		V/17 X/17 Y/17 Z/17 } do Fatigues	C.J.
	4		V/17 X/17 Y/17 Z/17 } do Advance party of one officer + 20 men went to ALBERT to arrange billets	C.J.

1875 Wt. W593/826 1,000,000 4/15 J.B.C. & A. A.D.S.S./Forms/C. 2118.

Instructions regarding War Diaries and Intelligence Summaries are contained in F. S. Regs., Part II. and the Staff Manual respectively. Title Pages will be prepared in manuscript.

WAR DIARY
or
INTELLIGENCE SUMMARY
(Erase heading not required.)

Army Form C. 2118

Place	Date	Hour	Summary of Events and Information	Remarks and references to Appendices
	1917 Mar 5		V/17 X/17 Y/17 Z/17 } Moved to ALBERT. Camped at ALBERT-BAPAUME road. C.J.	
	6		V/17 X/17 Y/17 Z/17 } at ALBERT camp. Fatigues. C.J.	
	7		V/17 at ALBERT Instructional parades.	
			X/17 Y/17 Z/17 } do 20 men left for fatigues at VIVIER.MILL. C.J.	
	8		V/17 do Instructional parades	
			X/17 Y/17 Z/17 } do 20 men on fatigues. C.J.	
	9		V/17 do Instructional parades	
			X/17 Y/17 Z/17 } do 20 men on fatigues C.J.	

1875 Wt. W593/826 1,000,000 4/15 J.B.C. & A. A.D.S.S./Forms/C. 2118.

Instructions regarding War Diaries and Intelligence Summaries are contained in F. S. Regs., Part II. and the Staff Manual respectively. Title Pages will be prepared in manuscript.

WAR DIARY
or
INTELLIGENCE SUMMARY
(Erase heading not required.)

Army Form C. 2118

Place	Date	Hour	Summary of Events and Information	Remarks and references to Appendices
	1917 Mar 10		V/17 at ALBERT. Instructional parades	
			X/17, Y/17, Z/17 } Fatigues C.J.	
	11		V/17 at ALBERT 20 men relieved men of XYZ on fatigues	
			X/17, Y/17, Z/17 } do. C.J.	
	12		V/17, X/17, Y/17, Z/17 } at ALBERT. Instructional parades, 20 men on fatigues C.J.	
	13		V/17, X/17, Y/17, Z/17 } at ALBERT. Instructional parades, 20 men on fatigues C.J.	
	14		V/17, X/17, Y/17, Z/17 } at ALBERT. Instructional parades, 20 men on fatigues C.J.	

1875 Wt. W593/826 1,000,000 4/15 J.B.C. & A. A.D.S.S./Forms/C. 2118.

Army Form C. 2118

WAR DIARY
or
INTELLIGENCE SUMMARY
(Erase heading not required.)

Instructions regarding War Diaries and Intelligence Summaries are contained in F. S. Regs., Part II. and the Staff Manual respectively. Title Pages will be prepared in manuscript.

Place	Date	Hour	Summary of Events and Information	Remarks and references to Appendices
	1917 Mar 15		V/17 X/17 Y/17 Z/17 At ALBERT. Instructional parades, pay, C.J.	
	Mar 16		V/17 X/17 Y/17 Z/17 At ALBERT do. C.J.	
	Mar 17		V/17 X/17 Y/17 Z/17 At ALBERT. do. Billetting party left for FONTAINE C.J.	
	Mar 18		V/17 X/17 Y/17 Z/17 Moved to PUCHEVILLERS. C.J.	

1875 Wt. W593/826 1,000,000 4/15 J.B.C. & A. A.D.S.S./Forms/C. 2118.

Instructions regarding War Diaries and Intelligence Summaries are contained in F. S. Regs., Part II. and the Staff Manual respectively. Title pages will be prepared in manuscript.

WAR DIARY
or
INTELLIGENCE SUMMARY.
(Erase heading not required.)

Army Form C. 2118.

Place	Date	Hour	Summary of Events and Information	Remarks and references to Appendices
	1917 Mar 19		V/17, X/17, Y/17, Z/17 } at PUCHEVILLERS. Instructional parade	CJ
	Mar 20		V/17, X/17, Y/17, Z/17 } Moved to FROHEN le PETIT.	CJ
	Mar 21		V/17, X/17, Y/17, Z/17 } at FROHEN le PETIT.	CJ
	Mar 22		V/17, X/17, Y/17, Z/17 } At FROHEN le PETIT, cleaning stores	CJ

A5834 Wt. W4973/M687 750,000 8/16 D. D. & L. Ltd. Forms/C.2118/13.

Instructions regarding War Diaries and Intelligence Summaries are contained in F. S. Regs., Part II. and the Staff Manual respectively. Title pages will be prepared in manuscript.

WAR DIARY
or
INTELLIGENCE SUMMARY.
(Erase heading not required.)

Army Form C. 2118.

Place	Date	Hour	Summary of Events and Information	Remarks and references to Appendices
	1917 Mar 23		V/17 X/17 Y/17 Z/17 } Intensive training at FROHEN le PETIT, 22 reinforcements joined the brigade	C.J.
	Mar 24		V/17 X/17 Y/17 Z/17 } Marched to MONCHEL.	C.J.
	Mar 25		V/17 X/17 Y/17 Z/17 } Marched to St MICHEL	C.J.
	Mar 26		V/17 X/17 Y/17 Z/17 } Marched to BRAY camped at camp SW of BRAY	C.J.

A5834 Wt. W4973/M687 750,000 8/16 D. D. & L. Ltd. Forms/C.2118/13.

Instructions regarding War Diaries and Intelligence Summaries are contained in F. S. Regs., Part II. and the Staff Manual respectively. Title pages will be prepared in manuscript.

WAR DIARY
or
INTELLIGENCE SUMMARY.
(Erase heading not required.)

Army Form C. 2118.

Place	Date	Hour	Summary of Events and Information	Remarks and references to Appendices
	1917 Mar 27		V/17, X/17, Y/17, Z/17 } Fatigues, instructional parades. C.J.	

A5834 Wt. W4973/M687 750,000 8/16 D. D. & L. Ltd. Forms/C.2118/13.

Instructions regarding War Diaries and Intelligence Summaries are contained in F. S. Regs., Part II. and the Staff Manual respectively. Title pages will be prepared in manuscript.

WAR DIARY
or
INTELLIGENCE SUMMARY.
(Erase heading not required.)

Army Form C. 2118.

Place	Date	Hour	Summary of Events and Information	Remarks and references to Appendices
	1917 Mar 28	~~10~~	V/17 X/17 Y/17 Z/17 } Instructional parades at BRAY	C.J.
	Mar 29		V/17 X/17 Y/17 Z/17 } Instructional parades at BRAY.	C.J.
	Mar 30		V/17 X/17 Y/17 Z/17 } Instructional parades. 2/Lieut Tulloch & 11 men returned from 5th Army TM School	C.J.

A5834 Wt. W4973/M687 750,000 8/16 D. D. & L. Ltd. Forms/C.2118/13.

Instructions regarding War Diaries and Intelligence Summaries are contained in F. S. Regs., Part II. and the Staff Manual respectively. Title pages will be prepared in manuscript.

WAR DIARY
or
INTELLIGENCE SUMMARY.
(Erase heading not required.)

Army Form C. 2118.

14th T.M.'s
Vol 4

Place	Date	Hour	Summary of Events and Information	Remarks and references to Appendices
	1917 Mar 31		~~Instructional~~ parades at BRAY. Moved to ARRAS. V, X & Z prepared for action Y Batty held in reserve.	C.J.
	Apl 1.		V/17 Took over partially constructed positions and commenced work on them	
			X/17 do do do	
			Y/17 Supplied carrying parties for the batteries in action	
			Z/17 Took over position & started work on them.	C.J.
	2		V/17 Worked on positions and bomb stores Roclincourt sheet G 5 b.	
			X/17 do do	
			Z/17 do do	
			Y/17 Carrying parties & fatigues	C.J.
	3.		V/17 Registered on enemy trenches. Ammunition expended 3 rounds	
			X/17 Registered on enemy wire do 7 do	
			Z/17 do do do do 14 do	
			Y/17 Carrying parties. Casualties Killed 2.O.R Wounded 2 O.R.	C.J.

Army Form C. 2118.

WAR DIARY
or
INTELLIGENCE SUMMARY.
(*Erase heading not required.*)

Instructions regarding War Diaries and Intelligence Summaries are contained in F. S. Regs., Part II. and the Staff Manual respectively. Title pages will be prepared in manuscript.

Place	Date	Hour	Summary of Events and Information	Remarks and references to Appendices
	1917 Ap/4		V/17 In action. Ammunition expended, 10 rounds. Casualties, nil.	
			X/17 do do 111 rounds. do nil	
			Z/17 do do 101 rounds. do , nil	
			Y/17 In reserve. Carrying parties + fatigues. do , nil	C.J.
	5		V/17 In action. Ammunition expended 47 rounds. Casualties, nil.	
			X/17 do do 123 " . do Wounded 3 O.R	
			Z/17 do do 168 " . do nil	
			Y/17 In reserve. Carrying parties + fatigues. do nil	C.J.
	6		V/17 In action. Ammunition expended 20 rounds. Casualties, nil.	
			X/17 do do 70 " . do , nil	
			Z/17 do do 186 " . do Killed, 2 O.R Wounded, died of wounds 1 O.R	
			Y/17 In reserve. Carrying parties + fatigues.	C.J.

Instructions regarding War Diaries and Intelligence Summaries are contained in F. S. Regs., Part II. and the Staff Manual respectively. Title pages will be prepared in manuscript.

WAR DIARY
or
INTELLIGENCE SUMMARY.

(Erase heading not required.)

Army Form C. 2118.

Place	Date	Hour	Summary of Events and Information	Remarks and references to Appendices
	1917 Apl 7		V/17 In action. Ammunition expended, 12 rounds. Casualties, nil.	
			X/17 do do 176 " do ~~nil~~ Wounded 1 off	
			Z/17 do do 169 ~~149~~ do nil	
			Y/17 In reserve, Carrying parties & fatigues. do nil	
	8		V/17 In action. Ammunition expended, 20 rounds. Casualties, nil	
			X/17 do do 103 " do, nil.	
			Z/17 do do 152 do, nil.	
			Y/17 In reserve Carrying parties & fatigues do nil.	
	9		V/17 In action. Ammunition expended 2 rounds. Casualties, nil.	
			X/17 do do 3 " do, nil	
			Z/17 do do 2 do, nil	
			Y/17 In reserve. Carrying parties & fatigues do, nil	
			Personnel was withdrawn from the trenches and returned to ARRAS. Guard left on positions of V, X & Z batteries. 62 O.R. attached to 78th & 79th Brigades RFA	

A5834 Wt. W4973/M687 750,000 8/16 D. D. & L. Ltd. Forms/C.2118/13.

Instructions regarding War Diaries and Intelligence Summaries are contained in F. S. Regs., Part II. and the Staff Manual respectively. Title pages will be prepared in manuscript.

WAR DIARY
or
INTELLIGENCE SUMMARY.
(Erase heading not required.)

Army Form C. 2118.

Place	Date	Hour	Summary of Events and Information	Remarks and references to Appendices
	1917 Ap/10		V/17 In ARRAS. 2/Lt Galsworthy admitted to hospital.	
			X/17 do } general fatigues. 25 O.R. attached to 78th & 79th Bde R.F.A.	
			Y/17 do	
			Z/17 do	[illegible]
	11		V/17, X/17, Y/17, Z/17 } A battery of 4 german light Minenwerfer was found in the captured area and a supply of ammunition.	[illegible]
	12		V/17, X/17, Y/17, Z/17 } A carrying party was employed all day removing 2" T.Ms from the trenches and digging out buried guns. 30 O.R. returned from RFA Bdes	[illegible]
	13		V/17, X/17, Y/17, Z/17 } Remaining 2" T.Ms and 9.45 T.M. were brought out of action and taken to ARRAS. 30 ~~Remainder~~ of O.R.s returned from R.F.A Bdes	[illegible]

A5834 Wt. W4973/M687 750,000 8/16 D. D. & L. Ltd. Forms/C.2118/13.

Instructions regarding War Diaries and Intelligence Summaries are contained in F. S. Regs., Part II. and the Staff Manual respectively. Title pages will be prepared in manuscript.

WAR DIARY
or
INTELLIGENCE SUMMARY.
(Erase heading not required.)

Army Form C. 2118.

Place	Date	Hour	Summary of Events and Information	Remarks and references to Appendices
	1917 Apl 14		V/17 ~~Cle~~ Instructional parades &c.	
			X/17 Cleaning guns and stores. 2/Lt ADAMSON transferred to R.F.C.	
			Y/17 do	
			Z/17 do	CJ
	15		V/17 4 German light Minenwerfers were removed from the trenches	
			X/17 to ARRAS and 156 rounds of ammunition was saved	
			Y/17 Cleaning fatigues & parades in Arras	
			Z/17	CJ
	16		V/17 Cleaning fatigues & parades	
			X/17 do	
			Y/17 do	
			Z/17 do	CJ
	17		V/17 Cleaning stores & parades	
			X/17 do	
			Y/17 do	
			Z/17 do	CJ

A5834 Wt. W4973/M687 750,000 8/16 D. D. & L. Ltd. Forms/C.2118/13.

Instructions regarding War Diaries and Intelligence Summaries are contained in F. S. Regs., Part II. and the Staff Manual respectively. Title pages will be prepared in manuscript.

WAR DIARY
or
INTELLIGENCE SUMMARY.
(Erase heading not required.)

Army Form C. 2118.

Place	Date	Hour	Summary of Events and Information	Remarks and references to Appendices
	1917 Apl 18		Capt Beasley & 2 officers examined a German dugout in the captured area & discovered a supply of ammunition for the light Minenwerfer.	
			2 Officers carried out a reconnaissance of battle position from which to shoot on the enemy front line with the Minenwerfer.	
	19		Capt Beasley & 2 officers continued reconnaissance of position near MONCHY les Preux.	
			2 officers were sent to 3rd Army school & H.Q. to obtain information concerning the German Minenwerfer & ammunition but were unsuccessful in obtaining any further information.	
	20		3 light Minenwerfer were carried up to gun positions and dug in. Ammunition was carried up and the guns were placed in position ready to fire by 3 a.m. on the morning of the 21st. Casualties, Killed 1 O.R. Wounded 1 O.R.	
	21		All guns were registered on the enemy trench between I31.a.1.4 and I25 c 15.20. Ammunition expended 51 rounds. Casualties nil	
	22		During the morning a lively bombardment of the enemy trench was carried out with successful results. The personnel of the T.M.s were withdrawn to ARRAS after the bombardment. Ammunition expended 286 rounds. Casualties, nil.	

A5834 Wt. W4973/M687 750,000 8/16 D. D. & L. Ltd. Forms/C.2118/13.

Army Form C. 2118.

Instructions regarding War Diaries and Intelligence Summaries are contained in F. S. Regs., Part II. and the Staff Manual respectively. Title pages will be prepared in manuscript.

WAR DIARY
or
INTELLIGENCE SUMMARY.

(Erase heading not required.)

Place	Date	Hour	Summary of Events and Information	Remarks and references to Appendices
	1917 Apl 23		V/17 X/17 Y/17 Z/17 } Parades, cleaning fatigues. CJ	
	24		V/17 X/17 Y/17 Z/17 } Parades for instruction. 30 men sent to DAC for fatigues at ammunition dump. CJ	
	25		V/17 X/17 Y/17 Z/17 } Instructional parades, fatigue supplied for work on ammunition dump. CJ	
	26		V/17 X/17 Y/17 Z/17 } Instructional parade. CJ	
	27		V/17 X/17 Y/17 Z/17 } Cleaning up billets &c. CJ	

A5834 Wt. W4973/M687 750,000 8/16 D. D. & L. Ltd. Forms/C.2118/13.

Instructions regarding War Diaries and Intelligence Summaries are contained in F. S. Regs., Part II. and the Staff Manual respectively. Title pages will be prepared in manuscript.

WAR DIARY
or
INTELLIGENCE SUMMARY.
(Erase heading not required.)

Army Form C. 2118.

Place	Date	Hour	Summary of Events and Information	Remarks and references to Appendices
	1917 Apl 28		V/17 X/17 Y/17 Z/17 } Moved from ARRAS to IVERGNY by lorry.	C.J.
	29		V/17 X/17 Y/17 Z/17 } Cleaning equipment, billets &c.	C.J.
	30		V/17 X/17 Y/17 Z/17 } Parades, Marching drill, rifle drill, signallers parades &c.	C.J.

A5834 Wt. W4973/M687 750,000 8/16 D. D. & L. Ltd. Forms/C.2118/13.

Instructions regarding War Diaries and Intelligence Summaries are contained in F. S. Regs., Part II. and the Staff Manual respectively. Title pages will be prepared in manuscript.

WAR DIARY
or
INTELLIGENCE SUMMARY.
(Erase heading not required.)

Army Form C. 2118.

1/1st Divl. Trench Mortars.

Vol 5

Place	Date	Hour		Summary of Events and Information	Remarks and references to Appendices
	1917 1st May		V 17 X 17 Y 17 Z 17	Instructional parade & Kit Inspection	
	2nd		V 17 X 17 Y 17 Z 17	March from IVERGNY to ARRAS by lorry	
	3rd		V 17 X 17 Y 17 Z 17	Cleaning equipment & billets	
	4th		V 17 X 17 Y 17 Z 17	Moved to new billets in ARRAS	
	5th		V 17 X 17 Y 17 Z 17	Rifle & Marching Drill General fatigues & Signallers [illegible]	
	6th		V 17 X 17 Y 17 Z 17	Church Parade & Fatigues. Casualties by Shell Fire in ARRAS. 1 O.R. killed 1 O.R. [illegible] wounded	
	7th		V 17 X 17 Y 17 Z 17	Move to Race Course. General fatigues	

A5834 Wt. W4973/M687 750,000 8/16 D. D. & L. Ltd. Forms/C.2118/13.

Instructions regarding War Diaries and Intelligence Summaries are contained in F. S. Regs., Part II. and the Staff Manual respectively. Title pages will be prepared in manuscript.

WAR DIARY
or
INTELLIGENCE SUMMARY.
(Erase heading not required.)

Army Form C. 2118.

Place	Date	Hour	Summary of Events and Information	Remarks and references to Appendices
	1917 8th		V 17 X 17 Y 17 Z 17 } 2 Officers + V/17 Fatigues on Ammunition Dumps. X17 Y17 - Z17 Signalling Rifle + Marching Drill. 2/Lt A.H. Watkins joined + Posted to V/17 T.M.B.	
	9th		V17 Rifle + Marching Drill. Kit Inspections. X Y + Z 17 2 Officers + men Fatigues on Ammunition Dumps.	
	10th		V17 2 Off. + 30 O.R. sent to 3rd Army Trench Mortar School. X Y + Z 17 2 Off + 15 O.R. sent to 3rd " " " " Remainder Fatigues.	
	11th		4 Officers + 64 O.R. attached to 51st + 52nd Field Ambulance as Stretcher Bearers.	
	12th		— Nil —	
	13th		— Nil —	
	14th		— Nil —	
	15th		— Nil —	
	16th		— Nil —	
	17		— Nil —	

A5834 Wt. W4973/M687 750,000 8/16 D. D. & L. Ltd. Forms/C.2118/13.

Army Form C. 2118.

WAR DIARY
or
INTELLIGENCE SUMMARY.
(*Erase heading not required.*)

Instructions regarding War Diaries and Intelligence Summaries are contained in F. S. Regs., Part II. and the Staff Manual respectively. Title pages will be prepared in manuscript.

Place	Date	Hour	Summary of Events and Information	Remarks and references to Appendices
	May 18th		— Nil —	
	19th		4 Officers & 43 O.R. return from the 3rd Army Trench Mortar School	
	20th		V 17, X 17, Y 17, Z 17 } Kit Inspection & Gen[eral] Fatigues	
	21st		Reconnaissance was carried out by D.T.M.O. of a front line & position was chosen close to bombing sap CURSE. I 1 a 45.35. Y/17 commence work on 2 2" positions. V X & Z/17 carrying parties for material and ammunition.	
	22nd		Work continued on positions.	
	23rd		V 17, X 17, Y 17, Z 17 } Work continued on positions	
	14		V 17, X 17, Y 17, Z 17 } Work continued on positions	
	25th		V 17, X 17, Y 17, Z 17 } Work continued on positions. Reconnaissance was carried out by D.T.M.O. & position was chosen at I 7 c 8.5.8.	
	26th		V 17, X 17 } Commence work on new position. Y 17, Z 17 } Continue work on do position	

A5834 Wt. W4973/M687 750,000 8/16 D. D. & L. Ltd. Forms/C.2118/13.

Instructions regarding War Diaries and Intelligence Summaries are contained in F. S. Regs., Part II. and the Staff Manual respectively. Title pages will be prepared in manuscript.

WAR DIARY
or
INTELLIGENCE SUMMAR[Y]
(Erase heading not required.)

Place	Date	Hour	Summary of Events and Inform[ation]
	27th		V 17 X 17 Y 17 Z 17 — Work continued on positions
	28th		V 17 X 17 Y 17 Z 17 — Work continued on positions
	29th		V 17 X 17 Y 17 Z 17 — Work continued on positions
	30th		V 17 X 17 Y 17 Z 17 — Work continued on positions
	31st		V 17 X 17 Y 17 Z 17 — Work continued on positions

A5834 Wt. W4973/M687 750,000 8/16 D. D& L. Ltd. Forms/C.2118/13.

Instructions regarding War Diaries and Intelligence Summaries are contained in F. S. Regs., Part II. and the Staff Manual respectively. Title pages will be prepared in manuscript.

WAR DIARY
or
INTELLIGENCE SUMMARY.
(Erase heading not required.)

Army Form C. 2118.

17th Divisional Trench Mortars.

Vol 6

Place	Date	Hour	Summary of Events and Information	Remarks and references to Appendices
	June 1st	V 17, X 17, Y 17, Z 17	Site of Camp changed owing to danger from Rifle Range. Guns parked in Arras. V. 1 Officer 4 OR attached to Gun Park	[illegible]
	2nd	V 17, X 17, Y 17, Z 17	Rifle & Marching Drill.	[illegible]
	3rd	V 17, X 17, Y 17, Z 17	Kit inspection.	[illegible]
	4th	V 17, X 17, Y 17, Z 17	Instructional Parades	[illegible]
	5th	V 17, X 17, Y 17, Z 17	Instructional Parades	[illegible]
	6th	V 17, X 17, Y 17, Z 17	Instructional Parades	[illegible]
	7th	V 17, X 17, Y 17, Z 17	Instructional Parades	[illegible]

A5834 Wt. W4973/M687 750,000 8/16 D. D. & L. Ltd. Forms/C.2118/13.

Instructions regarding War Diaries and Intelligence Summaries are contained in F. S. Regs., Part II. and the Staff Manual respectively. Title pages will be prepared in manuscript.

WAR DIARY
or
INTELLIGENCE SUMMARY.
(Erase heading not required.)

Army Form C. 2118.

Place	Date	Hour	Summary of Events and Information	Remarks and references to Appendices
	June			
	8th		V 17, X 17, Y 17, Z 17 } Rifle & Marching Drill	H.G.A.
	9th		V 17, X 17, Y 17, Z 17 } Gas Parade & Gas Helmet Inspection.	H.G.A.
	10th		V 17, X 17, Y 17, Z 17 } Church Parade.	H.G.A.
	11th		V 17, X 17, Y 17, Z 17 } Cleaning Parades & Fatigues.	H.G.A.
	12th		V 17, X 17, Y 17, Z 17 } Marching Drill, rifle drill, & signallers parades.	H.G.A.
	13th		V 17, X 17, Y 17, Z 17 } Parades. Physical Exercises, Marching drill	H.G.A.

A5834 Wt. W4973/M687 750,000 8/16 D. D. & L. Ltd. Forms/C.2118/13.

Instructions regarding War Diaries and Intelligence Summaries are contained in F. S. Regs., Part II. and the Staff Manual respectively. Title pages will be prepared in manuscript.

WAR DIARY
or
INTELLIGENCE SUMMARY.
(Erase heading not required.)

Army Form C. 2118.

Place	Date	Hour	Summary of Events and Information	Remarks and references to Appendices
	June			
	14th	V 17 X 17 Y 17 Z 17	Instructional & Pay Parades	HGH
	15th	V 17 X 17 Y 17 Z 17	Marching & Rifle Drill Shooting on Range	HGH
	16th	V 17 X 17 Y 17 Z 17	G.O.C. inspection	HGH
	17th	V 17 X 17 Y 17 Z 17	Changed Camp from VI Corps to XVII Corps area.	HGH
	18th	V 17 X 17 Y 17 Z 17	Instructional Parades & Fatigues	HGH
	19th	V 17 X 17 Y 17 Z 17	Parades. Gas Helmet Drill Physical Exercises	HGH

A5834 Wt. W4973/M687 750,000 8/16 D. D. & L. Ltd. Forms/C.2118/13.

Instructions regarding War Diaries and Intelligence Summaries are contained in F. S. Regs., Part II. and the Staff Manual respectively. Title pages will be prepared in manuscript.

WAR DIARY
or
INTELLIGENCE SUMMARY.
(Erase heading not required.)

Army Form C. 2118.

Place	Date	Hour	Summary of Events and Information	Remarks and references to Appendices
	June 20		Marching & Rifle Drill	[illegible]
	21st	V 17 X 17 Y 17 Z 17	Instructional Parades	[illegible]
	22nd	V 17 X 17 Y 17 Z 17	Instructional Parades Physical exercises Rifle & Marching Drill 2" Flow drill X & Y Bty: took over gun position from 34th Div in 1.1 d.4.4 & 1.1.6.1.7	[illegible]
	23rd		Camp moved from Anzac Road to Blangy. Work started on Positions at CIVIL 1.1.6.1.7 Positions reconnoitred at Conrad 1.1.6.5.3	[illegible]
	24th		Material carried up & work continued	[illegible]
	25th		Material carried up & work continued Z Bty relieved Y Bty	[illegible]

A5834 Wt. W4973/M687 750,000 8/16 D. D. & L. Ltd. Forms/C.2118/13.

Instructions regarding War Diaries and Intelligence Summaries are contained in F. S. Regs., Part II. and the Staff Manual respectively. Title pages will be prepared in manuscript.

WAR DIARY
or
INTELLIGENCE SUMMARY.
(Erase heading not required.)

Army Form C. 2118.

Place	Date	Hour	Summary of Events and Information	Remarks and references to Appendices
	June			
	26		X Bty Positions changed to take on Gun Pits at 1.1.6.7.2	[initials]
	27		Gun got into action at Y Bty position Bombs carried to Bty	[initials]
	28		V Bty relief Work continued	[initials]
	29		Y Bty relieved Z Bty	[initials]
	30		Carrying material Work continued	[initials]

A5834 Wt. W4973/M687 750,000 8/16 D. D. & L. Ltd. Forms/C.2118/13.

Instructions regarding War Diaries and Intelligence Summaries are contained in F. S. Regs., Part II. and the Staff Manual respectively. Title pages will be prepared in manuscript.

WAR DIARY
or
INTELLIGENCE SUMMARY.
(Erase heading not required.)

Army Form C. 2118.

17th Div'l T.M.s.

Vol 7

Place	Date	Hour	Summary of Events and Information	Remarks and references to Appendices
	July			
	1-6		X/17, Y/17, Z/17 } Work on positions continued. Casualties:- 5/7/17. X/17 – 3 O.R. wounded.	CDM
	7.	8P.M.	X/17 started registration from CURSE. 4 rounds fired at WIT TRENCH at I 2 c. 1.6. Covering fire by 78 F.A.B.	CDM
			Y/17 has both guns in action.	
	8	7.30P.M.	X/17 Fired 6 rounds registration. Then fired 5 rounds on junction WIT and WISH.	
			Z/17 has both guns in action	CDM
	9	morn.	Y/17 registered with 10 rounds.	
	10		X/17, Y/17, Z/17 } Wire cutting ~~cutting~~ was begun along WIT between I.P.6. 55.90 to I.2.c. 20.45 in accordance with orders of 51st Inf. Brigade. Amm. Expended. 20 rounds.	CDM. CDM.
	~~11-12~~		2LT. N.D.L. STOCKIN R.F.A. posted to Z Battery.	

T.2134. Wt. W708–776. 500,000. 4/15. Sir J. C. & S.

Army Form C. 2118.

Instructions regarding War Diaries and Intelligence Summaries are contained in F. S. Regs., Part II. and the Staff Manual respectively. Title pages will be prepared in manuscript.

WAR DIARY
or
INTELLIGENCE SUMMARY.

(Erase heading not required.)

Place	Date	Hour	Summary of Events and Information	Remarks and references to Appendices
	JULY		~~V/17. Work continued~~.	
	11 ~~17~~		X/17, Y/17, Z/17. 105 rounds fired on wire in front of WIT. Gaps were made all along the sector between I 1.b.60.80 – I 2.a.10.60. M.G. emplacements engaged at I.1.b.99.15. + at I 2.a.10.95.	CDM
			DTMO + OC V/17 carried out reconnaissance for position for heavy T.M. in CROW TRENCH at I 13.b.60.25	

T2134. Wt. W708–776. 500000. 4/15. Sir J. C. & S.

Army Form C. 2118.

Instructions regarding War Diaries and Intelligence Summaries are contained in F. S. Regs., Part II. and the Staff Manual respectively. Title pages will be prepared in manuscript.

WAR DIARY
or
INTELLIGENCE SUMMARY.

(Erase heading not required.)

Place	Date	Hour	Summary of Events and Information	Remarks and references to Appendices
	July. 12.		~~V/17 started work on new position in CROW trench~~	
			X/17, Y/17, Z/17: Bombardment continued on WIT TRENCH. MG. emplacements + wire. Ammunition expended: 100 rounds. Casualties NIL. CDM	CDM.
			5 O.R. joined from D.A.C.	
	13.		X/17, Z/17: continued destructive fire on wire + MG. emplacements on WIT TRENCH from I2.c.2.4. to I2.a.1.2.	
			Y/17 re-registered No1 gun, on sap at I1.b.5.8., + joined in the bombardment of this sap + MG. emplacement, with 4.5 Hows.	CDM.
			Ammunition expended. 60 rounds. Casualties. NIL.	
			DTMO + O.C. V/17 reconnoitred a position for one 9.45" Heavy TM. in CROW TRENCH. S. of the RAILWAY at I13.b.8.1.	
	14.	~~10pm~~	V/17 ~~Started~~ continued work upon new position in CROW TRENCH.	
		10PM	X/17 fired 12 rounds, in support of an Infantry Raid on WIT TRENCH., between Zero + Zero + 20	CDM
			Z/17 fired 20 rounds ditto.	

A5834 Wt. W4973/M687 750,000 8/16 D. D. & L. Ltd. Forms/C.2118/13.

Instructions regarding War Diaries and Intelligence Summaries are contained in F. S. Regs., Part II. and the Staff Manual respectively. Title pages will be prepared in manuscript.

WAR DIARY
or
INTELLIGENCE SUMMARY.
(Erase heading not required.)

Army Form C. 2118.

Place	Date	Hour	Summary of Events and Information	Remarks and references to Appendices
	July 15.		V/17. Continued work on position in CROW. X/17 O C X17 made a reconnaissance of German MINENWERFER positions between CHARLIE + CUBA at I7d. 20.55; and found three pieces to be apparently fit for action. Also about 180 rounds of ammunition. Y/17 } Z/17 } Work on improvement of positions. Casualties - NIL.	CDH.
	July 16		V/17 X/17 Y/17 Z/17 } Continued work on positions. Casualties NIL.	CDH.
	17.		V/17 Continued work on position in CROW. X/17 Y/17 Z/17 } Work on improvement of positions. D.T.M.O. reconnoitred 2" positions in CHARLIE, COSTA, CURLY + COCK. ~~Casualties NIL~~ Casualties. Y/17 - 2 OR died of Gas poisoning. 6 O.R. gassed. 1 officer gassed.	CDH.

A5834 Wt. W4973/M687 750,000 8/16 D. D. & L. Ltd. Forms/C.2118/13.

Army Form C. 2118.

Instructions regarding War Diaries and Intelligence Summaries are contained in F. S. Regs., Part II. and the Staff Manual respectively. Title pages will be prepared in manuscript.

WAR DIARY
or
INTELLIGENCE SUMMARY.
(Erase heading not required.)

Place	Date	Hour	Summary of Events and Information	Remarks and references to Appendices
	July 18		V/17, X/17, Y/17, Z/17 } Worked on positions. Casualties, NIL.	C.D.M.
	19		V/17 Continued work on position.	
			X/17, Y/17, Z/17 } Fired 70 rounds on WIT TRENCH. Casualties NIL.	C.D.M.
	20.	10-30.	V/17 - Continued work on position.	
			X/17 Fired 12 rounds in support of Infantry raid on WART TRENCH. between Zero & Zero +14.	C.D.M.
			Y/17 Fired 7 rounds ditto.	
			Z/17 " " " ".	
			Casualties NIL.	
	21st		V/17, X/17, Y/17, Z/17 Continued work on position	C.D.M.

A5834 Wt. W4973/M687 750,000 8/16 D. D. & L. Ltd. Forms/C.2118/13.

Instructions regarding War Diaries and Intelligence Summaries are contained in F. S. Regs., Part II. and the Staff Manual respectively. Title pages will be prepared in manuscript.

WAR DIARY
or
INTELLIGENCE SUMMARY.
(Erase heading not required.)

Army Form C. 2118.

Place	Date	Hour	Summary of Events and Information	Remarks and references to Appendices
	22nd		V/17 Work continued on position X/17 10 rounds fired on WHIT Casualties Nil Y/17, Z/17 } Positions improved	C.D.h.
	23rd		Reconnaissance by D.T.M.O for two positions in CUPID + COCOA X/17 15 rounds fired on WHIT No 2 Gun had a premature – Casualties – 1 OR wounded. Y/17 Work continued on position Z/17 } Work started on two positions in COCOA + CUPID Casualties NIL	C.D.h.
	24th		V/17, X/17, Z/17 } Work continued on new positions	C.D.h.
	25th		X/17 9.45 T.M. taken up and put into position V/17 X/17 Y/17, Z/17 } Work continued on new position	C.D.h.
	26th		V/17 Work continued X/17 V/17 Fired 10 rounds on WHIT TRENCH Z/17 Y + Z/17 Continued work on Position	C.D.h.

A5834 Wt. W4973/M687 750,000 8/16 D. D. & L. Ltd. Forms/C.2118/13.

Instructions regarding War Diaries and Intelligence Summaries are contained in F. S. Regs., Part II. and the Staff Manual respectively. Title pages will be prepared in manuscript.

WAR DIARY
or
INTELLIGENCE SUMMARY.
(Erase heading not required.)

Army Form C. 2118.

Place	Date	Hour	Summary of Events and Information	Remarks and references to Appendices
	27th		V/17 Work continued X/17 - 10 rounds expended. Y/17 Z/17 Guns in CUPID + COCOA registered on wire North + South of railway cutting 7 rounds fired	CDn.
	28th		X/17 } Y/17 } Z/17 } 105 rounds fired on WIT + WART trenches, + wire in front of them - Fire maintained throughout day, and in support of raid on RAILWAY CUTTING - from Zero (at 12:30 AM 29/7/17) to Zero + 30. Two guns in COCOA + CUPID continued wire-cutting + firing 132 rounds. V/17. Work Continued.	CDn.
	29		X/17 } Y/17 } Z/17 } V/17 } Work on positions.	CDn

A5834 Wt. W4973/M687 750,000 8/16 D. D. & L. Ltd. Forms/C.2118/13.

Instructions regarding War Diaries and Intelligence Summaries are contained in F. S. Regs., Part II. and the Staff Manual respectively. Title pages will be prepared in manuscript.

WAR DIARY
or
INTELLIGENCE SUMMARY.
(Erase heading not required.)

Army Form C. 2118.

Place	Date	Hour	Summary of Events and Information	Remarks and references to Appendices
	29/7/17.		CAPT OUSELEY, D.T.M.O. was posted to T.M. School, Third ARMY. ~~CAPT. ROBINSON~~	ODh.
	30		V/17, X/17, Y/17, Z/17 } Work on positions continued.	ODh.

Instructions regarding War Diaries and Intelligence Summaries are contained in F. S. Regs., Part II. and the Staff Manual respectively. Title pages will be prepared in manuscript.

WAR DIARY
or
INTELLIGENCE SUMMARY.
(Erase heading not required.)

Army Form C. 2118.

Place	Date	Hour	Summary of Events and Information	Remarks and references to Appendices
	31		V/17 } X/17 } work continued. Y/17 fired 10 rounds on WIT trench + wire. Z/17 " " " " " " " " a/DTMO carried out a reconnaissance of positions for additional 2" T.M.'s: (1) South of CARBUNCLE trench at I 14. c 45.60 ; (2) West of COCKBURN Trench at I 14. a. 25.95 ; (3) North of COSTA trench at I 7. b. 70.10 ; (4) East of CHARLIE Trench at I 7 b. 45.70 ; (5) North of a new C.T. at I 7 b. 60.80.	CBn

Instructions regarding War Diaries and Intelligence Summaries are contained in F. S. Regs., Part II. and the Staff Manual respectively. Title pages will be prepared in manuscript.

WAR DIARY
or
INTELLIGENCE SUMMARY.
(Erase heading not required.)

17th Divl. Trench Mortars

Army Form C. 2118.

Vol 8

Place	Date	Hour	Summary of Events and Information	Remarks and references to Appendices
	1917			
	Aug 1		Work continued on Medium positions in COCOA + CURLY and on Heavy Battery position in CROW.	CDM.
			~~20 rounds 2" fired on wire and trench I 16.69. + I 16.74.~~	
	Aug 2		Work continued on 9.45 position in CROW.	
			Work commenced on new 2" position in CARBUNCLE.	
			Gun + emplacement (medium) in CURLY at I 7d. 7.5 destroyed by enemy shell-fire.	CDM
	Aug 3		25 rounds 2" on enemy wire at I 16.60.50 + I 2a.35.20	
			15 " " on strong point at I 1d. 8.4.	
			Work commenced on new medium positions in COCKBURN, COSTA, CHARLIE, + NEW C.T.	CDM.
	Aug 4		60 rounds 2" fired at enemy wire, particularly at I 16.60.50 – 80 and I 2c.00.90 to I 16.95.30, and junction WIT + WISH. One gun in CONRAD buried; no casualty to personnel or Equipment.	CDM.
			2Lt N.D.L. STOCKEN slightly wounded on carrying party, remains at duty.	

Instructions regarding War Diaries and Intelligence Summaries are contained in F. S. Regs., Part II. and the Staff Manual respectively. Title pages will be prepared in manuscript.

WAR DIARY
or
INTELLIGENCE SUMMARY.
(Erase heading not required.)

Army Form C. 2118.

Place	Date	Hour	Summary of Events and Information	Remarks and references to Appendices
	Aug. 5.		50 rounds 2" on I 2c 00.85 – 95, I 1c 70.70 & I 16.95.30; and on WIG at I 14 b. 25.75.	CDM.
	6		27 rounds 2" fired on wire in front of WIT & WISH.	CDM.
	7		47 rounds 2" fired at enemy trench & wire at I 16.60.80, wire at I 2c.05.90. I 2c. 00.80; New works at I 19.80.20, wire in front of WIT at I 16.80.80.	CDM
			Casualties – 1 OR slightly wounded remaining at duty.	
			Work commenced on second emplacement in CARBUNCLE at I.14.c. 45.60.	CDM.
			Gun & ammunition pit at CURSE buried, but no damage done.	
	8.		15 rounds 2" fired at junct WIT & WISH. – Wire at I 16.95.05 & I 16.80.45.	CDM
	9		25 rounds fired on wire in front of WIT.	CDM.

Instructions regarding War Diaries and Intelligence Summaries are contained in F. S. Regs., Part II. and the Staff Manual respectively. Title pages will be prepared in manuscript.

WAR DIARY
or
INTELLIGENCE SUMMARY.
(Erase heading not required.)

Army Form C. 2118.

Place	Date	Hour	Summary of Events and Information	Remarks and references to Appendices
	10		73 rounds 2" fired on wire in front of CUB, S of Ry cutting, in front of WIG No of Ry cutting, & wire junction WANT & ~~WASH~~ WIT.	
			Casualties – 1 Sergt wounded. CDM.	
	11		112 rounds 2" fired on wire in front of WANT & WIT junction, junct. WOOL & WIT, & on wire repaired in front of CUB & CRUST.	
			New 2" T.M. brought into action in CARBUNCLE. I 14 c. 45.60 CDM	
	12		75 rounds 2" fired on wire in front of CUB & CRUST, & WIT & WOOL. CJM.	
	13		40 rounds 2" fired on wire at junction of WIT & WANT & WIT & WOOL. CDM.	
	14		76 rounds 2" fired on wire in front of junct. WIT & WANT, junction WIT & WOOL, and in front of CUB & CRUST. CDM.	
			Second 2" mortar in action in COLON I 4 c. 48.60	
			30 men from D.A.C. attached for duty.	

T.2134. Wt. W708-776. 500,000. 4/15. Sir J. C. & S.

Instructions regarding War Diaries and Intelligence Summaries are contained in F. S. Regs., Part II. and the Staff Manual respectively. Title pages will be prepared in manuscript.

WAR DIARY
or
INTELLIGENCE SUMMARY.
(Erase heading not required.)

Army Form C. 2118.

Place	Date	Hour	Summary of Events and Information	Remarks and references to Appendices
	15.		152 rounds 2" fired on enemy wire by day, and by night as per scheme. CDM	
	16		114 rounds 2" fired wire cutting in front of WIT CUB & CRUST. CDM	
	17.		107 rounds 2" fired as follows: Wire cutting in front of CUB & CRUST & WIT. On ~~CUB &~~ CRUST trench; and on junction of WIT & WANT & on I 2 a. 05.20 & at I 1 d. 95.50. Casualties: One OR wounded (accidentally). CDM	
	18.		150 rounds 2" fired on wire in front of CUB & CRUST & trench NO. of WHIP CROSS ROADS; and on WIT TRENCH. CDM	
	19.		134 rounds fired on wire in front of CUB, CRUST & WIT and on CRUST Trench & shell holes at I 14 b. 10.75. CDM	
	20.		112 rounds 2" fired on wire in front of WIT, CUB & CRUST; & on Minenwerfer emplacements in railway cutting. CDM	

T2134. Wt. W708–776. 500000. 4/15. Sir J. C. & S.

Instructions regarding War Diaries and Intelligence Summaries are contained in F. S. Regs., Part II. and the Staff Manual respectively. Title pages will be prepared in manuscript.

WAR DIARY
or
INTELLIGENCE SUMMARY.
(Erase heading not required.)

Army Form C. 2118.

Place	Date	Hour	Summary of Events and Information	Remarks and references to Appendices
	21.		80 rounds 2" fired on enemy wire, strong points & organized shell-holes. CDM.	
	22.		87 rounds 2" fired on enemy wire & strong points. 4 Signallers RE attached for reorganization of communications. CDM.	
	23.	5PM 5.30PM	86 rounds 2" on wire in front of WIT; on M.G. Emplacement at I1.d.95.55; on CUB & CRUS trenches; and on RAILWAY CUTTING at I14.b.10.75 (39 rounds fired from 2 guns during Artillery bombardment.	
		5–5.30PM	9.45" HTM fired 7 rounds at WINDMILL COPSE during artillery bombardment from [struck out] dummy position. In action for first time. CDM.	
	24.		55 rounds 2" fired on RY. CUTTING & Adjacent trenches & on wire in front of WIT during gas bombardment at 10PM. 23/8/17. 2 rounds 9.45" fired on WINDMILL COPSE at same time	
			Work begun by RE's on new position in CASH. CDM	

T2134. Wt. W708–776. 500000. 4/15. Sir J. C. & S.

Army Form C. 2118.

Instructions regarding War Diaries and Intelligence Summaries are contained in F. S. Regs., Part II. and the Staff Manual respectively. Title pages will be prepared in manuscript.

WAR DIARY
or
INTELLIGENCE SUMMARY.
(Erase heading not required.)

Place	Date	Hour	Summary of Events and Information	Remarks and references to Appendices
	25		130 rounds 2" fired on Enemy trenches & wire, & at suspected T.M. emplacements. CDM	
			Heavy retaliation by 4.2 & light minnies.	
	26.		45 rounds 2" fired at wire & trenches.	
			2 Lt N.D.L. STOCKEN RFA slightly wounded (at duty)	
			New emplacement completed at I 7 b 45 70 & gun in action. CDM	
	27.		60 rounds 2" fired at Enemy wire trenches & MG emplacements in GREENLAND HILL SECTOR (and) on RY CUTTING & T.M. emplacements in CHEMICAL WORKS SECTOR. German minenwerfer put in action in CROW. CDM	
	28		105 rounds 2" fired	
			R. SECTOR — on RY cutting & on COB & CRUST	
			L SECTOR. — wire in front of WIT & WART	
			Emplacement in NEW CUT at I 7 b 65 50 completed, & gun in action CDM	
	25–28		2" ammunition successfully taken up by pack mules by night across the open to CRY TRENCH	

Instructions regarding War Diaries and Intelligence Summaries are contained in F. S. Regs., Part II. and the Staff Manual respectively. Title pages will be prepared in manuscript.

WAR DIARY
or
INTELLIGENCE SUMMARY.
(Erase heading not required.)

Army Form C. 2118.

Place	Date	Hour	Summary of Events and Information	Remarks and references to Appendices
	28		2nd LT. J.A. OLD R.F.A. reported for duty at XVII Corps Infantry Training School	
	29		85 rounds 2" fired –	
			L. SECTOR – on enemy wire in front of W.T. & WART.	
			R. SECTOR – on RY Cutting & on CRUST & CUB.	
			4 rounds 9.45" MK. I on WINDMILL CORSE – three appeared to be blinds.	
			1 75 mm. Minenwerfer brought into action on CROW to enfilade CLOD. 1 round fired …	
	30		Medium Trench Mortars and 9.45 MK I co-operated wi…	
			bombardment of Railway Cutting and enemy trenches …	
			Mortars fired 129 Rounds 9.45 MK I fired 8 Roun…	
			New position in COSTA at I 7 b 75 1½ completed …	
	31		Medium Trench Mortars co-operated with Field …	
			trenches & wire, firing 165 rounds.	
			German MINENWERFER mounted …	

T.134. Wt. W708–776. 50,000. 4/15. Sir J. C. & S.

Instructions regarding War Diaries and Intelligence Summaries are contained in F. S. Regs., Part II. and the Staff Manual respectively. Title pages will be prepared in manuscript.

WAR DIARY
or
INTELLIGENCE SUMMARY.
(Erase heading not required.)

Army Form C. 2118.

1st Aust Trench Mortars

Vol 9

Place	Date	Hour	Summary of Events and Information	Remarks and references to Appendices
	1917			
	Sept 1		Y Battery went to 3rd Army School. Cocoa position repaired	
	Sept 2		Medium T.Ms continued fire on enemy's wire & for registration purposes. German Minenwerfer in Crow continued registration. Ammn Expended 48 rounds	
	Sept 3		Medium T.Ms fired 15 rounds on Enemy's Wire.	
	Sept 4th		Medium T.Ms continued fire in GREENLAND HILL Sector. Fire at night was directed on a Machine Gun position at I.1.d 95.35 & on wire at I.8a 25.75. Fire during the day was directed on wire in front of WIT with good effect. Am expended 366 Rounds	
	Sept 5		A Bombardment by T.Ms in conjunction with Field Artillery was carried out in the CHEMICAL WORKS SECTOR. Four M.T.Ms one H.T.M & a German Minenwerfer took part but one M.T.M out of action through the bed cracking. Fire very effective & considerable damage done to enemy's trenches & large burst of black smoke after one of 9.45 shells exploded in Railway Cutting. Machine guns co-operated. Am Expended MTM 72 Rds, HTM 9, Minen 54	

T2134. Wt. W708–776. 500000. 4/15. Sir J. C. & S.

Instructions regarding War Diaries and Intelligence Summaries are contained in F. S. Regs., Part II. and the Staff Manual respectively. Title pages will be prepared in manuscript.

WAR DIARY
or
INTELLIGENCE SUMMARY.
(Erase heading not required.)

Army Form C. 2118.

Place	Date	Hour	Summary of Events and Information	Remarks and references to Appendices
	1917 Sept 6th		Organised bombardment of enemy defences & wire by MTMs Stokes & Field Artillery 171 Rds were fired from 8 Med. Guns, 6 Rds from 9.45 on 18c 55.85 & 18d 10.60 throwing up much timber & material 56 Rds were fired from Minenwerfer on HAUSA WOOD 2/Lt T BOWMAN reported for duty instead of 2/Lt GORDON	
	Sept 7th		Continued fire on enemy fire. Party of Germans seen to run down WOOL when fire opened. Many stretcher cases reported from previous days bombardment & Infantry report MEDIUM MINENWERFER blown up Am Expended 46 Rds 2/Lt T BOWMAN reported sick	
	Sept 8th		Wire cutting continued on wire at junction WIT. WOOL.	
	Sept [illegible]		Trench Mortars co-operated with Field & Heavy Artillery in a bombardment of enemy defences. Also continued wire cutting in preparation for projected raid on WIT & WOOL Am Expended 2" 172 Rds 9.45 6	

T2134. Wt. W708–776. 500000. 4/15. Sir J. C. & S.

Instructions regarding War Diaries and Intelligence Summaries are contained in F. S. Regs., Part II. and the Staff Manual respectively. Title pages will be prepared in manuscript.

WAR DIARY
or
INTELLIGENCE SUMMARY.
(Erase heading not required.)

Army Form C. 2118.

Place	Date	Hour	Summary of Events and Information	Remarks and references to Appendices
	1917			
	Sept 9th		Trench Mortars fired on the night 8/9 during raid on WIT. WOOL Am Expended 99 Rds. Minenwerfer 63 9.45 4	
	Sept 10		M.T.M's continued firing on enemy defences Reported Machine gun & whistles blown for stretcher bearers. Direct hit obtained on emplacement or dugouts 41 Rds Expended	silenced
	Sept 11		Continued fire on enemy wire & for registration purposes Expended 42 Rds	
	Sept 12		Wire cutting continued & hostile T.M's engaged Amt Ex 65 Rds	
	Sept 13		Retaliation & Wire cutting 167 Rds	
	Sept 14		176 Rds expended on WIT. WANT WOOL WEASEL CUB & CRUST Trenches	

Instructions regarding War Diaries and Intelligence Summaries are contained in F. S. Regs., Part II. and the Staff Manual respectively. Title pages will be prepared in manuscript.

WAR DIARY
or
INTELLIGENCE SUMMARY.
(Erase heading not required.)

Army Form C. 2118.

Place	Date	Hour	Summary of Events and Information	Remarks and references to Appendices
	1917 Sept 15		Wire cutting continued. Heavy retaliation from Boche MINENWERFERS & CONRAD 2 & CORFU 2 blocked with debris & temporarily out of action. 9.45 MK III fired 2 Rds	
	Sept 16		147 Rds fired from MT Ms. Amn Expended 205 Rds. Over 100 4.2s fired at CORFU & trench & dug out entrance badly damaged	
	Sept 17		MTMs co-operated with RFA during raids by Manchesters & Sherwoods firing on the flanks of raiders. Amn Expended 184 Rds	
	Sept 18		Continued firing during night on enemy defences & by day for registration. 9.45 2 Rds, MTM 34	
	Sept 19		MTMs fired 20 Rds on wire & for registration. 9.45 3. 9.45 6 Rds	

Army Form C. 2118.

Instructions regarding War Diaries and Intelligence Summaries are contained in F. S. Regs., Part II. and the Staff Manual respectively. Title pages will be prepared in manuscript.

WAR DIARY
or
INTELLIGENCE SUMMARY.
(Erase heading not required.)

Place	Date	Hour	Summary of Events and Information	Remarks and references to Appendices
	1917			
	Sept 20		32 Rds from 2" fired on hostile T Ms & Mach guns	[illegible]
			4 " from 9.45	
	Sept 21		75 Rds from 2" & 7 from 9.45 fired on enemy's defences	[illegible]
	Sept 22		63 Rds fired on enemy's defences	[illegible]
	Sept 23		36 Rds fired on Working Parties & hostile T Ms	[illegible]
			9.45 Mk III fired 6 Rds	
	Sept 24		Dummy raid on night 23/24 84 rounds expended	[illegible]
			6 Rds were fired from 9.45 on Railway Cutting	
	Sept 25		Med T Ms fired 36 Rds on Enemy wire & defences	[illegible]
	Sept 26		M T Ms fired 35 Rds on enemy defences	[illegible]
	Sept 27		15 Rds fired on CRUST & CUB	[illegible]
			Relief carried out by 61st Div at 8 p.m	

A5834 Wt. W4973/M687 750,000 8/16 D. D. & L. Ltd. Forms/C.2118/13.

Army Form C. 2118.

Instructions regarding War Diaries and Intelligence Summaries are contained in F. S. Regs., Part II. and the Staff Manual respectively. Title pages will be prepared in manuscript.

WAR DIARY
or
INTELLIGENCE SUMMARY.

(Erase heading not required.)

Place	Date	Hour	Summary of Events and Information	Remarks and references to Appendices
	Sept 28		Equipment & Stores overhauled	
	29		Kit & ~~[illegible]~~ inspections	
	30		Rifle & Gas helmet inspection	

A5834 Wt. W4973/M687 750,000 8/16 D. D. & L. Ltd. Forms/C.2118/13.

Instructions regarding War Diaries and Intelligence Summaries are contained in F. S. Regs., Part II. and the Staff Manual respectively. Title pages will be prepared in manuscript.

WAR DIARY
or
~~INTELLIGENCE SUMMARY.~~
(Erase heading not required.)

Army Form C. 2118.

17 D T M Bty

Trench Mortars 17 Div

Vol 10

Place	Date	Hour	Summary of Events and Information	Remarks and references to Appendices
	Oct 1		Fatigues in Camp preparatory to removal from BLANGY	[illegible]
	2		Brigade entrained at ARRAS	[illegible]
	3		Detrained: V Batt GODEWAERSVELDE: Med Batts at CASSEL Brigade marched to ~~PROVEN~~ PROVEN	[illegible]
	4		V Batt inoculated	[illegible]
	5		Brigade marched to ONDANK: Fatigue party of 1 Off + 60 O.R. detailed to report to ELVERDINGHE siding at 5-30 pm.	[illegible]
	6		Fatigue party of 1 Off + 60 O.R. to ELVERDINGHE siding 4-30 pm	[illegible]
	7		Fatigue party of 1 Off + 60 O.R. to " " 2nd Lt GORDON H.W. reported to D 79 for duty	[illegible]
	8		Fatigue party of 1 Off + 60 O.R. to ELVERDINGHE siding 5-0 am Building Bivouacs at Camp	[illegible]
	9		Checking of stores. Cleaning guns & gun parts Fatigue party 1 Off + 30 O.R. to ELVERDINGHE at 9-0 pm	[illegible]
	10		2nd Lt ATKINSON E.H. attached to 78th Brigade Fatigue party of 6 O.R. for 78 Brigade Parades: Inspection & Drill. Signallers class. Officers Class: Lecture	[illegible]
	11		Parades: Inspection & Drill. Signallers class. Officers Class: Lecture Fatigue for 78 Brigade continued	[illegible]
	12		Parades: Drill. Signallers class. Officers Class: Lecture	

A5834 Wt. W4973/M687 750,000 8/16 D. D. & L. Ltd. Forms/C.2118/13.

Instructions regarding War Diaries and Intelligence Summaries are contained in F. S. Regs., Part II. and the Staff Manual respectively. Title pages will be prepared in manuscript.

WAR DIARY
or
INTELLIGENCE SUMMARY.
(Erase heading not required.)

Army Form C. 2118.

Place	Date	Hour	Summary of Events and Information	Remarks and references to Appendices
	Oct. 13		Fatigue party 13 O.R. to D.A.C Fatigue for 78 Bde continued X + Y Batteries inoculated Parades: Men not inoculated Drill NCOs redrilling Baths Fatigue 1 Off + 20 O.R. reported at XIV Corps Ammn Park 2 Lt BOWMAN posted to 11 Div	SR.
	14		Parades: Drill. Signallers Class Z Battery inoculated Fatigues 1 Off + 20 O.R. at XIV C.A.P Casualties: 2 O.R. wounded (Bomb splinters) at XIV C.A.P.	SR.
	15		Parades: Drill. Signallers Class 2 Lt BAREHAM reported to 79 Brigade for duty Fatigues 1 Off 20 O.R at XIV C.A.P	SR.
	16		Parades: Drill. Signallers Class 2 Lt BAREHAM rejoined from 79 Brigade Fatigues 1 Off 20 O.R at XIV C.A.P	SR.
	17		Parades Drill. Signallers Class Fatigues: 1 Off 20 O.R at XIV C.A.P	SR.
	18		Parades: Drill Signallers Class Fatigues 1 Off 20 O.R. at XIV C.A.P 1 NCO 12 O.R. reported to D/79	SR.

A5834 Wt. W4973/M687 750,000 8/16 D. D. & L. Ltd. Forms/C.2118/13.

Instructions regarding War Diaries and Intelligence Summaries are contained in F. S. Regs., Part II. and the Staff Manual respectively. Title pages will be prepared in manuscript.

WAR DIARY
or
~~INTELLIGENCE~~ SUMMARY.

(Erase heading not required.)

Army Form C. 2118.

Place	Date	Hour	Summary of Events and Information	Remarks and references to Appendices
	Oct 19		Parades: Drill. Signallers Class Fatigues: 1 Off 20 O.R. at XIV C.A.P. 1 N.C.O. 12 O.R. at D/79	G.R.
	20		Parades: Cleaning Guns etc Inspection of Signallers & telephone equipment Fatigues: 1 Off 20 O.R. at XIV C.A.P 1 N.C.O. 12 O.R. at D/79	G.R.
	21		Fatigues: 1 Off 20 O.R. at XIV C.A.P 1 N.C.O. 12 O.R. at D/79 1 Off. 3 NCOs & 30 O.R. reported to 104th Field Ambulance	G.R.
	22		Fatigues: 1 Off 20 O.R. at XIV C.A.P. 1 N.C.O. 12 O.R. returned from D/79 1 Off 3 NCOs & 30 O.R. at 104 F.A. 2 Off 50 O.R. ~~reported to~~ detailed for D/79 at 2.0 am 23/10/17	G.R.
	23		Fatigues: 1 Off 20 O.R. at XIV C.A.P 1 Off 3 NCOs & 30 O.R. at 104 F.A. 2 Off 50 O.R. reported to D/79 at 2.0 am.	G.R.

A5834 Wt. W4973/M687 750,000 8/16 D. D. & L. Ltd. Forms/C.2118/13.

Army Form C. 2118.

Instructions regarding War Diaries and Intelligence Summaries are contained in F. S. Regs., Part II. and the Staff Manual respectively. Title pages will be prepared in manuscript.

WAR DIARY
or
~~INTELLIGENCE~~ SUMMARY.

(Erase heading not required.)

Place	Date	Hour	Summary of Events and Information	Remarks and references to Appendices
	Oct 24		Parades Cleaning Guns Fatigues: 1 OFF. 20 O.R. at XIV C.A.P. ~~1 Off 3 NCO~~ 2 Off 50 O.R. reported to D/79 1 Off 3 NCO & 30 O.R. rejoined from 104 F.A.	[illegible]
	25		Parades: Cleaning Guns Fatigues 2 Off 50 O.R. reported to D/79 at 9-0 pm 1 Off 20 O.R. at XIV C.A.P.	[illegible]
			Casualties 1 O.R. wounded (Shell Forearm & Breast)	
	26		Fatigues 1 Off 20 O.R. at XIV C.A.P.	[illegible]
	27		Fatigues 1 Off 20 O.R. at XIV C.A.P.	[illegible]
	28		Parades Drill Parade for Baths. 2 Lt McCLELLAN rejoined D.A.C. Fatigues 1 Off & 50 O.R. detailed for D/79 at 4-15 am 29/10/17 1 Off 20 O.R. at XIV C.A.P.	[illegible]
	29		Fatigues 1 Off 20 O.R. at XIV C.A.P. 1 Off 50 O.R. reported to D/79 at 4-15 am	[illegible]

A5834 Wt. W4973/M687 750,000 8/16 D. D. & L. Ltd. Forms/C.2118/13.

Army Form C. 2118.

Instructions regarding War Diaries and Intelligence Summaries are contained in F. S. Regs., Part II. and the Staff Manual respectively. Title pages will be prepared in manuscript.

WAR DIARY

or

~~INTELLIGENCE SUMMARY.~~

(Erase heading not required.)

Place	Date	Hour	Summary of Events and Information	Remarks and references to Appendices
	Oct 30		Parade: Drill Fatigues: 1 Off 20 O.R. at XIV CAP.	[illegible]
	31		Parades: Drill. Telephone Class Fatigues: 1 Off 20 O.R. at XIV CAP.	[illegible]

A5834 Wt. W4973/M687 750,000 8/16 D. D. & L. Ltd. Forms/C.2118/13.

Instructions regarding War Diaries and Intelligence Summaries are contained in F. S. Regs., Part II. and the Staff Manual respectively. Title pages will be prepared in manuscript.

WAR DIARY
or
~~INTELLIGENCE~~ SUMMARY.

of 17 Divisional Trench Mortars

(Erase heading not required.)

Army Form C. 2118.

Vol 11

Place	Date	Hour	Summary of Events and Information	Remarks and references to Appendices
	1917 Nov 1		Parade for Kit Inspection. Inoculation of men not previously inoculated	
	2		Inspection of Gas Helmets. Gas Drill Fatigues: 1 Off & 50 OR at ADELPHI HOUSE	
	3			
	4		Rifle Inspection & Drill Fatigues: 2 Off & 70 OR at ADELPHI HOUSE	
	5		Inspection of Gas Helmets. Gas Drill. Lecture: Trench Feet	
	6		Drill	
	7		Drill	
	8		Brigade marched to PLUMSTEAD CAMP PROVEN	
	9		Brigade marched to NOORDPEENE	
	10		Cleaning Kit etc	
	11		Inspection parade 2 Lt E.H. GLAISBY attached to Y Battery for duty	
	12		"	
	13		"	
	14		Parade (Inspection)	
	15		Bathing parade at ARNEKE. Inspection parade Drill	
	16		Inspection of Gas Helmets Gas Drill	
	17		Marching Drill. Physical Drill. Saluting Drill	

Instructions regarding War Diaries and Intelligence Summaries are contained in F. S. Regs., Part II. and the Staff Manual respectively. Title pages will be prepared in manuscript.

WAR DIARY

17 Divisional Trench Mortars

or ~~INTELLIGENCE SUMMARY.~~

(Erase heading not required.)

Army Form C. 2118.

Place	Date	Hour	Summary of Events and Information	Remarks and references to Appendices
	1917 Nov 18		Marching Drill. Physical Drill. Saluting Drill	
	19		C.Os Parade. Marching Drill. Physical Drill. Saluting Drill	
	20		Marching Drill. Physical Drill. Rifle Drill. X & Z Batteries proceed to 5 Army T.M. School.	
	21		Marching Drill. Physical Drill. Gas Drill. 1 NCO & 9 OR employed at Divnl Fatigue	
	22		" " "	
	23		Marching Drill. Physical Drill. Guard Mounting Drill. Cleaning Guns etc	
	24		Cleaning Guns. Marching & Physical Drill. Rifle Drill. Signallers Class	
	25		Voluntary Church Parade	
	26		Marching Drill. Gas Drill. Physical Drill. Guard Mounting. Signallers Class	
	27		Bathing Parade. Lt TULLOCH attached 5th Army Anti-Aircraft. 2nd LT. G.B. STORR & 2 Lt D.C. MASON posted to Y & X Batteries respectively	
	28		Inspection of Box Respirators by Gas NCO. Physical Drill. Guard Mounting. Signallers Class	
	29		Marching & Rifle Drill. Physical Drill. Saluting Drill. Signallers Class	
	30		Rifle Inspection & Drill. Physical Drill. Rifle Aiming Drill	

Gleeson C. Holman

Capt R.F.A.

DTMO 17 Div

A5834 Wt. W4973/M687 750,000 8/16 D. D. & L. Ltd. Forms/C.2118/13.

Instructions regarding War Diaries and Intelligence Summaries are contained in F. S. Regs., Part II. and the Staff Manual respectively. Title pages will be prepared in manuscript.

WAR DIARY

or

~~INTELLIGENCE SUMMARY.~~

(Erase heading not required.)

Army Form C. 2118.

Trench Mortars
17th Divisional Arty.

VM 12

Place	Date 1917	Hour	Summary of Events and Information	Remarks and references to Appendices
	Dec 1		Marching Drill; Physical Drill; Fire Drill; Signalling Class.	
	3		Marching Drill; Physical Drill; Gas Drill; Signalling Class.	
	4		Physical Drill; Signalling Class.	
	5		Rifle Inspection; Cleaning Guns; Physical Drill.	
	6		Inspection of Clothing; Physical Drill; Signalling Class.	
	7		Physical Drill.	
	8		Inspection of Gas Helmets; Gun Drill; Physical Drill; Signalling Class.	
	9		Service for R.C's. in OCHTEZEELE Church.	
	10		Inspection of Rifles; Bath Parade; Gun Drill, one 18 pdr. and one 4.5" How. for instructional purposes.	
	11		Gun Drill – one 18 pdr and one 4.5" How. for instructional purposes.	
	12		" " " " " " " "	
	13		" " " " " " " " " " " 3 Officers and 43 Other Ranks rejoined from 5th Army T.M. School.	
	14		Gun Drill – 18 pdr. and 4.5" How.	
	15		Rifle Inspection; Gas Helmet Inspection; Gun Drill – 18 pdr. & 4.5" How. One 18 pdr. and one 4.5" How returned to their respective units.	
	16		1 Officer and 16 Other Ranks proceeded to 2nd Army T.M. School. Brigade moved from OCHTEZEELE to CLERTY.	

(A7092). Wt. W12839/M1293. 750,000. 1/17. D. D. & L., Ltd. Forms/C.2118/14.

Army Form C. 2118.

Instructions regarding War Diaries and Intelligence Summaries are contained in F. S. Regs., Part II. and the Staff Manual respectively. Title pages will be prepared in manuscript.

WAR DIARY
or
~~INTELLIGENCE SUMMARY.~~ Trench Mortars 17th Divisional Artillery
(*Erase heading not required.*)

Place	Date	Hour	Summary of Events and Information	Remarks and references to Appendices
	1917 Dec. 17		Brigade moved from CLERTY to BELVAL.	
	19		" " " BELVAL to ETREE-WAMIN.	
	21		" " " ETREE-WAMIN to AVESNES-LE-COMTE.	
	24		" " " AVESNES-LE-COMTE to COURCELLES-LE-COMTE	
	25		" " " COURCELLES-LE-COMTE to BEAULENCOURT	
	26		" " " BEAULENCOURT to MANANCOURT	
	27		D.T.M.O. made reconnaissance of Line held by 6th Div Lt. HUCKSTEP and part of Z Battery proceeded to front line to take over. V Battery took over Heavy Gun position in course of construction Inspection of Gas Helmets	
	28		Lt. H. NOËL PAUL, R.F.A. posted to X Battery.	
	29		Rifle Inspection, Marching Drill. 1 N.C.O and 3 men proceeded to 6th DIV. T.M. Camp to guard guns and equipment Am Expended 3 Rounds 6" T.M.	
	30		Kit Inspection; Cleaning of Rifles + Fire orders read out. Am Exp. 30 rounds 6" T.M.	
	31		X Battery relieved Z Battery in trenches Am Exp. 10 rounds 6" T.M.	

Gleeson E. Robinson
Capt R.F.A. D.T.M.O. 17 Div

(A7092). Wt. W12839/M1293. 750,000. 1/17. D. D. & L., Ltd. Forms/C.2118/14.

Instructions regarding War Diaries and Intelligence Summaries are contained in F. S. Regs., Part II. and the Staff Manual respectively. Title pages will be prepared in manuscript.

WAR DIARY

or

~~INTELLIGENCE SUMMARY.~~

(Erase heading not required.)

Army Form C. 2118.

Trench Mortars, 17th Divisional Artillery.

Page 1

Vol 13

Place	1918 Date January	Hour	Summary of Events and Information	Remarks and references to Appendices
	1		Work continued on emplacements for 6" Newton T.M. and Heavy T.M. Parades :- Rifle Inspection and Marching Drill. Ammunition Expended :- 10 rounds 6" T.M.	HWP
	2.		Amm. Exp. 30 rounds 6" T.M. HWP	
	3.		Amm. Exp. 20 rounds 6" T.M. HWP	
	4		Handed over positions and guns in action to the 6th Division. Took over positions and guns from 2nd Division. Brigade moved from MANANCOURT to J 35 d 6.8, camp vacated by 2nd Division T.M's.	HWP
	7		Amm. exp. 2 rounds 6" T.M. HWP	
	8		Amm. exp. 13 rounds 6" T.M. HWP	
	9		Casualties 1 O.R. Z/17 T.M.B. wounded in the leg (shell). HWP	
	11		Amm. exp. 41 rounds 6" T.M. HWP	
	12		Amm. exp. 20 rounds 6" T.M. HWP	
	13		Amm. Exp. 8 rounds 6" T.M. HWP	
	14		Amm. Exp. 32 rounds 6" T.M. HWP	
	15		Amm. exp. 18 rounds 6" T.M. HWP	
	16		Lieut. T.F. RIVE R.F.A. reported and attached to Y Battery. 16 O.R. reported from the Base and posted as follows :- 11 to V Battery, 3 to Y Battery and 2 to Z Battery.	HWP

(A7092). Wt. W12839/M1293. 750,000. 1/17. D. D. & L., Ltd. Forms/C.2118/14.

Army Form C. 2118.

WAR DIARY

~~or~~

~~INTELLIGENCE SUMMARY.~~

(Erase heading not required.)

Instructions regarding War Diaries and Intelligence Summaries are contained in F. S. Regs., Part II. and the Staff Manual respectively. Title pages will be prepared in manuscript.

Trench Mortars, 17th Divisional Artillery.

Page 2

Place	Date 1918 January.	Hour	Summary of Events and Information	Remarks and references to Appendices
	19		Captain G.A. PURTON R.F.A. and 17 O.R. V/17, proceeded to Third Army Trench Mortar School of Instruction. Brigade moved from J35 d 6·8 to P4 a 6·5	HWP
	23.		Amm. Exp. 52 rounds 6" T.M. 2Lieut F.A. MARGRY R.F.A. reported and attached to Z Battery	HWP
	24		2Lieut T. ANDERTON R.F.A. reported and attached to X Battery. 15 O.R. reported from 17th D.A.C and attached to V Battery. Amm. Exp.:- 36 rounds 6" T.M. Casualties:- 2Lieut N.D.L. STOCKEN R.F.A. of Z Battery and 28 O.R. wounded gassed (shell)	HWP
	25		1 N.C.O of Y and 1 N.C.O. of Z Battery proceeded to BELLE EGLISE on course of Instruction in Gas. Amm. Exp:- 15 rounds 6" T.M. ~~Casualties:- 3 O.R. wounded gassed (shell)~~.	HWP
	~~26~~ 27.		15 O.R. reported from 17th D.A.C. and attached to V Battery.	HWP
	28		2Lieut T. ANDERTON RFA X Battery and 6 O.R. wounded gassed (shell) Amm. Exp:- 35 rounds 6" T.M.	HWP
	29		Brigade moved from P4 a 6.5 to J34 d 9.2. 2Lieut H.R. HEWETSON R.F.A. reported and attached to Z Battery Amm. Exp.:- 44 rounds 6" T.M. - Casualties 1 O.R. wounded in the leg (shell)	HWP
	31		1 N.C.O of Y and 1 N.C.O. Z Battery rejoined from course of Instruction in gas. Amm. Exp.:- 31 rounds 6" T.M.	HWP

[illegible signature] Capt. R.F.A.
D.T.M.O. 17th DIVISION

Wt. W12659/M1293. 750,000. 1/17. D. D. & L., Ltd. Forms C.2118/14.

Instructions regarding War Diaries and Intelligence Summaries are contained in F. S. Regs., Part II. and the Staff Manual respectively. Title pages will be prepared in manuscript.

WAR DIARY
or
~~INTELLIGENCE SUMMARY.~~ Trench Mortars. 17th Divisional Artillery.

(Erase heading not required.)

Army Form C. 2118.

VBL 14

Place	Date	Hour	Summary of Events and Information	Remarks and references to Appendices
	1918 FEB.			
	1		Work continued on emplacements for 6" T.M's. and 9.45 T.M. in forward area & at HERMIES. 6" NEWTON T.M's fired 20 rounds on enemy trenches.	HW
	2.		10 O.R. proceeded to 3rd ARMY T.M. School. 8 O.R. attached to this Brigade from 17 D.A.C. 6" NEWTON T.M's fired 15 rounds on enemy trenches.	HW
	3.		CAPT. G.A. PURTON. R.F.A. and 17 O.R. returned from 3rd ARMY T.M. School. 6" NEWTON TM's fired 38 rounds on MINENWERFER emplacements.	HW
	4		6" NEWTON T.M's fired 34 rounds on MINENWERFER emplacements & M.G. in K3C7740	HW
	6		200 rounds T.M.G. received from 47th Div A.R.P.	HW
	7		17 Reinforcements reported from the Base. 6" NEWTON T.M's fired 41 rounds on enemy M.G. post at K2D84, BOMBING POST and TRENCH in K3C1.2 to 2.1	HW
	8		6" NEWTON T.M's fired 20 rounds on MINENWERFER emplacement in K3A7015 CASUALTIES:- 1 O.R. wounded Leg M.G. bullet.	HW
	9		6" NEWTON T.M's fired 35 rounds on MINENWERFER emplacement at K3C7740 and enemy trenches.	HW

(A7092). Wt. W12839/M1293. 750,000. 1/17. D. D. & L., Ltd. Forms/C.2118/14.

Army Form C. 2118.

WAR DIARY

~~or~~

~~INTELLIGENCE SUMMARY.~~ Trench Mortars. 17 Divisional Artillery

(Erase heading not required.)

2.

Instructions regarding War Diaries and Intelligence Summaries are contained in F. S. Regs., Part II. and the Staff Manual respectively. Title pages will be prepared in manuscript.

Place	Date 1918	Hour	Summary of Events and Information	Remarks and references to Appendices
	FEB 10.		6" NEWTON T.M's fired 42 rounds on enemy trenches in K3C 5035 to 7060 – MINENWERFER emplacement K3C7752 – M.G. K3C84.	[illegible]
	11.		6" NEWTON T.M's fired 37 rounds on new works K3A 5535 – M.G's K3C6370 – 6078. 2" T.M's complete with stores forwarded to 3rd ARMY GUN PARK.	[illegible]
	12.		6" NEWTON T.M's fired 35 rounds on MINENWERFER in K3C7540 – M.G. K3C8040	[illegible]
	15		6" NEWTON T.M's fired 6 rounds on MINENWERFER in K3C1530 – K3C7740	[illegible]
	17		6" NEWTON T.M's fired 23 rounds on SCOTT – STONE posts + MINENWERFER K3C1530	[illegible]
	18		6" NEWTON T.M's fired 3 rounds on MINENWERFER in K3C7740 [illegible] 1 Reinforcement reported from Base.	
	19		6" NEWTON T.M's fired 40 rounds TMC SOS. 1 N.C.O. (R.G.A.) and 4 OR (R.G.A.) proceeded to 3rd Army School on H.T.M. Course	[illegible]
	20		6" NEWTON T.M's fired 30 rounds on MINENWERFER emplacements in K3A and K3C. and trench junction at K3C4540 [illegible] 300 rounds T.M.G. received from 17th A.R.P.	
	21		6" NEWTON T.M's fired 25 rounds on T.M.C. S.O.S. [illegible] 10 O.R. returned from 3rd ARMY T.M. School.	

(A7092). Wt. W12839/M1293. 750,000. 1/17. D. D. & L., Ltd. Forms/C.2118/14.

Instructions regarding War Diaries and Intelligence Summaries are contained in F. S. Regs., Part II. and the Staff Manual respectively. Title pages will be prepared in manuscript.

WAR DIARY
~~or~~
~~INTELLIGENCE~~ SUMMARY.
(Erase heading not required.)

Army Form C. 2118.

Trench Mortars
17th Divisional Artillery
3.

Place	Date	Hour	Summary of Events and Information	Remarks and references to Appendices
	1918 FEB 22		6" NEWTON T.M's fired 57 rounds on TMC SOS HWP	
	24		6" NEWTON T.M's fired 105 rounds on STONE POST – MINENWERFER K3C7540, K3C1532, K3C7515. HWP 1 N.C.O. proceeded on course at V CORPS GAS SCHOOL 6" T.M. emplacements at HERMIES handed over to 47th Division.	
	26		6" NEWTON T.M's fired 37 rounds on MINENWERFER at K3C7540, K3C1532	HWP
	27		6" NEWTON T.M's fired 20 rounds HWP	
	28		Reorganization of MEDIUM T.M. Batteries R.G.A. N.C.O.s and men proceeded to BARASTRE to join V Corps H.T.M. Battery. Stores of V/17 handed over to V/V H.T.M. Battery.	HWP

Glenn E. Robinson
Capt. R.F.A.
D.T.M.O. 17 Div.

(A7092). Wt. W12839/M1293. 750,000. 1/17. D. D. & L., Ltd. Forms/C.2118/14.

17th Div.

17th DIVISIONAL TRENCH MORTAR BATTERIES.

M A R C H

1 9 1 8

Instructions regarding War Diaries and Intelligence Summaries are contained in F. S. Regs., Part II. and the Staff Manual respectively. Title pages will be prepared in manuscript.

WAR DIARY
or
~~INTELLIGENCE SUMMARY.~~

(Erase heading not required.)

Army Form C. 2118.

Trench Mortars.
17th Divisional Artillery.

Vol 15

Place	1918 Date March	Hour	Summary of Events and Information	Remarks and references to Appendices
	1		Work continued on 6" Newton T.M. Emplacements	
	3		6" Newton T.M's fired on German MINENWERFER emplacement at K3a 7515 Ammunition expended = 17 rounds. T.M.G.	
	4		6" Newton T.M's fired on enemy O.P. K3c 7080, emplacements K3c 1532, K3c 7740. Amm. expended = 61 rounds T.M.G.	
	5		6" Newton T.M's fired on MINENWERFER K3c 1532. Amm. expended = 22 rounds. T.M.G.	
	6		6" Newton T.M's fired on MINENWERFER K3c 7540 Amm. exp. = 36 rounds. T.M.G.	
	7.		Reconnaisance by D.T.M.O 6" Newton T.M's fired on ALLEN POST in K3C. Amm. exp. = 28 rounds T.M.G.	
	8.		6" Newton T.M's fired on BRIDGEHEAD K9b 3590 Amm. exp. = 28 rounds T.M.G.	
	9		6" Newton T.M's fired on MINENWERFER emplacements K3c 1532, K3d 7225 Amm. exp. = 36 rounds T.M.G.	
	10		6" Newton T.M's fired on K10a 9075, K10a 8262. Amm exp. = 24 rounds T.M.G.	
	11		" " " " M.G. post. K3c 13·32 " " = 16 " "	
	12		" " " " Trench mortars in K3C " " = 69 " "	
	13		" " " " " " " " = 21 " "	
	14		" " " " MINENWERFER K3c 7540 " " = 16 " " Reconnaisance by D.T.M.O.	

(A7092). Wt. W12839/M1293. 750,000. 1/17. D. D. & L., Ltd. Forms/C.2118/14.

Army Form C. 2118.

WAR DIARY

or

~~INTELLIGENCE SUMMARY.~~

(*Erase heading not required.*)

Instructions regarding War Diaries and Intelligence Summaries are contained in F. S. Regs., Part II. and the Staff Manual respectively. Title pages will be prepared in manuscript.

TRENCH MORTARS.
17th DIVISIONAL ARTILLERY
– 2 –

Place	1918 Date March	Hour	Summary of Events and Information	Remarks and references to Appendices
	15	—	6" Newton T.M's fired on enemy emplacement K3c 1532. Amm. Exp. 47 rounds T.M.	
	16	—	" " " " " " in K3c + K4c. " " 61 " "	
	17	—	" " " " " " " K3c " " 10 " "	
	18		" " " " " " " K3c and CAT TRENCH K3d73 to K4c94 " " 78 " "	
	19		" " " " " " in K3c + d and Trenches + Junction in K4c " " 71 " "	
	20		" " " " " " K3c 7540, PUPPY TRENCH and wire " " 86 " "	
	21		Enemy attack E. of CANAL DU NORD caught by 6" Newton Barrage, and suffered heavy casualties. Casualties 2 OR. KILLED (SHELL) – 2 OR. WOUNDED (SHELL)	
	22		Orders received to evacuate positions, and bring out or destroy guns. Remaining Ammunition Expended and guns destroyed as they could not be removed. Batteries fell back on HERMIES and HAVRINCOURT. 3 gun positions in HERMIES found unoccupied and were manned by Y Battery. X Battery took over 2 positions in HAVRINCOURT from 19th DIV. T.M's and also manned position constructed between HAVRINCOURT and CANAL DU NORD. Fired on S.O.S. lines during enemy attacks. Casualties :– 1 OR WOUNDED (SHRAPNEL)	

(A7092). Wt. W12839/M1293. 750,000. 1/17. D. D. & L., Ltd. Forms/C.2118/14.

Instructions regarding War Diaries and Intelligence Summaries are contained in F. S. Regs., Part II. and the Staff Manual respectively. Title pages will be prepared in manuscript.

WAR DIARY
or
~~INTELLIGENCE SUMMARY.~~

(*Erase heading not required.*)

Army Form C. 2118.

Trench Mortars
17th Divisional Artillery
— 3 —

Place	1918 Date March	Hour	Summary of Events and Information	Remarks and references to Appendices
	23		Ammunition almost expended when orders received to remove or destroy guns and evacuate positions. 3 guns E. of CANAL DU NORD were removed — 2 of which were put on a G.S. wagon in charge of 19th DIV. T.M's the other was brought back to camp. As the Infantry were withdrawing from HERMIES, there was no time to bring down the guns, which were destroyed. Orders were received from the C.R.A. for the Brigade to leave Camp and get away as best it could. No transport was available, and the gun in Camp was therefore destroyed, and the greater part of Equipment and Kits abandoned. Joined 17th D.A.C. at BEAULENCOURT, and moved with them to COURCELETTE	[illegible]
	24		Brigade moved with D.A.C. to HENENCOURT.	[illegible]
	25		" " " CONTAY Casualties 1 O.R. KILLED (SHELL)	[illegible]
	26		Brigade moved with D.A.C. to PUICHVILLERS via ACHEUX	[illegible]
	29		" " " " " PIERREGOT.	[illegible]
	30		" " " " " VADENCOURT.	[illegible]
	31		Personnel employed in D.A.C.	[illegible]

Glenn C. Robinson
Capt RFA.
D.T.M.O. 17 Div

(A7092). Wt. W12839/M1293. 750,000. 1/17. D. D. & L., Ltd. Forms/C.2118/14.

17th Divisional Artillery

WAR
DIARY

17th DIVISIONAL TRENCH MORTARS

APRIL 1 9 1 8

Instructions regarding War Diaries and Intelligence Summaries are contained in F. S. Regs., Part II. and the Staff Manual respectively. Title pages will be prepared in manuscript.

WAR DIARY
or
~~INTELLIGENCE SUMMARY.~~
(Erase heading not required.)

Trench Mortars
17 Division

Vol 16

Army Form C. 2118.

Place	Date 1918 April	Hour	Summary of Events and Information	Remarks and references to Appendices
In the field	1		Personnel attached to D.A.C GH	
	2		do do GH	
	3		do do GH	
	4		do do GH	
	5		do do GH	
	6		do do GH	
	7		Headquarters removed from No 2 Section D.A.C to MIRVAUX GH	
	8			
	9			
	10			
	11			
	12			
	13		20 Reinforcements posted	
	14		2Lt J A Oed posted to 17 D.A.C from X/17 T.M.B	
	15		Received 4 guns and 8 beds from I.O.M	
	16			

Personnel employed with D.A.C (8–16) GH

(A7092). Wt. W12839/M1293. 750,000. 1/17. D. D. & L., Ltd. Forms/C.2118/14.

Instructions regarding War Diaries and Intelligence Summaries are contained in F. S. Regs., Part II. and the Staff Manual respectively. Title pages will be prepared in manuscript.

WAR DIARY
or
~~INTELLIGENCE SUMMARY.~~
(Erase heading not required.)

Trench Mortars
17th Division

Army Form C. 2118.

Place	1918 Date April	Hour	Summary of Events and Information	Remarks and references to Appendices
In the Field	17		Headquarters removed to VARENNES. Took over from 63rd Division In Line 3 Guns. 3 Beds, 160 rounds T.M.G at Billet 9 Guns. 33 Beds	G.H.
	18		Work continued on 3 gun positions	G.H.
	19		Reconnaissance by D.T.M.O for 3 additional Gun positions in forward Zone Work continued on existing positions	G.H.
	20		Reconnaissance by D.T.M.O for 6 gun positions in defensive zone Work continued on existing positions 2 guns + 4 beds received from Ordnance	G.H.
	21		Work commenced on 9 new positions approved. Work continued on existing positions. Ammunition expended 57 rounds	G.H.
	22		Work continued on all positions Ammunition expended 30 rounds	G.H.
	23		Work continued on gun positions 4 O.R. returned from Div H.Q 5 guns + 10 beds handed to 35 D.A	G.H.
	24		Damaged T.M sent to I.O.M	G.H.

(A7092). Wt. W12839/M1293. 750,000. 1/17. D. D. & L., Ltd. Forms/C.2118/14.

Instructions regarding War Diaries and Intelligence Summaries are contained in F. S. Regs., Part II. and the Staff Manual respectively. Title pages will be prepared in manuscript.

WAR DIARY

~~or~~

~~INTELLIGENCE SUMMARY.~~

(Erase heading not required.)

Trench Mortars
17th Division

Army Form C. 2118.

Place	1918 Date April	Hour	Summary of Events and Information	Remarks and references to Appendices
In the field	25		Work continued on Gun positions 1. O.R. Wounded Shell fire [illegible]	
	26		Work continued on Gun positions Amm expended 11 rounds [illegible] 1 Gun & 2 beds handed to 63rd D.A. 12 beds returned to 3rd Army Gun Park	
	27		Work continued on Gun positions Ammunition Expended 15 rounds [illegible]	
	28		Work continued on Gun positions. 1. O.R. Wounded Shell fire [illegible] Amm. expended 26 rounds	
	29		Work continued on Gun positions Amm Expended 25 rounds [illegible]	
	30		Work continued on Gun positions [illegible]	

[illegible]
Capt R.F.A.
D.T.M.O.
17th Div

(A7092). Wt. W12839/M1293. 750,000. 1/17. D. D. & L., Ltd. Forms/C.2118 14.

Army Form C. 2118.

Instructions regarding War Diaries and Intelligence Summaries are contained in F. S. Regs., Part II. and the Staff Manual respectively. Title pages will be prepared in manuscript.

WAR DIARY
~~or~~
~~INTELLIGENCE SUMMARY.~~

(Erase heading not required.)

Trench Mortars
17 Division

Vol 17

Place	Date 1918	Hour	Summary of Events and Information	Remarks and references to Appendices
In the field	May 1		H. Qrs VARENNES. Work continued on construction of Trench Mortar emplacements.	S.H.
	2		Work continued on Gun positions. Ammunition Expended 35 rounds	S.H.
	3		Work continued. Ammunition expended 54 rounds.	S.H.
	4		Work continued. Ammunition expended 42 rounds.	S.H.
	5		Work continued. Ammunition expended 56 rounds.	S.H.
	6		Work continued. 2 Corporal Reinforcements arrived from 40th Div. Ammunition expended 50 rounds.	S.H.

(A7092). Wt. W12839/M1293. 750,000. 1/17. D. D. & L., Ltd. Forms/C.2118/14.

Instructions regarding War Diaries and Intelligence Summaries are contained in F. S. Regs., Part II. and the Staff Manual respectively. Title pages will be prepared in manuscript.

WAR DIARY
or
~~INTELLIGENCE SUMMARY.~~
(Erase heading not required.)

Trench Mortars
17th Division

Army Form C. 2118.

Place	Date 1918	Hour	Summary of Events and Information	Remarks and references to Appendices
In the field	May 7		Work continued	
			Ammunition expended 37 rounds	[illegible]
	8		Handed over to 63rd Div :-	
			9 Guns 11 Beds (in line) + 821 rounds Ammunition	
			3 " 13 " (at HQ)	
			Ammunition expended 51 rounds.	[illegible]
			Personnel moved to HARPONVILLE	
			Took over 3 Guns + 6 Beds from 63rd Div	
	9		Took over from 63rd Div 12 Beds. HQrs with personnel from HARPONVILLE moved to ARQUEVES	[illegible]
	10		Drill Parades	[illegible]
	11		do.	[illegible]
	12		do.	[illegible]
	13		do.	[illegible]

(A7092). Wt. W12839/M1293. 750,000. 1/17. D. D. & L., Ltd. Forms/C.2118/14.

Instructions regarding War Diaries and Intelligence Summaries are contained in F. S. Regs., Part II. and the Staff Manual respectively. Title pages will be prepared in manuscript.

WAR DIARY
or
~~INTELLIGENCE SUMMARY.~~
(Erase heading not required.)

Trench Mortars
17th Division

Army Form C. 2118.

Place	Date 1918	Hour	Summary of Events and Information	Remarks and references to Appendices
In the Field	May 14		Drill Parades.	[illegible]
	15		do	[illegible]
	16.		do . Received 9 Guns, 6 Beds + 3 Clinos from 63rd D.A.	[illegible]
			Received 2 Sub-beds from D.A.D.O.S.	[illegible]
	17		Drill Parades	[illegible]
	18		do	[illegible]
	19		do	
	20		do	[illegible]
	21		do 15 Reinforcements arrived from 39th T.M.B.	[illegible]
	22		do 3. O.R. proceeded to join 74 Div Arty	[illegible]
	23		do 6 Guns handed to 63rd T.M.	[illegible]
	24		do	[illegible]

(A7092). Wt. W12839/M1293. 750,000. 1/17. D. D. & L., Ltd. Forms/C.2118 14.

Instructions regarding War Diaries and Intelligence Summaries are contained in F. S. Regs., Part II. and the Staff Manual respectively. Title pages will be prepared in manuscript.

WAR DIARY
~~or~~
~~INTELLIGENCE SUMMARY.~~
(Erase heading not required.)

Trench Mortars
17th Division

Army Form C. 2118.

Place	Date 1918	Hour	Summary of Events and Information	Remarks and references to Appendices
In the field	May 25		Drill Parades	ER.
	26		Relieved 12th Div in action	
			Took over :- 12 Guns, 12 Beds, 9 Sub-beds (8 in line), 1000 rds Amm.	ER.
			Handed over :- 6 Guns, 12 Beds (6 without guys),	
			H.Qrs moved to (57 D.S.E.) P16 A1.9	
	27		Work continued on Gun positions	ER.
	28		do do	ER.
			Ammunition expended 19 rounds	ER.
			Reconnaissance by D.T.M.O to select new gun positions	
	29		Reconnaissance continued	ER.
			Work continued on gun positions	
	30		Work continued on gun positions	
	"		Ammunition expended 32 rounds.	ER.
	31		Work continued on gun positions	
			Ammunition expended 26 rounds.	ER.

Gleeson E. T. Robinson
Capt R.F.A. D.T.M.O. 17 Div

(A7092). Wt. W12839/M1293. 750,000. 1/17. D. D. & L., Ltd. Forms/C.2118/14.

Instructions regarding War Diaries and Intelligence Summaries are contained in F. S. Regs., Part II. and the Staff Manual respectively. Title pages will be prepared in manuscript.

WAR DIARY
or
~~INTELLIGENCE SUMMARY.~~
(Erase heading not required.)

Trench Mortars
17 Div
VI 18

Army Form C. 2118.

Place	Date 1918	Hour	Summary of Events and Information	Remarks and references to Appendices
In the Field	June 1		Work continued on Gun positions 48 rounds expended	S.H.
	2		do 55 do	S.H.
	3		do 50 do	S.H.
	4		do 120 do	S.H.
	5		do — —	S.H.
	6		do 23 do 2 Sdr Signallers & one Gunner Reinforcements	S.H.
	7		Work continued on Gun positions 28 rounds expended	S.H.
	8		Do Supported raid by 50th Infantry Bde 90 do	S.H.
	9		Work continued on Gun positions 373 do.	S.H.
	10		do. 45 rounds expended	S.H.
	11		do 59 do	S.H.

(A7092). Wt. W12839/M1293. 750,000. 1/17. D. D. & L., Ltd. Forms/C.2118/14.

Instructions regarding War Diaries and Intelligence Summaries are contained in F. S. Regs., Part II. and the Staff Manual respectively. Title pages will be prepared in manuscript.

WAR DIARY
or
~~INTELLIGENCE~~ SUMMARY.

(*Erase heading not required.*)

Army Form C. 2118.

French Mortars
17 Div

Place	Date 1918	Hour	Summary of Events and Information	Remarks and references to Appendices
Interpied	June 12		Work continued on Gun positions 232 rounds expended	S.H.
	13		do 67 do	S.H.
	14		do 80 do	S.H.
	15		do 60 do	S.H.
	16		do – –	S.H.
			Gun Reinforcement.	
	17		Work continued on Gun positions 78 do	S.H.
	18		do (4 RE Sappers attached) 100 do	S.H.
	19		do 52 do	S.H.
	20		do 61 do	S.H.
	21		do 75 do	S.H.
	22		do 52 do	S.H.

(A7092). Wt. W12839/M1293. 750,000. 1/17. D. D. & L., Ltd. Forms/C.2118/14.

Army Form C. 2118.

WAR DIARY
or
INTELLIGENCE SUMMARY.
(*Erase heading not required.*)

Trench Mortars
17 Div

Instructions regarding War Diaries and Intelligence Summaries are contained in F. S. Regs., Part II. and the Staff Manual respectively. Title pages will be prepared in manuscript.

Place	Date 1918	Hour	Summary of Events and Information	Remarks and references to Appendices
In the Field	June 23		Work continued on Gun Positions 80 rds expended	[illegible]
			63rd Div took over in Line	
	24		Handed over to 63rd Div :- 1345 rounds Ammunition	
			12 Guns with beds complete	
			11 Sub-beds	
			Took over :- 9 Guns 8 Beds 3 Sub-beds (at RUBEMPRE	[illegible]
			3 " 4 " at Le Mobile Workshop	
			4 Sub-beds (on loan to 35th Div)	
			HQrs & personnel removed to RUBEMPRE	
	25		Drill Parades	[illegible]
	26		do	[illegible]
	27		do	[illegible]
	28		do	[illegible]
	29		do 1 officer & 4 detachments proceeded with guns to line to assist in operation by 12th Div	[illegible]
	30		~~Drill Parades~~ Church services	[illegible]

(A7092). Wt. W12839/M1293. 750,000. 1/17. D. D. & L., Ltd. Forms/C.2118/14.

Army Form C. 2118.

Instructions regarding War Diaries and Intelligence Summaries are contained in F. S. Regs., Part II. and the Staff Manual respectively. Title pages will be prepared in manuscript.

WAR DIARY
or
~~INTELLIGENCE~~ SUMMARY.
(*Erase heading not required.*)

Trench Mortars 17 Division

Vol 19

Place	Date 1918	Hour	Summary of Events and Information	Remarks and references to Appendices
In the field	July 1		Drill Parades.	S.H.
	2		D°	S.H.
	3		D°	S.H.
	4		D°	S.H.
	5		D°	S.H.
	6		D°	S.H.
	7		D° Lieut F.N. Strickland posted to 78 Bde.	S.H.
	8		D°	S.H.
	9		D° 3 Reinforcements posted from 17 D.A.C.	S.H.
	10		D.T.M.O took over from 12th Div D.T.M.O in line	S.H.
	11		Drill Parades.	S.H.
	12		D°	S.H.
	13		Personnel + Stores moved to WARLOY to relieve 12th Div	S.H.
	14		Completed Relief Reconnaisance by D.T.M.O	S.H.
			Work continued on Gun positions, Dug-outs &c 35 rounds expended	S.H.

(A7092). Wt. W12839/M1293. 750,000. 1/17. D. D. & L., Ltd. Forms/C.2118 14.

Army Form C. 2118.

WAR DIARY
or
INTELLIGENCE SUMMARY.
(Erase heading not required.) French Mortars 17 Div.

Instructions regarding War Diaries and Intelligence Summaries are contained in F. S. Regs., Part II. and the Staff Manual respectively. Title pages will be prepared in manuscript.

Place	Date 1918	Hour	Summary of Events and Information	Remarks and references to Appendices
In the field	July 15		Work continued on Gun positions + Dug-outs 45 rounds expended	S.H.
	16		Work continued 25 rounds expended	S.H.
	17		Work continued 70 rounds expended	S.H.
	18		Work continued D.T.M.O. took over Y/38 T.M.B. – Reconnaissance by him of this battery in line 56 rounds expended	S.H.
	19		Work continued 2Lt Playfair and 2Lt Baily posted from Base 87 rounds expended	S.H.
	20		Work continued 96 rounds expended	S.H.

(A7092). Wt. W12839/M1293. 750,000. 1/17. D. D. & L., Ltd. Forms/C.2118/14.

Instructions regarding War Diaries and Intelligence Summaries are contained in F. S. Regs., Part II. and the Staff Manual respectively. Title pages will be prepared in manuscript.

Army Form C. 2118.

WAR DIARY
or
~~INTELLIGENCE~~ SUMMARY.
(*Erase heading not required.*)

French Mortars 17 Div.

Place	Date 1918	Hour	Summary of Events and Information	Remarks and references to Appendices
In the field	July 21		Work continued 60 rounds expended	[illegible]
	22		Work continued 2 Lt. Hewetson admitted to hospital Sick 78 rounds expended	[illegible]
	23		Work continued 2 Lt Huckstep attached A.A. 250 rounds expended	[illegible]
	24		Work continued 189 rounds expended	[illegible]
	25		Work continued 127 rounds expended	[illegible]
	26		Work continued 171 rounds expended	[illegible]

(A7092). Wt. W12839/M1293. 750,000. 1/17. D. D. & L., Ltd. Forms/C.2118/14.

Army Form C. 2118.

Instructions regarding War Diaries and Intelligence Summaries are contained in F. S. Regs., Part II. and the Staff Manual respectively. Title pages will be prepared in manuscript.

WAR DIARY
or
INTELLIGENCE SUMMARY.

(Erase heading not required.) Trench Mortars 17 Div.

Place	Date 1918	Hour	Summary of Events and Information	Remarks and references to Appendices
In the field	July 27		Work continued 185 rounds expended	FM
	28		Work continued 126 rounds expended	FM
	29		Work continued 244 rounds expended	FM
	30		Work continued Trench Mortar operation order No 18. – Bombardment of enemy defences.	FM
	–		Y/63 T.M.B. took over Left Brigade front from Y/38 T.M.B. 777 rounds expended	
	31		Work continued 211 rounds expended.	FM

Glenn C. Robinson
Capt RFA
D.T.M.O. 17 Div

(A7092). Wt. W12839/M1293. 750,000. 1/17. D. D. & L., Ltd. Forms/C.2118/14.

17th Divl.
Artillery.

D. T. M. O.

17th DIVISION,

AUGUST 1918.

24

Instructions regarding War Diaries and Intelligence Summaries are contained in F. S. Regs., Part II. and the Staff Manual respectively. Title pages will be prepared in manuscript.

WAR DIARY or ~~INTELLIGENCE SUMMARY.~~

(Erase heading not required.)

of. 6" Trench Mortars. 17th Divisional Artillery

Army Form C. 2118.

VII 20

Place	Date 1918	Hour	Summary of Events and Information	Remarks and references to Appendices
	Aug.			
	1		6" Newtons fired 185 rounds.	[illegible]
	2		" " 550 "	[illegible]
	3		" " 151 " — Ammunition Received 480 rounds T.M.G. Divisional front evacuated by the enemy.	[illegible]
	4		Guns out of range.	[illegible]
	5		LT. A.H. WATKINS joined and posted to X Battery. (from Base)	[illegible]
	6		Brigade relieved by 38th Div. T.M's.	[illegible]
	8		Brigade moved to BLANGY TRONVILLE. 1 O.R. admitted to Hospital. 2/LT. H.R. HEWETSON R.F.A. rejoined from Hospital	[illegible]
	10		2/LT. D.C. MASON R.F.A. rejoined from 2nd Army T.M. School.	
			Inspection of Kit, Rifles, stores	[illegible]
	12		Brigade moved to Q7C22 (62D) to relieve 3rd Australian Divn. Guns out of range	[illegible]
	13		1 O.R. to ENGLAND for tour of duty	
	17		Brigade relieved by 5th Australian Divn. — Brigade moved to VEQUEMONT.	[illegible]
	19		Brigade moved to TOUTTENCOURT	[illegible]
	20		1 O.R. admitted to hospital	[illegible]
	21		Inspections of Kit, Rifles, stores.	[illegible]
	22		Gun Drill — Marching Drill — Gas Helmet Drill	[illegible]
	23		Gun Drill — Rifle Drill — Gas Helmet Drill.	[illegible]

(A7092). Wt. W12839/M1293. 750,000. 1/17. D. D. & L., Ltd. Forms/C.2118/14.

Instructions regarding War Diaries and Intelligence Summaries are contained in F. S. Regs., Part II. and the Staff Manual respectively. Title pages will be prepared in manuscript.

WAR DIARY

~~INTELLIGENCE SUMMARY.~~

(Erase heading not required.)

Trench Mortars
17th Divisional Artillery

Army Form C. 2118.

Place	Date	Hour	Summary of Events and Information	Remarks and references to Appendices
	1918 Aug. 24		Laying tests, Gun Drill, Rifle Drill, Gas Helmet drill. D.T.M.O. rejoined from leave. Brigade moved to join 17th D.A.C. at P23 D 88. 1 Mobile T.M. bed received.	[initials]
	25		T.M. Headquarters moved to Q28 A95. 1 O.R. accidentally wounded. Personnel attached to D.A.C. for duty.	[initials]
	27		Lieut H.G. HUCKSTEP R.F.A. and 1 O.R. posted to 229 A.A. Section. T.M. Headquarters moved to X86 68	[initials]
	28		1 mobile T.M. bed taken forward into line	[initials]
	29		Am. Expended 14 rds	[initials]
	30		T.M. Headquarters moved to R29 C22. 1 mobile T.M. bed received + taken forward into line. Am. Expended 5 rds	[initials]
	31		1 O.R. Killed (shell)	[initials]

Gleeson C. Robinson
Capt R.F.A.
D.T.M.O. 17 Div

(A7092). Wt. W12839/M1293. 750,000. 1/17. D. D. & L., Ltd. Forms/C.2118/14.

Instructions regarding War Diaries and Intelligence Summaries are contained in F. S. Regs., Part II. and the Staff Manual respectively. Title pages will be prepared in manuscript.

WAR DIARY
~~or~~
~~INTELLIGENCE SUMMARY.~~
(Erase heading not required.)

Trench Mortars
17th Division

Army Form C. 2118.

VR 21

Place	Date 1918	Hour	Summary of Events and Information	Remarks and references to Appendices
	Sept. 1		2 Mobile Guns in action – 1 O.R. wounded (shell) – Amm. Expended 20 rounds.	H
	2		Ammunition Expended 35 rounds.	H
	3		1 O.R. wounded (shell) – Camp moved to LE TRANSLOY – Amm. Exp. 11 rds.	H
	4		1 Mobile Gun out of action, Carriage broken. – Amm. Expended 21 rounds.	H
	5		2 N.C.Os & 14 men recalled from D.A.C. – 1 O.R. rejoined from BASE. – Amm. Exp. 17 rounds.	H
	7		Ammunition Expended 19 rounds.	H
	10		2 Lieut H. R. Hewetson posted to 79 Bde. R.F.A. – Brigade relieved by 38th Div T.M.	H
	13		Camp moved to LECHELLE – 1 O.R. admitted to Hosp.	H
	14		Remainder of Brigade rejoined from D.A.C. – Y Bty. went into action att. 38th Div.	H
	15		X Bty. into action. Y38 T.M.B. attached.	H
	17		21st Div. Trench Mortars attached	H
	18		1 O.R. wounded (shell) – Amm. Exp. 370 rounds.	H
	19		1 O.R. wounded (shell) – Two Mobile Guns in action – Amm. Exp. 15 rounds.	H
	20		Ammunition Expended 21 rounds	H
	21		2 Lieut. F. A. MARGRY posted to 17 D.A.C. – 2 Lieut J. ANDERTON posted to Brigade (from D.A.C.) Ammunition Expended 50 rounds.	H

D. D. & L., London, E.C.
(A10266) Wt W5300/P713 750,000 2/18 Sch. 52 Forms/C2118/16

Instructions regarding War Diaries and Intelligence Summaries are contained in F. S. Regs., Part II. and the Staff Manual respectively. Title pages will be prepared in manuscript.

WAR DIARY

~~or~~

~~INTELLIGENCE~~ SUMMARY.

(*Erase heading not required.*)

Army Form C. 2118.

Trench Mortars
17th Division.

Place	Date 1918	Hour	Summary of Events and Information	Remarks and references to Appendices
	Sept. 22		1 O.R. wounded at Duty.	
	25		Ammunition expended 34 rounds	
	26		1 O.R. wounded at Duty – Amm. Exp. 30 rounds.	
	27		Amm. Exp. 180. – 2 Lieut V.A. BAREHAM leave to U.K. – Lieut WAINSWORTH joined from BASE.	
	28		Fired on S.O.S lines. – Amm. Exp. 57 rounds	
	29		Taking fixed gun out & reassembling sub. beds. 1 Mobile gun in action	
	30		do. do. do. do.	

Edwin E. Robinson
Capt R.F.A.
D.T.M.O. 17 Div

D. D. & L., London, E.C.
(A10266) Wt W5300/P713 750,000 2/18 Sch. 52 Forms/C2118/16

16

Army Form C. 2118.

WAR DIARY
or
~~INTELLIGENCE SUMMARY.~~
(Erase heading not required.)

17 Division Trench Mortars

Instructions regarding War Diaries and Intelligence Summaries are contained in F. S. Regs., Part II. and the Staff Manual respectively. Title pages will be prepared in manuscript.

VR 22

Place	Date	Hour	Summary of Events and Information	Remarks and references to Appendices
In the field	Oct 1		Rear HQrs LECHELLE	
			In action with Mobile T M S	
	2		Rear HQrs moved to FINS - GOUZEAUCOURT ROAD (Q 34 D 5 5)	
			In action with Mobile T M S	
	3		Do 15 rounds expended	
	4		Do 44 do	
	5		Do 3 ORs accidentally wounded	
	6		Do Rear HQrs moved to Q 36 A 1 2	
	7		Do	
	8		Do	
	9		Do Rear HQrs moved to BANTOEUZELLE	
	10		Do do do to ESNES	
	11		Do do do MONTIGNY J 25 D 2 2	
	12		Do 60 rounds expended	

D. D. & L., London, E.C.
(A10266) Wt W5300/P713 750,000 2/18 Sch. 52 Forms/C2118/16

Army Form C. 2118.

Instructions regarding War Diaries and Intelligence Summaries are contained in F. S. Regs., Part II. and the Staff Manual respectively. Title pages will be prepared in manuscript.

WAR DIARY
or
~~INTELLIGENCE SUMMARY.~~

(*Erase heading not required.*) 17 Division Trench Mortars

Place	Date	Hour	Summary of Events and Information	Remarks and references to Appendices
In the field	Oct 13		In action with Mobile T.M.S	
	14		Do Do 2 Officers, 17 ORs and 8 mules attached from 21st D.A 50 rounds expended	
	15		In action with Mobile T.M.s 77 rounds expended	
	16		In action with Mobile T.M.S 96 rounds expended	
	17		Do Do 30 Officers + ORs attached from 62nd L.T.M.B 62 rounds expended	
	18		In action with Mobile T.M.S 5 ORs wounded	
	19		Do 71 rounds expended	
	20		Do co-operated with Artillery in attack by 17 Div. 854 rounds expended	
	21		Do	
	22		Do	

D. D. & L., London, E.C.
(A10266) Wt W5300/P713 750,000 2/18 Sch. 52 Forms/C2118/16

Instructions regarding War Diaries and Intelligence Summaries are contained in F. S. Regs., Part II. and the Staff Manual respectively. Title pages will be prepared in manuscript.

WAR DIARY

or

~~INTELLIGENCE SUMMARY.~~

(*Erase heading not required.*) 17 Division Trench Mortars

Army Form C. 2118.

Place	Date	Hour	Summary of Events and Information	Remarks and references to Appendices
On the field	Oct 23		Rear HQrs & equipment etc moved to OVILLERS	
			Mobile T.M.s standing to	
	24		do	
	25		do	
	26		2 Mobile T.Ms taken in action & laid on S.O.S. lines	
			Capt G E Robinson RFA DTMO wounded	
	~~27~~ 27		2 guns in action & laid on S.O.S lines	
	28		3 do do	
	29		Relieved by 21st Div 3 guns brought down to Rear HQrs	
	30		OVILLERS Drill Parades	
	31		Do Drill Parades	

[signature]

Lieut RFA
for DTMO 17 Div

(A7092). Wt W12839/M1293 75,0 0. 1/17. D. D. & L., Ltd. Forms/C.2118/14.

Army Form C. 2118.

WAR DIARY
or
INTELLIGENCE SUMMARY.
(Erase heading not required.)

17 Division Trench Mortars

Vol 2

Instructions regarding War Diaries and Intelligence Summaries are contained in F. S. Regs., Part II. and the Staff Manual respectively. Title pages will be prepared in manuscript.

Place	Date 1918	Hour	Summary of Events and Information	Remarks and references to Appendices
Inchefield	Nov 1		Rear Hdqrs. OVILLERS Drill Parades.	
	2		Do 4 Mobile Guns in action. POIS DU NORD	
	3		Do Do ENGLEFONTAINE	
	4		Do Do Do	
			2nd Lt. A A R Baily and one OR (X/17 T M B) killed in action	
			3. ORs wounded.	
			88 rds expended in support of attack by 17 Division	
	5		Rear Hdqrs moved to POIS-DU-NORD	
			Guns standing to	
	6		Rear H.Qrs POIS-DU-NORD	
			2Lt A A R Baily, and Bombardier Howard E. buried in Military Cemetery, alongside Civilian Cemetery (Sheet 51 A) X.28 Central (POIS DU NORD) at 4 pm,	
			Guns standing to.	

D. D. & L., London, E.C.
(A10266) Wt W5300/P713 750,000 2/18 Sch. 52 Forms/C2118/16

Instructions regarding War Diaries and Intelligence Summaries are contained in F. S. Regs., Part II. and the Staff Manual respectively. Title pages will be prepared in manuscript.

WAR DIARY

~~or~~

~~INTELLIGENCE SUMMARY.~~

(Erase heading not required.) 17 Division Trench Mortars

Army Form C. 2118.

Place	Date 1918	Hour	Summary of Events and Information	Remarks and references to Appendices
In the field	Nov 7		Guns moved forward under 51st Inf Bde in relief of 21st Division	[initials]
			Rear HQrs moved to BERLAIMONT	
	8		Rear HQrs. BERLAIMONT	[initials]
			Guns standing to	
	9		Rear H.Qrs moved to AYMERIES	[initials]
			D.T.M.O. returned from hospital	
	10		AYMERIES	[initials]
	11		Cessation of hostilities	[initials]
			personnel & guns came down to Rear HQrs AYMERIES	
	12		moved to AULNOYE	[initials]
	13		do VENDEGIES	[initials]
	14		do CLARY	[initials]

D. D. & L., London, E.C.
(A10266) Wt W5300/P713 750,000 2/18 Sch. 52 Forms/C2118/16

Army Form C. 2118.

WAR DIARY
or
INTELLIGENCE SUMMARY.
(Erase heading not required.)

Instructions regarding War Diaries and Intelligence Summaries are contained in F. S. Regs., Part II. and the Staff Manual respectively. Title pages will be prepared in manuscript.

Place	Date 1918	Hour	Summary of Events and Information	Remarks and references to Appendices
Lithefield	Nov 15		Moved to LE-GRAND-PONT ESNES	[illegible]
	16		LE-GRAND-PONT Drill parades	[illegible]
	17		Do Do	[illegible]
	18		Do Do	[illegible]
	19		Do Do	[illegible]
	20		Do Do	[illegible]
	21		Do Do	[illegible]
	22		Do Do	[illegible]
	23		Do Do	[illegible]
	24		Do Do	[illegible]
	25		Do Do	[illegible]

D. D. & L., London, E.C.
(A10266) Wt W5300/P713 750,000 2/18 Sch. 52 Forms/C2118/16

Army Form C. 2118.

WAR DIARY
or
~~INTELLIGENCE~~ SUMMARY.

(*Erase heading not required.*) 17 Division Trench Mortars

Instructions regarding War Diaries and Intelligence Summaries are contained in F. S. Regs., Part II. and the Staff Manual respectively. Title pages will be prepared in manuscript.

Place	Date 1918	Hour	Summary of Events and Information	Remarks and references to Appendices
In the field	Nov 26		LE-GRAND-PONT Drill parades.	
	27		Do Do.	
	28		Do Do.	
			3 Mobile 6" T M s drawn from Third Army Gun Park in exchange for 3 Sub beds and 3 beds.	
	29		LE-GRAND-PONT Drill parades.	
	30		Do Do.	

[illegible] Capt R.F.A.
DTMO 17th Division

D. D. & L., London, E.C.
(A10266) Wt W5300/P713 750,000 2/18 Sch. 52 Forms/C2118/16

Instructions regarding War Diaries and Intelligence Summaries are contained in F. S. Regs., Part II. and the Staff Manual respectively. Title pages will be prepared in manuscript.

WAR DIARY
or
~~INTELLIGENCE SUMMARY.~~

(Erase heading not required.)

Army Form C. 2118.

17 Division Trench Mortars

Place	Date	Hour	Summary of Events and Information	Remarks and references to Appendices
In the field	Dec 1		LE-GRAND-PONT. Drill Parades. [illegible]	VR 24
	2		D° D°. [illegible]	
	3		D° D°. [illegible]	
	4		D° D°. [illegible]	
	5		D° D°. [illegible]	
	6		D° D°. [illegible]	
	7		Moved to ETRICOURT. [illegible]	
	8		do MEAULTE. [illegible]	
	9		do ALLONVILLE [illegible]	
	10		do AIRAINES [illegible]	
	11		AIRAINES Drill Parades. [illegible]	

D. D. & L., London, E.C.
(A10266) Wt W5300/P713 750,000 2/18 Sch. 52 Forms/C2118/16

Instructions regarding War Diaries and Intelligence Summaries are contained in F. S. Regs., Part II. and the Staff Manual respectively. Title pages will be prepared in manuscript.

WAR DIARY
or
~~INTELLIGENCE SUMMARY.~~
(Erase heading not required.) 17 Division Trench Mortars

Army Form C. 2118.

Place	Date	Hour	Summary of Events and Information	Remarks and references to Appendices
In the field	Dec 12		AIRAINES — Drill Parades.	
	13		do — do	
	14		do — do	
	15		do — ~~Inspection Parade~~ do	
	16		do — R.E. Fatigues	
	17		do — do	
	18		do — do	
	19		do. — do.	
	20		do — Drill Parades	
	21		do — do	
	22		do — ~~Inspection Parade~~ do	
	23		do — ~~Drill Parade~~ do	
	24		do — do.	
	25		do — Christmas Services (Voluntary)	
	26		do. — ←	

D. D. & L., London, E.C.
(A10266) Wt W5300/P713 750,000 2/18 Sch. 52 Forms/C2118/16

Army Form C. 2118.

Instructions regarding War Diaries and Intelligence Summaries are contained in F. S. Regs., Part II. and the Staff Manual respectively. Title pages will be prepared in manuscript.

WAR DIARY
or
INTELLIGENCE SUMMARY.

(*Erase heading not required.*) 17 Division Trench Mortars

Place	Date 1918	Hour	Summary of Events and Information	Remarks and references to Appendices
In the field	Dec 27		AIRAINES Drill Parades [illegible]	
	28		do do [illegible]	
	29		do Inspection Parade [illegible]	
	30		do Drill Parade [illegible]	
	31.		do do [illegible]	

[illegible signature]
Capt R.F.A.
D.T.M.O. 17 Div.

D. D. & L., London, E.C.
(A10266) Wt W5300/P713 750,000 2/18 Sch. 52 Forms/C2118/16

www.ingramcontent.com/pod-product-compliance
Lightning Source LLC
Chambersburg PA
CBHW081426300426
44108CB00016BA/2311
* 9 7 8 1 4 7 4 5 1 0 3 1 8 *